The
Good
Life

The Good Life

History of the Frank H Russell Family

William Russell

authorHOUSE®

AuthorHouse™
1663 Liberty Drive
Bloomington, IN 47403
www.authorhouse.com
Phone: 1-800-839-8640

Published by AuthorHouse   09/07/2012

ISBN: 978-1-4772-5549-0 (sc)
ISBN: 978-1-4772-5548-3 (e)

Any people depicted in stock imagery provided by Thinkstock are models, and such images are being
used for illustrative purposes only.
Certain stock imagery © Thinkstock.

This book is printed on acid-free paper.

TABLE OF CONTENTS

DEDICATION

To Joanne, my partner and devoted wife of 54 years who brought wit, wisdom, and intelligence to every day with an eternal optimism that contributed mightily to our joyous life together.

INTRODUCTION

My intent, when I started this book, was simply to write a history of the Russell family starting with my father's birth in 1880. However, as the book developed, I felt that just an account of who begat who and when was not enough. I found myself including philosophy of the family, which started with my father's inspiring leadership in freethinking as fundamental to enjoying the best of life's gifts.

As the book unfolded, the title became obvious, as our family has enjoyed the good life in every respect. Why, and how you might ask? I have attempted to answer that question and hope that the reader will find value in these writings and ideas to improve their own full share of life's riches.

During the period covered by my book, there have been numerous wars and religions have come and gone. Millions of innocents have been slaughtered in the name of religion. We must ask the simple question, "Why can't we get along?" That subject will be addressed in this book.

Can we as a people learn to live without the enslavement of religious superstition? Cannot life be better when we depend upon our brains using logic and reason for solutions to life's problems rather than falling back to the dark ages myths perpetuated by religions?

We so often hear, "It was God's plan" or "God will provide". This is little more than abdication of responsibility for one's actions in solving problems. Taking responsibility is an essential step in facing life's problems and successfully solving them. We must learn to tax our intellect and not depend upon mystical powers These subjects will be addressed.

In writing a family history book, I may have revealed more philosophy than should be necessary. But there it is.

PREFACE

The most significant development in our country during this book's period has been the rise of the black race from total poverty, virtual slavery, illiteracy, and rejection and considered an inferior race by large segments of the white population to today when blacks have attained unprecedented achievement and equality. A generation ago, this would have seemed impossible. This book addresses this subject.

Another subject is to reveal religion for what it is—a waste of time and resources, creating divisiveness among peoples, an obstacle to the principles of humanism, standing in the way of individual development, and impeding scientific progress. The United States is probably the most religious country in the Western world. Our forebears left Europe because of religious persecution yet we now face a growing strict religious environment making secularism not so subtlety ostracized and religion often divisive, intrusive, and restrictive of scientific truths. Many religions stand firmly opposed to population control, the use of condoms, stem cell research, gay marriage, and abortion to name just a few current legal practices that are being actively opposed by many religions. Many religions also are homophobic in their support of gay bashing and the lack of support for the equality of women.

The religions teach that prayer will bring answers to one's problems. This is one of the greatest fictions and leaves many unable to cope with life's normally challenging vicissitudes. Facing life's problems is essential to solving those problems and that can only be achieved by recognizing the need to study, develop skills, and work with optimism and diligence to solve those problems. Prayer has absolutely nothing to do with solving problems or finding one's way through the jungle of obstacles impeding solutions. It is just talking to yourself, an insult to intelligence, and a waste of time. Those who need prayer for assistance in leading a full life need guidance. As Albert Einstein says in his book, <u>The World as I See It</u> *"such notions are for the fears of absurd egoism of feeble souls"*.

Every day in all the media, there are numerous religious programs preaching various versions of the so-called gospel. Few seem to complain. However, just let one article or program appear in the media of a secular, anti-religious or free-thinking nature and there is uproar of opposition. Atheists do not enjoy easily or comfortably freedom of speech or discussion of alternatives to religion. An atheist, today, could not be elected to public office. Hopefully this can be changed, someday. This book, doubtless, will be heavily criticized if it attains any reasonable distribution.

I have long been an advocate of population control since I first studied the subject in college and read Thomas Malthus, a philosopher of the 17th and 18th Centuries and Paul Ehrlich, the contemporary investigator.

We have heard the religious admonition, "Go Forth and Multiply" generated by biblical quotes as follows:

Genesis 1:22

"And God blessed them, saying, Be fruitful, and multiply, and fill the waters in the seas, and let fowl multiply in the earth."

Genesis 9:7

"And you, be ye fruitful, and multiply; bring forth abundantly in the earth, and multiply therein."

This faulted advice in the face of the recognized science of over-population continues. The Earth cannot sustain unlimited population growth without a serious reduction in quality of life.

Malthus has become widely known for his analysis according to which societal improvements result in population growth which, he states, sooner or later gets checked by famine, disease, and widespread mortality.

He wrote in the context of the popular view, in 18th century Europe, that saw society as improving, and in principle as perfectible. William Godwin and the Marquis de Condorcet, for example, believed in the possibility of almost limitless improvement of society. So, in a more complex way, did Jean-Jacques Rousseau, whose notions centered on the goodness of man and the liberty of citizens bound only by the social contract, a form of popular sovereignty.

Malthus thought the idea of endless progress towards a utopian society was impaired by the dangers of population growth: "The power of population is infinitely greater than the power in the earth to produce subsistence for man". Believing that one could not change human nature, and that egalitarian societies were prone to over-population, Malthus wrote in dramatic terms: "epidemics, pestilence and plague advance in terrific array, and sweep off thousands and tens of thousands. Should success be still incomplete, gigantic famine stalks in the rear, and with one mighty blow, levels the population with the food of the world".

Malthus became hugely influential, and controversial, in economic, political, social and scientific thought. Many of those whom subsequent centuries sometimes term "evolutionary biologists" also read him, notably Charles Darwin and Alfred Russel Wallace, for each of whom Malthusianism became an intellectual stepping-stone to the idea of natural selection. Malthus remains a writer of great significance, and the debate continues.

When I was a youth, there were about 2 billion people in the world. Today there are about 7 billion. Most scientists agree that this population explosion is not sustainable. Yet efforts to develop active population control programs and incentives are vigorously opposed by most of the religions and even today by political hacks such as Rick Santorum who ran unsuccessfully for Republican presidential nomination in 2012.

In 1938, Dr Paul Ehrlich wrote, "The Population Bomb, which was opposed by the religious then and continues to be opposed today by the same narrow parochial interests." Today, the population bomb is exploding, as predicted.

We worry today about global warming, loss of open space, pollution, loss of habitat for many wild species and the general degradation of quality of natural life. We must reduce population to correct these problems or suffer a continued reduced quality of life. The religions oppose all efforts to control population.

We also have many who believe that prayer should be included in the classroom curriculum. Even our recent past President Bush would have allowed and even encouraged it. To do so would be a tremendous mistake. Not only is prayer scientifically proven to be totally ineffective repeatedly in achieving objectives by numerous research studies but, it confuses a student who is in school to learn about science not myth and superstition that should be confined to the churches. What do you think would happen to the person who advocated that atheism should be taught in the public schools? So why should Christianity or any religious practice along with their mythical foundations be encouraged or allowed?

Evolution is a fact of science. There are several theories associated with it and the most important one was brought forth individually and separately by Darwin and Wallace. This is known as "Darwin's Theory of Evolution." It Is the theory of the mechanism of how evolution works, not evolution itself. Evolution evidences itself all around us and proves it is a scientific fact through simple observation. A recent best-selling book by Richard Dawkins, The Greatest Show On Earth is recommended reading on this important subject

One of the most obvious examples of evolution is the way the body becomes immune to certain drugs when taken over a period of time. At first the drugs are effective in controlling certain diseases. As they are continually administered, the body evolves an immunity to the drugs and they are no longer effective. There are many other examples of evolution occurring all around us on a regular basis. Those who "don't believe in evolution" are simply not observant or not willing to face the facts of their own observations. It is largely ignorance.

Christopher Hitchens has shown how blind salamanders make nonsense of creationists' claims. A quote from him explains:

"It is extremely seldom that one has the opportunity to think a new thought about a familiar subject, let alone an original thought on a contested subject, so when I had a moment of **eureka** a few nights ago, my very first instinct was to distrust my very first instinct. To phrase it briefly, I was watching the astonishing TV series _Planet Earth_ (which, by the way, contains photography of the natural world of a sort that redefines the art) and had come to the segment that deals with life underground. The subterranean caverns and rivers of our world are one of the last unexplored frontiers, and the sheer extent of the discoveries, in Mexico and Indonesia particularly, is quite enough to stagger the mind. Various creatures were found doing their thing far away from the light, and as they were caught by the camera, I noticed—in particular of the salamanders—that they had typical faces. In other words, they had mouths and muzzles and eyes arranged in the same way as most animals. Except that the eyes were denoted only by little concavities or indentations. Even as I was grasping the implications of this, the fine voice of Sir David Attenborough was telling me how many millions of years it had taken for these denizens of the underworld to **lose** the eyes they had once possessed."

"If you follow the continuing argument between the advocates of Darwin's natural selection theory and the partisans of creationism or "intelligent design," you will instantly see what I am driving at." The creationists (to give them their proper name and to deny them their annoying annexation of the word **intelligent**) invariably speak of the eye in hushed tones. How, they demand to know, can such a sophisticated organ have gone through clumsy evolutionary stages in order to reach its current magnificence and versatility? The problem was best phrased by Darwin himself, in his essay "Organs of Extreme Perfection and Complication":

None the less, the creationists continue naively to put forth, "To suppose that the eye, with all its inimitable contrivances for adjusting the focus to different distances, for admitting different amounts of light, and for the correction of spherical and chromatic aberration, could have been formed by natural selection, seems absurd in the highest possible degree." These creationists are unable to face the facts of evolution. It is ignorance.

Many religions do not support evolution as a fact. There are even some school districts in the United States today under the pressures of local religious groups that do not permit the teaching of evolution in their public school systems. This is a tragedy for the children in those school systems and greatly handicaps their intellectual development and their preparation for the modern scientific world. This should not be countenanced in a free and secular country dedicated to scientific truths.

There are active religious groups insisting that Intelligent Design should be taught as an alternative to Evolution. Obviously, Intelligent Design is simply Creationism with a different name. It depends on the belief in a mystical God. To permit it in some school systems is certainly tragic and is one more example of the battle that continues to maintain the separation of state and religion. It parallels the belief that the "stork theory" should replace the theory of natural birth.

The Bible and the Koran were written at a time when people thought the Earth was flat, when the wheelbarrow was high tech. These writings were written by men who would be considered ignorant and uneducated by today's standards. Are their teachings applicable to the challenges we now face as a civilization in a modern world? Our modern world scientific knowledge makes these books and their ancient world irrelevant to the needs of a modern society. This pertains as well to other religious texts such as the Torah.

Religion has always been a threat to the progress of man. Today, however, in much of Europe and the United States, religion in general is being recognized by many for what it is . . . . a crutch to the weakest in our societies and has lost much of the importance it enjoyed only a few decades ago. However, there is a new threat to the modern development of mankind. It is Islam. Though over 1400 centuries old, this primitive religion has developed into an ideological theology that is said to have a following world-wide of over 1.3 billion believers. This book will also address this threat to the security of our civilization and suggest ways to keep it in check and reveal its intellectual irrelevancy and dangers to our civilization.

Much of what I've been talking about so far involves problem-solving. Certainly, we have problems in life, not the least of which is making a living. But, making a living is not the only aim in life. We have to set aside time to enjoy recreation, our hobbies, and our families. I have been more than adequately rewarded with ample time to enjoy my hobbies like skiing, sailing, mountaineering, and world travel with my family. We have spent a lot of time skiing and hiking in the Alps of Europe. I've been blessed to have had, perhaps, more than my share of such rewards.

Often, I have heard that a man, to have achieved fully in life, must have done four things. 1) Build a house 2) Raise a son 3) Start a business 4) Write a book. Up to the present, I had done all but the last and now this effort corrects that. I hope it fills a need.

My father was a physician-surgeon and a philosopher dedicated to the well-being of his fellow man and his community. He often quoted Sam Walter Foss's poetic line, "But let me live by the side of the road and be a friend to man." This was basic in my father's living philosophy and as a physician he was able to live it fully.

He and I were close and I held him in great esteem, so his life and philosophies are an important part of this book. This history starts with his birth in 1880 and his youth in the south following the American Civil War. His timeless and inspired philosophies have shaped my life and I hope, in this book, to reveal them for others' benefit.

Addendum.

Though this book is essentially about the period starting in 1880, my brother, Frank, has researched some decades before that and written it as follows:

This is the story of my grandfather, Frank H. Russell (1851 to 1889), accountant, of Yazoo city, Mississippi; as we have discovered in Arden, genealogy research. My father Frank H. Russell, M.D. (1880-1955) lost his father when he was nine years old. I question if he knew what we have now learned.

The Russell family has been traced to the mid-1600s in Boston, Massachusetts. It includes a number of distinguished members, ministers, physicians, soldiers, and statesmen. Some are buried in the old North Church burial grounds in Boston next to Samuel Adams, John Adams, Paul Revere and other notables of the time. John Russell (1729-1813), was a member of the Sons of liberty, who dressed up like Indians and pulled off the Boston Tea Party in 1775.

After the Civil War (1861 to 1865). The South was in great turmoil, particularly Yazoo County and Yazoo city. President Lincoln's assassination in 1865 by John Wilkes Booth, and following Andrew Johnson's (R—Tennessee) ascension to the White House, did not fare well for hopes for Southern Reconstruction. Some northern Mississippi counties were not all sympathetic to the Confederacy, and some even wanted to succeed from the Confederacy. Example: Jones County. Many of the populace even fought for the North or refused to carry arms for the South.

The area was a hotbed for federal sympathizers, carpetbaggers and Republicans. Now come the elections of 1876, when the Democrats hoped to recapture political powers and some of the ways of the "ol' South". The local confederates and Democrats were making it very clear that the Republicans who were the majority, we're not going to prevail in the local elections. Night riders with guns and ropes, "the clan", conducted hangings of opposing whites and blacks. Murder and intimidation was rampant. Letters to Gov. Adalbert, "a union war hero" pleaded for Army or National Guard protection, but the governor, turned carpetbagger, watched helplessly as did Pres. Grant who offered no help.

The black deputy sheriff, Charles E. Fawn was warned by Frank Russell in a letter the day before, October 25, 1875, "if you value your life, keep out of the Sheriff's office." On Tuesday, October 26, 1875 Frank, met Charles Fawn. They reportedly walked down the hall in the courthouse, when Russell drew a pistol and shot deputy Fawn in the head at 10:30 AM. Fawn dropped dead. Russell's father, Joshua Thompson Russell, a deputy with Fawn—both appointed by Sheriff Albert Morgan has said he would not continue as a deputy if Fawn was elected sheriff. He said Fawn was a "rascal and a God damned scoundrel" a witness, Robert Lewis, confirmed the story and shot at Russell who escaped after the shooting. Russell's employer, WC Craig confirmed the handwriting he knew well, was Russell's. The clan and the good ol' boys were back in power. Mississippi remained progressively, with the "Jim Crow" laws, and became a segregated state. It remained so until the 20th century when the civil rights legislation began to set things right again.

In the second Yazoo County District Court, after a five-day trial. Russell, the shooter, was tried, convicted, and sentenced to prison. He was later pardoned as not guilty on January, 1880. The family left Yazoo City and moved to a home in Leesburg, Florida owned by Elizabeth's father, Dr. James T. Green, M.D., a prominent Florida surgeon, (1834 to 1910). He was a major, C.S.A., Third infantry—field surgeon during the Civil War.

The Russell family grew up in Leesburg. Russell's son, Frank, my father, became a pharmacist and owned two drugstores. His education included three years of high school, night school and self teaching. He sold his drugstores. He rode a bicycle to Memphis Tennessee in 1913, took and passed entrance exams at the University of Tennessee medical school. In 1917 he earned his M.D. degree—he trained at New York Lying In and Bellevue Hospital, second Cornell Surgical Division. He practiced surgery in New York City, 1918 to 1937. In 1937 dad moved to Worcester and practiced surgery at the Doctors Hospital, which he owned, from 1938 to 1955 when he died on November 24, 1955. He is buried in Worcester Massachusetts

And now to the book about the Russell family from dad's birth in 1880.

CHAPTER 1

Life in the
Mississippi Delta

A golden morning sun slowly peeked above the horizon over the gently waving delta grasses on an already stifling morning: the intense rays creeping broadly in a cloudless sky raising the temperature to an almost unbearable level. Mississippi delta weather generates heat and humidity that makes the cotton flourish but daily living agonizing for those unable to escape it in those days long before air conditioning or even electricity was available.

The devastation of the Civil War could still be seen everywhere in 1880 when my father, Frank, was born. The South was in slow recovery but the life of the Negro had changed little since colonial days. Equality and freedom of the formerly black slaves was not an important priority for southern whites who looked upon Negroes as inferior in every way. The majority of southern whites stubbornly resisted the efforts of the north to integrate the races in the south. Though it was the law of the land, there still were no schools for Negroes. Illiteracy was the norm. Negros in the south were considered an inferior species and even the parsons from their pulpits supported and preached this fable. Even though slavery continues to be supported in the bible.

A small boy strolled dreamily along the delta embankment, as he often did in the early morning hours. He was bare footed with tousled blond hair and dressed in tattered shorts. He loved nature, and he especially loved to go to some quiet spot by himself to think and wonder at the scudding clouds above. As he walked along, he reveled in the abundance of nature surrounding him: the egret stalking its prey in the shallows: the soaring hawk seeking a new born duckling for breakfast; the lazing swans picking their morning meal in the shallows and there he saw a little black boy down in the water up to his knees bent over intently staring into the shallow waters. Suddenly the black boy dove in and clutched at something in the shallows.

"What are you doing?" the boy on the bank asked".

"Catchin frogs."

"Frogs? Why ya doin' that? Are they good for anything?

"They sure are. My momma cooks them at home, and they are really good eating-sweet and crackly. Don't yo'all like them?"

"I don't know, I never heard of eating frogs. Are they really good? What's your name?"

"Pete" the black boy answered. "Do you want to try to catch some? Come 'ere, this is a good spot."

The blond boy climbed down the bank and joined his newfound black friend to be quickly learning the art of catching frogs. "You learn fast. What's your name?" Pete asked.

"Frank Russell"

"Oh yeah, I know your name. Don't yo' daddy owns the plantation we all work on?"

"Well, he does manage it, but he doesn't own it. He's hired by the owner to do the management job. He's a hired business manager."

"Don't you know, you ain't supposed to be talking to me 'cause I'm a Nigger?"

"Yes, I know that but I don't like those kind a rules. Why should someone tell me who I can talk to? It's not right, don't you know?"

"It don't make no difference, if I agree or not. My daddy says, just do yo' work and keep yo' mouth shut. So that's what we all do. My daddy says it is better now than it was before the war. And we all hope it will get better. My preacher at our church says it will. So, we listen careful to him." Pete answered." What church do you go to?" Pete asked.

"Oh, we don't go to church. Not much anyway. My mom does sometimes, but me and my dad don't." Frank replied.

"Ain't you scared you ain't goin' to heaven?" Pete asked.

"Naw, my daddy says there is no heaven." Frank replied.

"No heaven? How could there be no heaven when my preacher and the Bible tells us that they sho' is?"

"Well, preachers can promise anything, but that doesn't make it true." Frank added, "My daddy says we make our own heaven right here on Earth"

"What about God? Do you believe in God?"

"Naw, my dad says there's no God"

"How could that be?"

"Well my dad says that the world is so full of wars, murder, an' people doing terrible things to other people that how could there be a God? He says God is supposed to be all powerful and all merciful. So how could He allow those things to happen? Naw, we don't believe in God"

"Well that may be okay for you because you're white but for us Niggers, it is no heaven, here. I'd say it's mo' like hell. And we need a God to help us and tell us what to do. Anyway, it's fun catchin' frogs and they are mighty fine to eat. Would you like to try some?" Pete asked.

"Well, maybe, but I doubt if my momma would cook them 'cuz they're kinda slimy."

"Naw, they ain't slimy. Here, I have enough right in this sack. So come on with me to my house. My momma would love to cook some for you an' me I'm sure." The two boys climbed out of the water and headed down the dusty jetty road. The bag of squirming frogs was dripping and moving. Pete had to hold tight on to it or they would sure get out. The sun was rising slowly promising another scorching day.

Soon they were at a small cluster of tiny unpainted buildings in bad repair. Really more shacks than houses. The windows were cracked and the front step was broken and sagging. "Here's where we live, Frank. Come on in. Momma, where are you?"

"Here I am child. Who have you got with you?" His mother asked as she appeared at a doorway.

"I got a new friend; this here is Frank—Frank Russell. We met in the Bayou, where I was catching frogs for breakfast. He ain't never et frogs before. Can you figur that? I told him you would cook some up for him Momma."

"Well, sure, honey, but you know, there are some rules around here. And I think Frank could get in a peck of trouble coming here to a Negro house. You know that ain't allowed by the company. We could get in trouble, too."

"Oh, that's okay 'cause Frank's daddy is the boss of the plantation. Ain't that somethin'?"

"He is? That is somethin'. Come here then, kids, and help me get things ready. Pete, you skin the frogs. Show Frank, how to do it, too, then set the table. Your daddy will be home soon, and we can all have fried frogs legs, grits, and biscuits, for breakfast. How does that sound?"

"That is just wonderful. I am sure that Frank will love the taste of these frogs as much as we do.

Suddenly there was a rumbling on the front steps. The door swung open and the doorway was filled by the huge figure of a black man. "Well good, I'm just in time for breakfast if my nose don't fail me. I got those logs cut so I can take a few minutes. Who's this?"

"Oh this here is young Frank Russell," Mama answered. "He's going to have frog legs with us for breakfast."

"This ain't the boss's son, is it?" he, asked.

"It sho is," Mama replied.

"Well, I sho am glad to meet you. You've got a fine daddy. We all like to work for him. Now where's those vittels? I am as hungry as a bear."

He almost looked like a bear, too, with a big head of hair and a full black beard, huge arms built up over the years swinging an axe and a hoe. The physiques of all the blacks was exceptional as they spent full-time in heavy labor.

"I hear your daddy got pardoned by the court. That's certainly right. He did what anyone would do. Those damn carpetbaggers from the North are just taking advantage of us down here in the South and shooting one of 'em is exactly what they should get. Your daddy is a brave man. He done the right thing"

"My mom doesn't want me to talk about that. But I do know what went on as some of the kids in school have told me. I guess everyone got behind my dad.

Carpetbaggers came south to seek opportunity. Many were crooked. By the 1860's carpetbags were carried by all most everyone, Men, Women, well to do, middle class and not so well to do when they traveled. Carpetbags were the first suitcases made in large numbers. When you traveled during the Civil War (1861-1865) and though the 1880's, you packed your Carpetbag. This became a way to identify an outsider.

During the Civil War Reconstruction Period many people from the Northern States went South because the south was so poor that there were many opportunities for a person with money even a little money. For example you could own a farm by paying the past due taxes for as little as $25. These opportunities attracted all sorts of people from honest hard working farmers, to crooks, charlatans, con artist and of course crooked politicians. All these outsiders (identified by their travel bags) were called Carpetbaggers and still are in many places. It became the term to refer to a Yankee who moved to the south and usually meant a "damn Yankee and one not to be trusted, a scoundrel". Probably the worst Carpetbaggers were the politicians who used their positions in the corrupt Reconstruction Government to enrich themselves through bribes, graft and other despicable acts at the expense of native Southerners.

Frankie's dad had shot one of these carpetbaggers during an altercation and was arraigned for it, but released by the court because the community was entirely behind his action which was considered acceptable.

This was the beginning of a friendship that would last a lifetime with Pete and Frank. Neither boy could begin to realize what the future had in store for them. They could only lead their daily lives taking what comes in this simple bayou back country. They did have to maintain what secrecy they could as the law of the delta country, prohibited any social contact between the races.

Even though Frank's dad was the manager of the plantation, he could lose his job if he did not follow the rules, which had been carefully laid down by the plantation owner. It was against the law for whites to have any social contact with blacks. This was normal in the south following the Civil War, as it was thought by the white leaders at this time that this was the only way to maintain order with the newly freed slaves. Current thinking among the white population was that any mixing of races would lead to social disruption. Also Negroes were not to be sent to school which was only for white children. There were no schools for Negros as they were considered an inferior race to whites. This idea was supported by the local clergy and most whites, at the time, in the country.

But there was another important element involved here, and that was the attitude of many whites who were afraid the negros would invade their segregated world and because blacks were willing to work for minimal wages, that they would steal the whites' jobs. The prejudice emanated from within all social levels of the white society.

Another problem was the lack of educational facilities for the negro population who were not permitted to go to school with whites. The only education they received was the little religious education that was available to them in their churches, which were segregated, too.

"Those frogs' legs were sure delicious. I just don't know if I've ever had anything any better. I'm going to have to tell my momma all about this" Frank said.

"Well, honey, be careful what you tell folks 'cause remember, you ain't supposed to be here with us"

"I won't tell anyone but my momma and daddy, and they will understand. So don't worry. I have to get along now and thanks again for a wonderful breakfast." Frank added.

Frank hurried home. He could not wait to tell his mom, of his new discovery and of his new found friend. His mom was in the garden, picking strawberries. "Hello Frankie, where have you been? We had to have breakfast without you"

"I found a new friend named Pete, who took me home to treat me to something really different, called fried frogs legs"

"That's French food that they eat in New Orleans, and also around here the negros eat it. Were you in a negro house?"

"Yeah, mom, and they were so welcoming."

"You know, that's against the rules don't you?" His mother asked." Your daddy could lose his job if the plantation owner found out and that is pretty serious. You just cannot see this boy, Pete, anymore. Do you hear?"

"Aw, mom, he's such a nice guy and his mom cooks the best fried frog's legs in the world."

"But, honey we're talking about your daddy's job. Do you know how important that is to us? Without that job, we would not be able to eat either. And we would be down there catching frogs for our meals, too."

Later that day Frank had an opportunity to talk with his father about the subject of socializing with negros. Frank's father was a very liberal person regarding the subject, but he did have to protect himself in a community that had very strong rules about mixing the races. He really could do little about it if he wanted to protect and maintain his own economic status. These rules dominated the community and made the development and integration of the races very difficult and almost impossible in the post-war south.

The two boys often went frog hunting together, these two boys from such different circumstances. It was unusual to see a white and black boy together in this highly segregated part of the country still recovering from the War Between the States that left the south in ruins and the large black population still in servitude. Though Emancipation was the law of the land, those former slaves had no education, were illiterate, had no money and generally worked as servants or sharecroppers on the plantations for meager subsistence wages. The owners provided them housing for which they charged them rent and then paid them so little that they never got out of debt and continued in poverty, without equality in the country for which the north had fought for equal status among all races.

There were no schools for black children, only black churches at this time. Black children worked in the fields like the adults and were required to do the same work as their elders but with less pay. It was still legal to sell black children to another plantation if their families got too far behind in their rent. Their former owners kept blacks illiterate so little had changed in the south since the war.

The two boys had developed a natural liking for one another even though the laws of the times in this place prohibited any social contact between the races.

"Don't you ever go to church?" Pete asked Frank.

"Heck, no," Frank answered. "My dad and me never go to church even though my momma does go once in a while, she says to keep up appearances, whatever that means."

"Our preacher says if you don't go to church, you're sure to go to hell. Don't you worry about going to hell?" Pete asked.

"That's silly," Frank answered, "my dad says so. He says you waste time going to church and praying to a God that does not exist. And he says, heaven and hell are what we make for ourselves right here on Earth as there is no heaven or hell, that's what my dad says"

"My preacher says the Bible says we have to go to church or else we sure will go to hell and burn forever, Pete added.

"The Bible says that it's alright to have slaves, too. What do you say to that?" Frank asked. "Dad says most preachers say that slavery is the word of God and that it is alright. What about that?"

"Well, I'll have to ask our preacher and see what he says, and he should know," Pete's voice raised up, "he should know."

"I know you can't read," Frank interjected, "but if you could read I could show you just what it says in the Bible about slavery being OK. As much as we both hate it and know it's wrong."

"Well, anyway, I have to get home." Frank added. "See you next week."

Frank's dad was called to the plantation owner's office. "You asked to see me Mr. Norman?" The windows of the small office were heavily draped even at mid day to keep the heat out, so a light was needed. There was a heavy ominous feeling in the darkened room. There was a large fan hanging from the ceiling with a cord to the hands of a black boy whose job was to keep the fan swinging to create air movement in the sweltering room.

"Yes, Russell. Sit down please. I've been wanting to talk to you for a long time and I'm sure you know what I'm talking about."

"I think I do but I'm not sure"

"Well, Russell, we've talked about this before. You know the rules of the corporation as well as I do. You have been doing a good job managing this plantation, but there is one thing I have told you before, and that is whites are not allowed to associate with the Negroes. I thought I made that clear."

"Mr. Franklin, I have told my family, many times what the rules are. And we do our best to follow them."

"But you know that your son Frank plays with that Negro boy Pete and that is just not allowable."

"They are just friends, and they think a lot of each other and after all, they're just little boys."

"Russell, don't you realize that we have to keep these Negroes in control? How can we do it if we allow our white children to play with their black children? It just will not work. It will destroy the discipline that is essential, if we're going to continue to run our business."

"The problem is, Mr. Norman, the Negro is still living the life of a slave. You know that, they do not get enough to eat, their housing is very primitive and their earnings are so meager that they cannot pay their rent. It is no wonder they are hard to control. I really feel very sorry for them."

"Russell, do you see this book? It is the holy Bible. I have heard you do not read it. However, if you did, you would know that the Lord God says that slavery is right. It is in Leviticus, and in other places in this holy Bible. These Negroes are slaves, or they ought to be and they would be if the damn Yankees hadn't overrun us."

"Well, Mr. Norman, the Negro is no longer a slave. It is the law of the land now. He has rights, just like the rest of us. And we've got to treat them like human beings."

"Don't you give me that stuff about human beings? Those Negroes are barely human. Look at the way they have kids-one after the other, and most of the kids don't even know who their father is. And look at the way they practice their voodoo and worship their savage gods. That is an abomination that no Christians will stand for. No, they are just slaves and savages and that is the way they are going to be forever no matter what the North says. In addition, you know what, the North needs our cotton believe me. They understand that these Negroes are essential to getting it picked. Therefore, law or no law, these Negroes are going to stay exactly where they are; out in the fields picking cotton, and nothing else. In addition, you are going to help me see to it. I hope I make myself perfectly clear. In addition, just because you do not go to church, and probably do not believe in the Bible either does not make you right. The government says we are supposed to have freedom of our religion, and that is what we have. Therefore, if you want to keep your job, you had better get your kid in line. And I suggest you start going to church, if you want to keep your job."

"I'll do my best, Mr. Norman, to follow the rules of the corporation. However, that does not mean that the corporation tells me how to live my life or what I am supposed to believe. There is also something called freedom from religion. We are all entitled to that and that is also the law of the land."

"Well, Russell. You can believe what you want, but you know what you have to do about your kid because that is the law around here. About going to church, that's your business, if you want to be a god damned atheist. You will just suffer eternal damnation and the fires of hell. I just feel sorry for you. You'll roast in hell. And I can just see God happy about all that."

Young Frank swung his house door open and seated himself at the kitchen table while his mother was busy at the stove. The fragrance of bacon frying and biscuits baking filled the air as she prepared breakfast.

"You been with Pete, again, Frank?" his mother asked. Without waiting for an answer she added, "You know your daddy has told you many times that you just can't do that. Do you understand?"

"I know, momma, but it don't hurt anyone. We were just jiggin' for frogs." He pleaded.

"Yes, but your father has strictly forbidden you to be with any Negro. In addition, you know why. It is the rule of the company that no whites associate with Negroes. Your father could lose his job." She pleaded. "If you don't mind me, I'll have to tell your father."

"Uh huh just one egg momma and could I have another glass of milk?" Frank was not a heavy eater. His slight frame and medium build was not that of an athlete but a student that he was.

"Here you are. Now, don't eat so fast."

"Mom," Frank asked, "do you think dad is right about the Bible sayin' slavery is alright? He told me it did but I have not actually seen it in the Book. Have you?"

"Yes, I have. It is in several places. Would you like to see it in writing? Wait a minute and I'll see if I can find the words." She went to the living room and found the Bible.

"Now, let's see, oh, here it is . . . . "Yes, I have it. It is in several places. Wait a minute and I will see if I can find the exact words. Here they are."

"As for your male and female slaves whom you may have; you may buy male and female slaves from among the nations that are round about you. You may also buy from among the strangers who sojourn with you and their families that are with you who have been born in your land; and they may be your property. You may bequeath them to your sons after you, to inherit as a possession forever; you may make slaves of them, but over your brethren the people of Israel you shall not rule, one over another, with harshness. LEVITICUS 25:44-46

"How come God would say that people can have slaves?" Frank asked. "Didn't the country just fight a war to stop slavery? How come the Bible still says that?

"You'll have to ask your father," his mother added, "when he gets home tonight. Meanwhile finish up and get up to your studies. But remember if your father catches you with a Negro, he'll be mad. Because he could lose his job with the company", his mother added. Frank finished his breakfast, put the Bible in his school bag with his books and went to his room to study.

The sound of horse hoofs were heard in the courtyard. Frank's father frequently supervised the plantation on horseback. Transportation by horse was at that time, the fastest way that man could get anywhere, as it had been for thousands of years. Slowly new forms of transportation, developed. Then, for many years, only the railroad was available. Then at the turn-of-the-century automobiles were invented and the world has never been the same.

Frank's father took the horse into the barn and unsaddled him; He filled his feed box and got water from the well. In those days, there was no running water, electricity, or central heating in homes. There were out houses instead of toilets. The world was so different in 1880 than it is today.

"Frank, your father is here. Why don't you ask him some of those questions?" His mother said.

His father always told him how important an education was and Frank listened carefully. He was very close to his dad. They often spoke of the problems of the south since the end of the civil war. Frank's dad never supported slavery and believed it was an abomination to civilization which was the belief of most of the founding fathers. He was often alone in his beliefs. Few in this society that had been raised with slavery felt that way. Therefore, he had to keep his thoughts to himself or risk reprisal and maybe even lose his managing job with the plantation.

"Son, you know how I feel about slavery and how I always believed that the Negros should be treated equally to whites but if I spoke out, I'd lose my job at the plantation. The owners do not feel as I and are only doing what was mandated by the Union Forces but not one bit more."

"I know dad. I know you're right, but what can we do about it?" Frank agreed.

"How come that the bible would say that people could have slaves?" Frank asked. "Didn't the government just fight a war to stop slavery? How come the Bible says that?"

"Well, son, there are a lot of inaccuracies in the bible. Remember it was written by numerous different people in different languages and at different times in history thousands of years ago by ignorant Arabs when most information was merely word of mouth and contained many inaccuracies. Many people do not believe in the accuracy of the Bible." He added. "And, there have been many translations of the Bible over the centuries so inaccuracies are bound to have accumulated. At best, the Bible is a history of sorts even though it's pretty inaccurate"

"Also, in those more primitive times, slavery was a norm in many societies. Whites were held as slaves, too. You remember the story of Spartacus the Greek slave. The world was emerging from a former savage state where the strong prevailed even if we consider it wrong today. Mores, traditions, and customs do change with time as mankind becomes more civilized. The bible has not changed. It continues to support philosophies that modern man has long since abandoned except for religious fundamentalists who say they believe every word of the bible which, of course, is ridiculous and only continues due to lack of education.

"Gosh, dad, I would think that would be a problem to all the people who go to church" Frank said.

"It sure is and the source of a lot of controversy and divisiveness," his dad added. "It's one of the important reasons why a lot of people just don't believe in all the mystical business that the churches teach. It's really the priests and pastors who keep it alive to serve their best interests so they can control others and fatten their coffers. So many of the stories and all the so-called miracles were simply invented by the priests and pastors to impress and put fear into the masses of uneducated believers, The mass of people still follow these ideas because they lack the education to rationalize and see reality and they are afraid of the unknown world of death."

"It is well documented that the priests developed machines secretly in their temples to impress the followers with magic that the priests said was divinely inspired. They were dealing with an uneducated, mostly illiterate superstitious populace who were easily influenced. The many so-called miracles were invented to create more magic in the universe. Not one of these miracles has ever been proven scientifically. It is said that one must have faith. It is only through having faith that one can be "saved" or so it goes. Just religious dogma and all untrue."

"Oh, dad, I want to ask you another question. You know I have a friend, Pete, who is a Negro and I know why you do not want me to see Negros but that is not my question. Is that the only reason we do not go to church or are there some others? Why don't we go to church like my friend, Pete?" Frank asked.

"Well, that is a longer story. Years ago, when I was a young man I read a book in the library by the great English scientist and author, Charles Darwin, who was one of the early discoverers of the theory of evolution, which explained where mankind came from. Science accepted this new theory but all the religions would not support the theory and many still do not. On further study, I concluded that the churches were wrong since what most religions were teaching was that a God formed all humanity all at once not through nature's natural workings of evolution. That God created man in his image was a completely wrong philosophy in the light of the scientific facts revealed by Darwin and numerous others. In fact, it was the other way around. Man created God in his image. The many fossils found throughout the world support Darwin's theory. Devine creation of mankind is simply unscientific foolishness perpetrated by the popes, pastors, and priests to maintain control of ignorant masses and, incidentally take their money."

"This whole subject fascinated me the more I read about the natural world. Thomas Huxley, another distinguished English author, also wrote extensively on the subject. I began to realize that religion was not the benign support of humankind but a source for hate and divisiveness in the world. Just about all the wars in the history of the world have been fought over religious differences. Then when you think of all the mayhem and murder that has gone on in the name of religion like the Spanish Inquisition and the burning of witches in Salem and many other examples of religious atrocities inciting cruelty to the people, it is very difficult to believe that religion can be something that helps people. In fact in my opinion, it is the worst idea of man"

"Anyway, after much study and thought I felt that religion was not a good idea for humanity. I moved eventually from that to my present position as an atheist. I do not believe in God or the hereafter. It makes no logical sense, so we do not go to church"

"Dad, does that mean I'm an atheist, too," Frank asked.

"Really, you have to make up your own mind. Everyone does but the facts seem obvious to me and at least I would say that church is a waste of time better spent in study of science, nature, and the natural world. Education is really the answer. Too many people have no education and blindly follow what they're told either by equally uneducated parents or by self-serving priests and pastors."

Frank's dad always seemed to have sensible answers.

"Why do so many people believe in going to church, and that God exists?" Frankie asked his dad.

"The answer to that really goes back a long way in history, son. Far back to the dawn of humankind, the powerful forces of nature, intimidated the early inhabitants on earth when the races called human first became aware of their environment. It was easy to believe that there was an unknown force in the heavens that created the lightning, storms, and the rains and floods. Primitive man invented gods hopefully for protection. Some of the leaders realized that they could gain power over others if they told the masses that they represented God's power on earth. Thus was born, the priesthood who has invented all the myths and false idols down through history none of which has ever been proven.

Over the centuries, there have been many gods. Certainly, there were hundreds of them in the various developing civilizations and many forgotten religions. The Greeks and the Romans all had multiple gods, each in charge of a particular problem of humanity. The priests held enormous power over their fellow man and churches continued to grow throughout the world. Just about every civilization has a culture of religion, and up until recently, if one did not follow a religion, they were outcasts in the community. The punishment was severe and frequently death. Even today in some countries the ruling religion prescribes death for dis-believers.

The idea of religion became an all-powerful institution throughout humankind's development. In addition, today still it is practiced by the majority of people, especially those with limited education. Things are changing; however, as we learn more about the true science of the world, we are beginning to learn about such forces as electricity as Benjamin Franklin was able to demonstrate with his kite flying experiment. I am sure in the future, we will add to this knowledge as science pushes back the curtains of ignorance.

Later that day after dinner, Frank went to the little house where Pete lived. "Hey, Pete, I have something to show you. Take a look at this here in the Bible. I know you can't read so I'll read it for you" Frank read the passage from Leviticus.

Pete could not believe it but he asked, "Could I borrow that book? I want to show it to my preacher." He asked. "In fact maybe you could come with me now and we'll go see him.

Pete could barely wait to get to the church. Their step quickened as they approached the steepled edifice. The door was partially open so they went in. The Reverend happened to be in. Pete and Frank presented the Bible quote from Leviticus.

"Well, Reverend, did you know that?" Pete asked.

"Yes, I did. Many people of faith do not believe that the Bible is always truthful. Others believe that every word in the Bible is accurate. There are many places where the Bible contradicts itself. Nevertheless, you can still have your faith even if you do not believe in every word in the Bible. The important thing is what can your faith do for you?

"I was trained as a minister at New York Seminary. After the war, when we graduated, we were trained by the government to come here to the south and help with the reconstruction. I was sent to New Orleans and finally here to Yazoo City to lead this parish and also to start schools for the Negros to teach them how to read"

"Can I learn to read?" Pete asked unbelieving.

"Sure you can. I am starting a class here at the church next Monday morning and you are invited," the minister offered.

"Oh, wonderful, I just can't wait, Reverend. I'll be there," Pete exclaimed with obvious joy.

Well, Pete was at the class every meeting he could be even at the expense of his work. He had to miss some hours but his dad covered for him because reading meant that for the first time in the history of their family someone was getting an opportunity to learn to read.

Days came and went in their world with little of consequence happening until one day; Frank's father came home early from his office with an ashen skin and pounding in his chest. He fell on the couch and within minutes was dead.

CHAPTER 2

The Facts of Life

Frank's world changed quickly. Though he was only 9 years old, he had to go to work to help his mother raise the family and help make ends meet. Frank was the oldest of four children. Between their two small incomes, and the help from his maternal grandfather, Dr James Green, a surgeon, from Leesburg, Florida, they were able to survive in a south that was in deep depression.

Frank's first job at age nine was helping to clean a local drugstore after school. He found he liked the store and became a favorite of the owner who soon promoted him to tending the fountain. Frank read as much as he could find on drug formulations and was eventually helping the owner compounding prescriptions. He had become a druggist through recognizing an opportunity and then working hard to learn the prescription business. Most professions in those early days had few academic requirements. Even medicine was practiced without a formal medical school degree. People learned their professional skills by working under an established practitioner.

At first, there was little time for anything but work. Frank's best friend was still Pete. Initially, Frank kept this completely to himself, but he soon found that the storeowner, John Morton, was unlike the plantation owners as he recognized that slavery was wrong and the blacks had been downtrodden in a cruel system that had to be stopped. However, he, too, had to keep his thoughts to himself or he really would not have a business. Southerners generally felt strongly about suppressing the black's new freedom and did not support it.

"Mr. Morton, I have a Negro friend, Pete, who needs a job. Could we use him to work in the store?" Frank asked. "He's real smart and I know he will work hard because he wants to get ahead in the world"

"Well, have him come in so I can talk to him," Mr Morton replied.

After work, Frank went to Pete's house. "Hey, Pete, I have what I think is some pretty good news for you. You know I've been working in a drugstore and the owner, Mr. Morton, says he might be interested in hiring you to help in the store, too."

"You really mean that I could maybe work in a white store?" Pete was incredulous. "I don't think no Negro could ever work in no white store."

However, Frank was convincing and Pete decided to go talk to Mr. Morton. He came to the store the following day. "Mr. Morton, Frank told me you might need some help around the store and I need a job. I am a hard worker. I will do any kind of work. I promise."

"Have you ever worked in a store before?" Mr. Morton asked.

"No, sir, but you can ask Frank, I learn fast and I'll do anything you ask just give me a chance."

"Okay, Pete, you have a trial job. Are you ready to start tomorrow?"

That started Pete on the long journey to an education. Frank helped him to learn to read in the evenings, Pete learned quickly and soon became a valuable addition in Mr. Morton's help in the store.

"Pete, do you know why I spend so much time at the library? Well, I have been doing some research on the subject of the races, especially here in the South, where the black race is relegated to an inferior position."

"Yes I know that, Frankie, and I've talked about it to my momma and daddy. They are really amazed that any white person would give a hoot about any black person."

"I don't blame them with a history that we see here for so many years of subjugation, but it should not have been like that. I'll give you an example; you know that in the Declaration of Independence in the original draft written by Thomas Jefferson in 1775 that he had a whole paragraph about how evil slavery was and how it should be done away with in the new United States, where everyone is "created equal.""

"Here's the original quotation that was in Thomas Jefferson's first draft, and which was deleted by the Continental Congress, because they were afraid that the Carolinas, would not go along with this language."

Here is the quote

> "He (Referring to King George) has waged cruel war against human nature itself, violating its most sacred rights of life and liberty in the persons of a distant people who never offended him, captivating and carrying them into slavery in another hemisphere, or to incur miserable death in their transportation thither. This piratical warfare, the opprobrium of infidel's powers, is for the warfare of the Christian king of Great Britain. He has prostituted his negative for suppressing every legislative attempt to prohibit or to restrain this execrable commerce determining to keep open a market where men should be bought and sold: and that this assemblage of horrors might want no fact of distinguished die, he is now exciting those very people to rise in arms among us, and to purchase that liberty of which he has deprived them, by murdering the people upon whom he also obtruded them: thus paying off former crimes committed against the liberties of one people, with crimes which he urges them to commit against the lives of another"

Not only Jefferson believed that slavery was an evil, but there are many followers of this idea, especially in the north. Subsequently, the North did away with slavery, and of course, it took a civil war to get rid of it in the South.

"The religions don't help. Even the bible says that slavery is allowed. Did you know that?" Frank asked.

"No, I'll have to ask our preacher."

"And now we still have the black race held in virtual slavery by not allowing universal education for everyone. There must be schools for blacks, and we must do away with illiteracy everywhere. To not do so is a disgrace for our civilization that fought so hard for freedoms for everyone."

"How are we going to get that done?" Pete asked. "Just about every Negro, I know, would love to go to school. But the whites don't want that and they think that we are inferior. How do you say, naturally, I think is a word which they use. I'm not sure if I understand exactly what that means, but I'm sure it has to do with the way things are in our world."

"Yes, it's certainly does. One of the things I intend to do in my lifetime is get the message out to as many people as I can that we are all equal and should all be treated the same as well as receiving the same opportunities for education and making a living. I know that during the past few years that some schools for blacks have opened."

"Yeah, but it is not enough we still can't go to school here in the south. That's what I want to do".

"I have a grandfather, who is a doctor and he has offered to help me go to medical school. I think I'm going to do it. So wish me luck."

Frank continued to help Pete in his reading.

After several years, Pete came to Mr. Morton. "Mr. Morton, you have been very good to me and have taught me about compounding. I want to do something with this knowledge and have investigated the US Army that has a special school for qualified black applicants to enter a black unit in the medical corps," Pete explained.

'I want to join as this would give me a chance to further increase my education." Pete said.

So Pete joined the army special unit for blacks and became a medical field orderly. WW I had started and Pete was transferred to France where he rescued and treated wounded soldiers. Frank was unable to join the forces as he had extremely bad eyes and needed heavy glasses

The Great War, as it became known, was largely fought in the trenches and Pete was called upon daily to work with wounded soldiers many of whom died in his arms.

One casualty turned out to be a man who felt such indebtedness to Pete that he offered to help Pete in his further medical education. After the war, Pete went back to finish his undergraduate education and ultimately graduated from Tuskegee Institute with a doctorate degree in medicine. He was eventually accepted in the internship program of Belleview Hospital in New York for surgical training in the Lying—In division.

CHAPTER 3

Frank Develops His
First Drugstore

Frank did well in Mr. Morton's drugstore. The owner eventually wanted to retire so he offered Frank a partnership. Frank finally bought out Mr. Morton's share leaving Frank owner of his first business with a silent partner, Ernest Berger.

This opened a completely new life for Frank. At last, he had his own business and because of his hard work, it prospered. Frank married a childhood sweetheart but in their first year of marriage, she developed tuberculosis.

"I think the only answer is for my wife and me to move to Colorado, where the climate is very dry," Frank confided with a friend, Ernest Berger.

"But what about our business?" Berger asked.

"I will just have to sell my share. I really don't know any other way. Sad as it is." Frank sold his share in the drugstore to Berger.

He packed up and Frank and his ill wife took the train to Denver. He found a drugstore to buy in Fort Collins, so they decided to move there.

Frank made an agreement with a drugstore owner in Fort Collins, allowing him to lease the store on a trial basis with the idea that he would eventually buy it. His ill wife, however, continued to deteriorate and within a year she was dead. She is buried in Fort Collins.

Frank terminated his drug store lease/purchase arrangement and moved back to Tampa where he called his friend Ernest and had a talk about what he wanted to do in the future.

Tampa was growing rapidly and was not so dependent on plantations and cotton growing so the black population was smaller and had started to become more integrated which was far different from the south Frank left behind in Yazoo City. Frank liked Tampa. Frank, like his father, could not abide the subjugation of the black race, which was still so prevalent in most of the South.

"They are human just like we are and should not be treated like animals," he told his close friend, Ernest. Ernest and Frank saw eye to eye on this subject like no other. Both realized fully the horror of slavery and even though the Civil War had abolished it legally, the black population of the South continued, still in practical bondage. Jim Crow laws mounted regularly.

Frank needed a business and the only one he knew was the drugstore business so he looked for one to buy and found one that he renamed, The Economical Drugstore. He always said he owned one of the early discount drugstores in the nation long before it had become so standard in that industry.

He merged with Earnest Berger giving Frank a second store with Berger as his partner. His commercial interest boomed and Frank began to gain a level of financial independence that he never dreamed possible.

Frank's grandfather, Dr James Green, the father of his mother, was a surgeon in Leesburg, Florida. Frank visited him often and became very interested in the study of medicine.

"Frank, it is so good to have you here in Florida. Your mother has been telling me about your progress in the drug business in Tampa. We are all so proud of you."

"Yes grandpa, I really have been very fortunate both to get into a field where I can help others by providing prescriptions and where I can make a good living as well." Frank added.

"Have you seen your mother recently? I understand she has not been well." Grandpa said.

"No, it has been a year since mother visited me in Tampa. I have asked her to come to live with me but she really wants to stay in Yazoo city at least for now." Frank added.

"With your interest in helping others, are you still considering a medical education?" Grandpa asked.

"Well, you know, I have. I have given it serious thought over the recent years." Frank added.

This was a subject Frank really had thought a lot about. He knew that his friend Pete had returned from the war and had gone to medical school but they had been out of touch. It did inspire him however as medicine seemed to Frank the very best way that one could contribute to society.

He was restless anyway and decided that he would go to medical school. He sold out his store interest to Berger and enrolled at The University of Tennessee Medical School in Memphis. In those days, an undergraduate degree was not required for admission. Frank was really self educated as he followed a heavy reading program. Frank bought a bicycle and rode to Memphis where there was a medical school that his grandfather had attended. He passed the entry exams for medical school easily.

CHAPTER 4

Frank Goes To
Medical School

D r Green, Frank's maternal grandfather, had graduated from The
University of Tennessee in Memphis so Frank applied there and
was accepted for the class to graduate in 1917.

He moved to Memphis and found a rooming house with someone named
Carltharp looking for a roommate who was only in college because his
father insisted he go. Carltharp was not a good student, Dad always told
us, and was always trying to skim by with a minimum of effort. Dad,
on the other hand was a very serious student who wanted very much to
succeed and graduate as a doctor. Carltharp failed and flunked out after
his freshman year. Dad told us this story often to reinforce his advice to
work hard and do your best in school.

Frank's basic interest was surgery. Every class choice he could make
that involved him with surgery. He also studied obstetrics. So, when he
graduated he was on his way to becoming a surgeon and obstetrician.
While in medical school, Frank was already beginning to gain a reputation
for helping others.

"Frank, there is a little Negro boy here asking for you."

"What does he want?"

"I don't know. I'll send him to talk to you."

"Thanks"

"Mr. Dr. Russell, I heard you helped black people out. Well, we have a problem. It is really my mama's problem."

"What is the problem?"

"Well, momma is having a baby and she jes don't know what to do. She's hurtin. We heard you have been very helpful to us Negroes, and we sure need help now."

"I'll do what I can. Where is your momma?"

"She's home, can you come real quick?"

"Sure, my roommate's horse is downstairs in the barn. He'll let me use it. Let's go." Frank mounted up together with the black boy sitting behind holding on for dear life.

The rain was coming down in buckets so the mud road was almost impossible to negotiate. They followed it towards West Memphis, into an area where only blacks lived.

"It's the house over there, Mr Dr. Russell, but we got to hurry."

The building was typical of Negro housing in that area. It was very run down, with no indoor facilities of any kind. The child and Frank went to the door, and were quickly at the woman's bedside.

She was the last stages of labor. Frank quickly appraised the situation and took over.

"Breathe deeply and push, he said even though it hurts. You got to give that little baby all the help he can get. Okay, deep breath, and push, push. Son, see if you can get me a basin of hot water and some toweling"

"Oh, oh, I feel it . . . . there it is." In moments, the newborn breech baby slipped into the Frank's waiting hands. It was a perfect child, dripping, gleaming black and ready for the world no matter what. Frank performed the regular post-delivery procedures.

"Now, you'll have to rest. Is there anyone here to take care of you?" Frank asked.

"No, no one just my little son here. He'll have to do."

"Who lives next door?"

"Yes, it's Mrs. James. Son, go get her." The little boy was out of the room and soon returned with Mrs. James.

"Oh, Lordy. Did you expect to do this all by yourself? Here give me that baby," as she quickly cleaned it and wrapped it ready for her mother's milk.

"Couldn't you find a local doctor here?" Frank asked.

"No, we ain't got no doctors here that takes care of us Negroes, and the only hospital here is for whites only. So, we just had to make do. We're so thankful that you could come. We heard about you and you sure are a blessing to us Negroes."

"Well, I'm happy to have been able to come and be a help to you. After you get rested, you may need some more assistance and your son knows where to find me."

Although Frank's first interest was surgery, he also studied and became qualified and licensed both as a general surgeon and an obstetrician.

After Frank graduated, he sought an internship. He knew he wanted to do it in a big city where he could get maximum experience.

Frank also had lived with the intense separation of the races in the South and had heard a lot about the North offering a much higher degree of equality to all races. Especially in New York City, where so many immigrants were arriving daily from all over the world to seek new opportunities in America. It really appealed to him and he looked for further training in this northern city.

Also his cousin, Henry Peers had moved with his wife, Emily, to New York City and had become a broker on the cotton exchange on Wall Street. Henry had told Frank how wonderful the opportunities were in the city and urged him to move there.

Frank graduated high in his class in 1917 and was accepted in a surgical internship at Bellevue Hospital in New York City.

He had always hated the way the south had treated its black people and wanted to leave the south for what he considered the more liberal north.

CHAPTER 5

Bellevue Hospital

For someone from a tiny southern village still functioning as if the world had stopped at the Civil War to experience New York City was a true cultural shock to Frank. He was astounded and at the same time delighted with the energy and optimism, he felt all around him.

He matriculated first in surgery and then in obstetrics so he was qualified eventually to practice in both disciplines when he completed his internship.

In one of his first classes at Bellevue, Frank thought he recognized someone and to his surprise, it was Pete Bean from Yazoo City, his black childhood friend.

Frank could hardly contain himself. "Is that you Pete?" Pete looked up in utter surprise.

"Frank, I can't believe it's you. I thought you were in the drug business in Tampa."

"I was for years and happily too but eventually I realized my real dream was to get into medicine." Frank explained "But how did you get here?" Frank asked.

"While I was a medical orderly in the war, I patched up a fella who was really in big trouble. He had been seriously hit by a piece of shrapnel. It turned out that he was a really wonderful man who very much appreciated what I had done for him. He learned of my interest in medicine so he offered to help me with what I do today. Further schooling if I wanted and of course, that was a marvelous opportunity, which I took", Pete explained.

"My early work compounding prescriptions in a drugstore and then being a medical orderly during the war really convinced me that medicine would be an ideal career for me to follow. Now that I had the possibility of someone to help me with the financing, I just had to go ahead. So I enrolled and then graduated from Tuskegee and came here for the surgical internship and residency."

"Pete, how lucky we are both ending up in medicine and in the same training program. It is amazing and how coincidental. I remember so often how we used to hunt frogs together when we first met and blacks and whites were not allowed to associate with each other. Your mother cooked me my first fried frogs legs and here we are now are in the same medical intern training class." Frank enthused.

"Yes, it is pretty wonderful. I guess you haven't heard, but my dad was shot dead by the plantation owner because he said dad was stealing something. Mother died of a broken heart. So I'm all alone. The plantation owner wasn't even punished after they discovered that it was somebody else, not my father, who did the stealing. It's typical of what goes on down there." The way the South treats the Negro is just not acceptable. The south still has not gotten over the civil war.

"Well, you're in the north now and things will be different." Frank offered.

"Yes, I've learned a lot by getting an education and one of the things that I'm sure will make you happy, I no longer attend church. It has finally entered my thick skull after being exposed to science for so many years that most of the things that are taught by the preachers are aimed at ignorant people without the opportunity that I had. It seemed so obvious, too, that the myths that the parsons teach really are Middle Ages inventions to allow the priests to dominate the uneducated masses while we're here now in the 20th century where we believe in science not myth and freedom for all without the oppression of the slavery of religion. The earth really isn't flat and the sun does not revolve around the earth. I will be forever grateful to you for getting me started down the right track."

Frank and Pete were almost inseparable as they worked practically day and night in the internship program where they both had an opportunity to see more serious medical problems in one month than they might have seen in a year in a smaller community because New York City has such a vast indigent population in need of medical care. Bellevue being a large city institution was very busy especially taking care of the newly arriving rapidly growing immigrant population.

"What are you going to do when you finish training?" Asked Pete.

"Well, Pete, this time that I have spent up north has really opened my eyes about how people of different backgrounds can get along." Frank said. "New York is a melting pot you know with people coming from every corner of the world and in every color, race, and religion. They all seem to manage to get along on this small island and even though there is some discrimination it's more that of ability and education than skin color or ethnicity, it seems to me."

"Yes, I have been aware of that. New York is so different from Yazoo City in so many ways. Here at the hospital they even let me sit at the same dining tables with whites. I could never do that in Yazoo even today." He explained. "We can't even drink from the same water fountain. Here in New York I am just another human being."

"It is true, this is a much more open and reasonable society. It's the way the South ought to be but it really isn't even though that terrible civil war was fought to offer some kind of equality among the races." Frank added.

"What are you going to do when you finish your internship?" Frank asked.

"Well, I'm torn between staying up north in this mostly free society or doing something for my people in the South where it really needs to be done. I'm thinking seriously about going back to Yazoo or someplace in that Mississippi Delta area and bringing medical care to my people. You know, they get very little care now and most die of the simplest illnesses that could have been easily cured if they had been treated early enough."

"I just knew you would say that," Frank offered. "The South needs you." Pete moved south, married and raised a family.

CHAPTER 6

Frank Develops a New York City Medical Practice

On completion of the internship program at Bellevue, Frank opened a surgical practice with offices at 219 West 44th street, New York City in the Astor Hotel annex. Dad eventually bought the annex building. Pete returned to Yazoo to be a physician to poor plantation blacks who needed medical care.

Frank's office was on Schubert's Alley in a brownstone attached to the Astor Hotel on Times Square. He lived in an apartment on the second floor with his office downstairs. In addition to a private practice, Frank was house surgeon for the Astor. The Astor was one of the best hotels in New York, if not, in the country and attracted many of the theatrical stars as they toured through the city as it was in the heart of the theatre district on Times Square.

Dad soon developed a busy practice in New York's theater district with members of the stage. Included as his many celebrity patients were Jimmy Durante, Gloria Swanson, George Burns, and Jack Dempsey, among many other show business and sports celebrities that I met as a young boy. My dad had become the theatre district's "show people's doctor".

One especially, was Charlotte McCoy, a young operatic contralto from Ohio a featured soloist at Carnegie Hall at the time and staying at the Astor. They met when she required medical attention. It was love at first sight and although he was 20 years older than she was, they married in 1923. They lived in the two floors above Frank's office on 44th Street in the brownstone over-looking Schubert's Alley as their first residence and started raising a family. I was born in Polyclinic Hospital in 1925.

Dad was on the surgical staffs of several New York Hospitals including Polyclinic, Bellevue, Lying-In, and NY City, with a busy surgical practice.

Life was good. Mother was still singing professionally throughout the East and in Hollywood where she sang with Lawrence Tibbett in the Hollywood Bowl. Sid Grauman of theatre fame was her accompanist when she sang in California. Frank Laforge was her voice coach. Star, Magel Norman was her friend and roommate in Hollywood. She even made a movie with Douglas Fairbanks, though her heart was with her husband in New York. She wanted a family, so she gave up the professional concert artist's life, and in 1925, bore a boy, William, (me) named after her father, William Wallace McCoy, a manufacturer and inventor who owned a shoe factory first in Cincinnati and later in Boston. Grandpa McCoy was the inventor of the Arch Preserver Shoe that he licensed out to others manufacturing shoes under the Red Cross patents which he owned and successfully licensed to several shoe manufacturing and marketing companies.

A second son, Frank Junior, was born in 1928.

Living in the Astor Annex, which was originally the home of the Astor's owner, Mushingheim, was exciting for the family and especially for us adventurous boys.

There it was at the end of the hall a doorway where Nana, our maid, placed our daily trash for pick-up. I had to pass the mysterious door every day and read the sign on it that read, "Caution Do Not Open except in Emergencies." It was merely an irresistible invitation as far as I was concerned and impossible for me to ignore. Mother had explained that it was there for use only in event of a fire and to stay away from it. To a six year old, that door was my center of mystery. Where did it go? What would happen if I opened it? What strange worlds may be behind that door?

One day an employee from the hotel was performing his duties, which included opening the door behind which he disappeared not to be seen again. I tried to be patient as I waited his re-appearance but to no avail. I tried the door handle with quivering hand. It turned slowly and I found it was not locked. I timidly opened the door to reveal a long darkened corridor. This was an emergency for me. A curiosity emergency that demanded satisfaction.

The door swung open and I stepped across the threshold into a darkened hall. Just being there thrilled me. I could tell as the hairs on my neck were standing straight up and I had goose bumps all over. The door slowly swung closed behind me and I was alone shrouded in an eerie silence that entirely enveloped me. Dim lighting came from skylights above that allowed me to barely see I was in a hallway from which there were several doors all closed to my inquisitive eyes.

Did I dare to open one of the doors?

I gathered my courage and slowly turned the knob of the first door. It turned with surprising ease and as it opened, a stairway was before me. The odor of food cooking filled the air. I descended the stairs into another huge room with bright red tapestries on the windows, filled with tables set with placements for a large group of diners and I was suddenly aware that I was not alone and that there were several men in waiters costume putting the final changes on the places at the tables. I was in the main ballroom of the Astor Hotel. They hurried from the main room through swinging doors returning with trays of water pitchers." It sure smells good." I wielded around and found my little brother Frankie behind me munching on a hard roll. He had somehow followed me.

"Shhh! someone will hear us" I warned, as we crouched under the white tablecloths. "Let's see what's behind those swinging doors."

"I'm scared." Frankie whispered, "we better get home"

"No, I want to see what's behind those doors", my bravado falsely speaking for me. "Follow me."

The swinging doors gave way before us and we were suddenly in the largest kitchen I had ever seen. It was full of busy people hardly noticing our intrusion.

"Hey! Look who's here? A couple of kids in their pajamas" roared a voice from under a tall white hat. He was a burly man. He looked like one of the men who delivered meals to the apartment where we lived. "What are you kids doing here?"

"Now we're go'na' get it." Frankie wailed and turned to run.

"Wait." I urged. "We're just from down the hall where we live." I tried to muster as much confidence as I could. "It sure smells good in here. What are you cooking?"

Who must have been the head man came over and took my hand. "You want to see how we cut up a pig?"

"Yeah", I tried to disguise my fright.

"OK, come with me" by now Frankie was by my side clutching my night shirt. "Tonight we're serving roast pork and the pigs have to be prepared and cooked. "Stand over there." He beckoned, "and don't get in the way." We did not need to be told twice.

The big man took a long knife and approached a pig hung above. So quickly he worked the knife through the flesh. Soon the whole pig was in parts and arranged on large cooking platters, which were soon put into giant ovens.

Then another man approached. "C'mon with me" such noise in the room made it hard to hear but we followed.

Here's where we prepare the vegetables. There were potatoes, carrots, salads, just too much to remember. There was even a large live turtle which was to be turtle soup. A small army of helpers rushed about each working at their assigned tasks and from this maze, meals were built.

There were racks upon racks of rolls, different varieties of bread and large cauldrons of soup. It was a food factory in every sense of the word but so wonderfully smelling, I would love to work here.

"You kids hungry?" our guide asked.

"Uh, no, but thanks anyway. I think we'd better get home"

"Here, try this." He handed me a small dark roll of shiny flesh that smelled of butter and garlic. He plopped it in my opened mouth.

"Did you like it?"

"Yeah, yeah, what was it?"

"A snail?" I couldn't believe it. Did I eat a snail? "Do you want one, Frankie?"

"Uh, no, no" He made a face.

"OK. How did you get here?" the big man asked.

"Through that door from the big room with all the tables."

"Joe! Take these kids back to the ballroom and find out where they came from. And, hey, kids, come back again when I have some time to show you around." He went back to work with his large knife.

We were soon back at the door marked CAUTION and back in our home having learned a lot about the huge kitchens needed to supply the Astor Hotel.

And I like snails. I guess I'll have to go back to that food factory.

Imagine that?

The next big question was should we tell our parents of our adventure? We decided not to tell them as we wanted to return to those exciting rooms behind that door someday and knew if we told, we'd be stopped. It was just too exciting.

Since my brother and I could look out our window to Schubert's Alley just below, we often found ourselves at the window when we were supposed to be sleeping, watching the theater crowds in the alley at intermission. It was a noisy busy scene with a lot of people, men dressed in tuxedos and women in long dresses. We both wondered what everyone was doing there until our mother told us that they were attending a theatrical play on the Schubert Theatre stage. It all sounded very exciting.

One night we decided to find out about what a play was so we sneaked down the rear stairs from our maid's room which emptied out on the alley. Just across was another door marked "Stage Door" That sounded interesting so we headed for it. When we entered there was an old man behind a big window sitting at a high desk. We ducked down below the window and went into the next room that was filled with numerous people mostly women dressed in all sorts of scanty costumes like bathing suits with feathers.

"Hey, look who's here. Two kids in their pajamas," one of the women with not much on screamed. Immediately we were surrounded by a bunch of women all asking questions. One of them seemed to be the head one.

"Where did you kids come from?" she asked. What's your name?"

"I'm Billy Russell and this is my brother, Frankie." I must admit I was scared.

"Is your dad the doctor across the alley?" one asked.

"Yes"

"They're Dr Russell's boys. I know him. He's the main doctor in the neighborhood. Everyone loves him. Do your parents know where you are?"

"Nope."

"Well, have you ever been in a theatre before?"

"I have," I answered, "but Frankie hasn't. I had seen my mother singing here in the city at Carnegie Hall.

"What theatre?"

"Carnegie Hall is where my mother sings."

"Really? Does she sing a lot?" she asked.

"Yes, dad and I love to hear her sing. She sang much more all over the country before she married my dad."

"Well you are lucky boys. Would you like to look around this theatre before we take you home?"

"We sure would. That would be great."

So the lady who knew our dad gave us a tour. It was a big space with several stages back behind one another. Our guide told us that this was so that scenes could be changed quickly. Then another lady asked if we would like some ice cream. Well we would but we thought we'd better get home before we were missed. The same lady took us home. She took us in our front door to dad's reception room where she used the phone to announce our presence. Our dad came down and, of course, was not too happy but he thanked our new friend and finally after giving us a talking to, got us back into bed. That was an adventure of a lifetime I have often thought about.

Life in our Astor Hotel annex was really ideal. We had our family privacy yet many of the services of the large hotel. That included ready cooked meals served when we wanted. Though we really liked mother's cooking the best, we took what was presented. And mother and dad liked the hotel food very much.

"Are you ready to go Billy boy?" dad asked.

"Are we going on house calls again? I like to do that" I answered. Dad frequently made house calls in those days. Occasionally he asked me to go along and I was always happy to do so. About twice a week, he went out on what he used to call pro bono calls. These were usually in the lower East side of New York where people lived in very crowded conditions. Sometimes two or three families lived in a single room and the only bathroom might be on the next floor and shared by numerous families. The buildings always had the smell of food cooking and other smells that were not so nice.

The people were always very happy to see my dad. And he said that this was one of the most important parts of his practice and really the main reason he went into medicine to help people who really needed help. One time I saw a baby born that my dad delivered.

He always introduced me as his assistant doctor which made me very proud because in those days that's all I thought about was being a doctor like my dad which continued for most of my young life up until the time I met Joanne, my future wife. I think she was the one that most influenced me about changing from medicine into some other field. I look back on that decision now and realize what a good life I've had and I'm glad I made that decision. Nevertheless, I can't help a little secret feeling of envy of my brother, Frank, who did make the decision to go into medicine. Certainly it is the best way I can think of to be helpful to those in greatest need. But I have had a perfect life with world travel as well as living and working abroad in France and England and lots of adventure so I am very happy with my decision and have no regrets.

Those calls to the slums of New York which in the late 20s and early 30s were in the depths of the great depression were a real education to me. I was able to see how fortunate I was to live such a comfortable life provided by our dad compared to the underprivileged children I met in those squalid circumstances.

CHAPTER 7

The Country Life in Riverdale

I t was soon obvious to father and mother that living in a less citified environment would be more conducive to us boys' healthful growth so they bought a house on the Dodge Estate in Riverdale at 242nd street.

The 1929 crash hit and money became very short. My dad's cousin, Henry Peers, whom we all called, Uncle Henry, met with financial disaster in the stock market where he was a broker and moved in with us in Riverdale with his wife, Emily, and children Bob, Marjorie, and Jacqueline from their former beautiful River Side Drive Manhattan apartment. We were lucky to have a very big house so there was plenty of room for all.

A daughter was born to mother in 1930. So, there were now three children in the family. Frankie and I had a new sister, Eleanor. We are still very close, I am happy to say and we are all well into our eighties.

Living in Riverdale was a real treat for us after being raised in Manhattan. We had a big yard on the estate and some of the most beautiful old trees one could imagine. This was originally an estate owned by the Dodge family of automobile fame. There was their huge mansion down on a bluff over-looking the Hudson River, which was the original Dodge family home. The Dodges started the car company by that name. Over the years, houses have been built on the property and sold individually. It was a private gated enclosure so we didn't have traffic to be worried about. As a result, we kids could wander freely everywhere in the beautiful surrounding forest. Even though it was only 30 minutes to Times Square where Dad kept his office, we lived a true rural life.

One of the great places to go was down to the Hudson River. The estate was built on a high bluff overlooking the river. Below us where the tracks of the New York Central Railroad following the river to Albany. We couldn't get down to the tracks as it was a very steep bluff but the view was wonderful. The river held interesting traffic with many barges loaded with all sorts of cargo.

Along the Hudson river banks right into Manhattan, there were many hundreds of shanties lived in by homeless families suffering from the Great Depression that was going on at that time. We were so fortunate with dad's busy practice, that we did not feel the effects of the sick economy. There always seemed to be a need for a doctor and some even paid their medical bills mother said.

This is my first experience also out in winter snows. One of dad's patients gave me a ski set, my first, so I started skiing at about age six or seven or so. It was a sport I was to perform actively all my life. Those first days in the snow I wandered through the beautiful forests near our house which was so quiet compared to the city. It's when I first learned about the beauties of cross-country skiing and I was so grateful for the opportunity. Cross-country skiing, and using skins for climbing has always been my first love. Fortunately Joanne liked this, as much as I and we have had an opportunity to do a lot of it especially when we lived in Europe.

One of the negative things I remember about our house in Riverdale was the way it was heated, by coal. Twice a day, it was my job to go to the basement and shovel coal into the furnace and then also take out the ashes and clinkers. It was a big and dirty job, but it had to be done. One of the things you have to do if you live in your own house, I learned. So living in the city was not all bad.

CHAPTER 8

Move to Central Park West

B y 1934, it became increasingly obvious to dad that the distance from Riverdale to the Manhattan Hospitals and his office made it very difficult for him to get home at reasonable hours, so the decision was made to move back into the city, which we did to Central Park West at 1 West 85th Street right on Central Park. Being at Central Park West, opened up the whole of Central Park as a personal playground right across the street so being back in the city was not so bad. Mother especially liked it because of her love of the theatre.

One of the wonderful things about living on Central Park West was the park right across the street. We children initially missed the country side in Riverdale which is truly wild by comparison with the park, but we soon learned to use the park. One of the exciting things to us at that time was kite flying. I think this is what spurred my initial interest in flying which exists to this day. I eventually learned to fly getting my pilot's license and obtained an instrument qualification. Flying a kite involved more than just putting something up into the sky. With a little imagination, there are all sorts of things that could be done. For example my brother and I would each have flight competition between each other. He had his kite and I had mine and we did battle.

Roller skating is another wonderful thing to do in central park where there are endless miles of perfect lanes and byways that are easy to skate on and they roll up and down gently enough so they all can be handled rather easily. Our biggest problems were skate wheels. We were always worrying about them. We skated so much we got to be very good at repairing and replacing roller skate wheels.

The next thing that was wonderful about Central Park West was every Thanksgiving Day Macy's held their Parade which started someplace north from where we lived at 85th St. and traversed all way down to the Macy's store at Herald Square. Since our apartment was on the fourth floor and had, little balconies we could open the windows, sit on the balconies, and practically touch the big balloons as they went by right in front of us on the street below. Mother always held a party on that day so her friends could comfortably enjoy the parade and we all had a marvelous time. We also ice skated on the big park ponds which were kept clear meticulously of the snows in winter.

The Natural History Museum at 72nd Street was also a wonderful nearby destination where giant dinosaurs lived. One of the important landmarks in my life started with my visits to the Museum. a short walk from our apartment at 85th Street. I was about 9-10 years old when our class in school visited the museum and I was exposed for the first time to the realities of evolution. Here was the proof that our dad had often talked to us about. It has always been amazing to me that there are so many people who don't believe in evolution especially as it is so obvious. They obviously have not been exposed to the facts of life.

The science of evolution fascinated me. The idea that dinosaurs roamed the earth 200 million years ago was simply astonishing to me. Then about 65 million years ago they became extinct. Today we are told that modern birds have dinosaurs as their ancestors. Modern crocodiles also are close relatives of the dinosaurs. The museum was full of information about the changes in the inhabitants of the earth over millions of years. Anyone who does not believe in evolution just has to go to the museum to see proof but there are still those who deny it in their ignorance. Most are blinded by their religions who teach faith rather than science.

It is always amusing to me that there are those who say, "it is only a theory." The theory of evolution is like the theory of gravity. They are both facts, but embody theories of their mechanisms. The following from Stephen J. Gould, "Evolution_as Fact and Theory"; is stating the prevailing view of the scientific community. In other words, the experts on evolution consider it to be a *fact*. This is not an idea that originated with Gould as the following quotations indicate:

> "Let me try to make crystal clear what is established beyond reasonable doubt, and what needs further study, about evolution. Evolution as a process that has always gone on in the history of the earth can be doubted only by those who are ignorant of the evidence or are resistant to evidence, owing to emotional blocks, influence of religion, or to plain bigotry and stupidity. By contrast, the mechanisms that bring evolution about certainly need study and clarification. There are no alternatives to evolution as history that can withstand critical examination. Yet we are constantly learning new and important facts about evolutionary mechanisms."

I have just completed an excellent new book by scientist and author, Dr. Richard Dawkins entitled, The Greatest Show on Earth" which further explains the facts of evolution. Dawkins also wrote the best seller, "The God Delusion" explaining the facts of atheism. That was always important in our family.

As a family, we went to church because dad had to as a doctor practicing in the city community. Our minister was Dr Ralph Sockman, of Christ's Church on Park Avenue who incidentally was a patient of dad's. Dad raised us children as non-believers, though mother and grandmother had some belief in a higher power but not organized religion. It was not a big issue in our family, however. But evolution and its theories were discussed on occasion.

The concept of evolution fascinated me. Dinosaurs were the dominant vertebrate animals of terrestrial ecosystems for over 160 million years, from the late Triassic period (about 230 million years ago) to the end of the Cretaceous period (65 million years ago), when most of them became extinct in the <u>Cretaceous-Tertiary extinction event</u>. The 10,000 living species of <u>birds</u> have been <u>classified</u> as having developed from dinosaurs.

The discovery in 1861 of *Archaeopteryx* first suggested a close relationship between dinosaurs and birds; aside from the presence of fossilized feather impressions, *Archaeopteryx* was very similar to the contemporary small predatory dinosaur *Compsognathus*. Research since the 1970s indicates that <u>theropod</u> dinosaurs are most likely the ancestors of <u>birds</u>; in fact, most paleontologists regard birds as the only surviving dinosaurs and some believe dinosaurs and birds should be put together under one biological class. <u>Crocodilians</u> are the other surviving close relatives of dinosaurs, and both groups are members of the <u>Archosauria</u>, a group of <u>reptiles</u> that first appeared in the very late <u>Permian</u> and became dominant in the mid-Triassic.

For about the first half of the 20th century, both scientists and the general public regarded dinosaurs as slow, unintelligent <u>cold-blooded</u> animals. However, the bulk of <u>research since the 1970s</u> has supported the view that they were active animals with elevated metabolisms, and often with adaptations for social interactions. This change of view was strongly influenced by evidence of the descent of birds from theropod dinosaurs.

The term "dinosaur" was first coined in 1842 by <u>Sir Richard Owen</u> and derives from <u>Greek</u> δεινός (*deinos*) "terrible, powerful, wondrous" + σαρος (*sauros*) "lizard". It is sometimes used informally to describe other prehistoric reptiles, such as the <u>pelycosaur</u> *Dimetrodon*, the winged <u>pterosaurs</u>, and the aquatic <u>ichthyosaurs</u>, <u>plesiosaurs</u> and <u>mosasaurs</u>, although none of these were dinosaurs.

With the above accepted science regarding dinosaurs, there are still fundamentalists (over 50% of the population) who believe the earth is only about 10,000 years old. An example of how religions mis-informs the uneducated with fanciful foolishness.

Our experience in Sunday school was frequently the subject of Sunday dinner discussions which were lively especially since our grandmother was a devout believer. Mother was less so but still was not able to take a position as strongly as my father regarding freethinking. Both mother and grandmother had not attended college. That was probably their problem.

Going to the New York Metropolitan Natural History Museum frequently reinforced my knowledge of the evolutionary changes that all life has undergone since the beginning of time. The fundamental ideas taught by some religions soon became very impossible to me in the light of the science that had been revealed to me at the museum. It has always been very strange to me that religious people can continue with their beliefs when science points out facts that are so very obvious, believable, and provable.

Moving back into the city offered many other advantages. The museum was just one. Central Park just across the street from our apartment was another that allowed us a lot of fun roller skating and visiting the zoo. Dad continued to feel that we needed more space so he bought a wonderful house on the water in Baldwin Harbor, which was on the south shore of Long Island only about an hour's drive from the city. Our house was on a canal which was deep enough for large boats to pull up to our dock. This was long before Jones Beach was developed. We were really in the country all summer. Long Island, then, was only large farms with no housing developments. Most people didn't have cars so there were no suburbs.

Dad also bought us a sailboat which was the center of our summer activity. We painted the boat red white and blue in honor of the Americas cup racing yachts that were then competing in Long Island sound. We spent endless days each summer on the protected bays near our house. We fished and dug clams and supplied the family with many seafood meals. Even mussels grew by the thousands on our dock pilings. It was my start of the love of the sea which has been with me all of my life through the many boats that I have owned. All of them sail boats until recently when I bought a power boat to explore the Connecticut River. Baldwin Harbor was especially good for young children because the bays are all quite shallow and there were many islands dotting the area so it was very hard to get into trouble.

The islands were full of thousands of bird nests on the ground. Every imaginable seabird nested there. Sometimes we would bring them home and keep them in a cage that we built for them on a flattened portion of the garage roof. Dad taught us how to nurse young birds with pellets of bread soaked in milk. They seemed to thrive on this diet. We kept them until their wings developed and then released them. It was a lesson in natural history that we could never have experienced in any other way.

Sometimes in the spring and in the fall we would go to the local Baldwin Harbor school instead of the New York public school which we attended in Manhattan. Somehow or other we were able to do this without being left back. It did give us a chance to extend our use of our summer house from March through October. The remainder of the school year we attended Manhattan public grade schools. Our family believed in public school education.

Dad was such a hard worker, that the pace in New York was getting to him. Traffic in New York was impossible according to dad. He yearned for a smaller community for his practice. He frequently commentated to mother that the city pace was going to kill him so the decision was made to move to a smaller city.

"Charlotte, we've talked a lot about my practice in the city, and it just doesn't get any better. If I keep up this intensity, it will kill me. I was talking to my friend. Dr. Walter Masters the other day, and he's getting tired of his city practice as well. We feel that maybe we should both look for a smaller city. What do you think about that?" dad asked mother.

"Darling, I know the problem well. I understand what both you and Walter are suffering with a big-city practice. Nan, (his wife) and I have discussed it often." The Masters were good friends from England. Nan was also a professional opera singer so mother and she had much in common. They lived on Long Island and he practiced medicine in the city.

"I was reading medical economics the other day and saw an advertisement for a practice in Worcester, Massachusetts for sale, which included a small private hospital. I really don't know much about Worcester, but

I've heard it is a nice, prosperous city in a lovely part of the country. What do you think if I look into it?" dad asked mother.

Dad did look into it and found a practice that seemed to suit him very well. So, with Whem Masters as a partner they bought the practice and the hospital in Worcester, Massachusetts from a Doctor LaLibertie.

CHAPTER 9

The Country Life
In Worcester

D ad was very excited about the prospects, because not only did it allow him to move to a smaller community without the pressures of New York City but it offered him an opportunity to do something contributory in the hospital field. One thing always bothered him. It was called the Closed Hospital System. Doctors were graduated from medical schools all over the country and for one reason or another do not complete their surgical internships. One of the important reasons was that they were members of certain minority groups like blacks and Jews so were unable to get internship assignments. So they could not get accepted to do surgery in many of the local hospitals. These are people who have their formal MD educations behind them and are licensed legally to practice medicine and perform surgery, but because they cannot operate in the local hospital they operate in the patient's home without supervision, and without the team back up the well equipped hospital provides. There were no laws then against this kind of practice, and as a result, the public suffered mightily. There were many unnecessary deaths.

Dad bought the hospital, and we moved to Worcester, where he and Dr Masters, his partner, were able to open the hospital facility to all graduate MDs and they could be supervised and trained by dad, as chief surgeon, and his staff so that the public received the kind of care that they otherwise would not have received.

The closed hospital system was inaugurated many years ago in an effort to raise the standards of medical care. It required that all doctors permitted to practice in certain hospitals be required to meet certain educational and training standards. There was also a strong element of minority prejudice. Especially since the majority of those doctors denied the use of major hospitals were either blacks or Jewish.

However, there are many doctors who graduated from recognized medical schools, who did not complete all of their internship training, but who did receive licenses to practice. Since they could not practice in a hospital, they had to do everything in the patient's home. This obviously did not provide the best service for all patients.

When Dad bought the Lincoln Hospital in Worcester Massachusetts, he decided to open it to all licensed doctors so that they would have the supervision and support of a well-trained hospital staff which dad developed and supervised.

Doctor's Hospital in Worcester, Mass.

The phone rang, one day and a frightened voice asked, "Doc can you come right away? It's an emergency."

"Of course, what's the address I'll be right there?" Dad was always quick to respond to emergencies of this kind.

The address was in the one black section of Worcester.

"Oh, are we glad to see you Doc? Here she is."

There was blood just about everywhere and Dad quickly realized it was the termination of a pregnancy. But unfortunately a breach birth. Fortunately Dad was also trained in OB GYN and Obstetrics.

"Doc, this here is Dr. Brown. He's been having trouble and needs some help." The patient's husband said. Dad went to work immediately and quickly made the necessary adjustments, turning the fetus around and delivering a healthy baby. "Dr. Brown, this should have been done in a hospital. Why did you take this on in the patient's home?"

"Well, Dr. Russell, I don't have hospital privileges. So this is the only place I could take care of my patient, and I just couldn't handle this breach birth."

"It looks like the patient is resting easy, and the baby seems healthy. Here's my card, you can give me a call. I would like to talk to you about a hospital appointment."

The venture was a success with dad, heading the surgical end of things and Whem Masters managed the administrative details. The hospital grew quickly. Its original name was Lincoln Hospital under the former owner, but dad changed the name to Doctors Hospital and it lasted for many years. Even well after dad died in 1955. I visited Worcester recently and it is still there on Lincoln Street, though much grown, as it has become a mental therapeutic institution. Mother sold the hospital after dad died in 1955 and moved to Long Island to be near Frank, Jr and Eleanor in Port Jefferson.

Our family moved to Worcester in 1938.

Dad bought a lovely large Queen Anne style home built in 1820 at 78 Burncoat Street in Worcester just across the street from a beautiful public park named, North Park with two lakes and a perfect ski hill adjacent to it named, Greenfield Hill. It could not have been a more perfect place for children to grow up. The house was one block to the grade school and 1 mile walking distance from dad's hospital so it was very convenient for dad and we began to see him for all meals finally. Life could not have been better.

78 Burncoat Street

The un-packing was barely finished when I asked, "Mom can I go over in the park?" North Park, just across Burncoat Street, had a lovely lake and it wasn't long before I got some heavy thread and a hook on which I impaled a wiggly worm and began fishing.

"Bart better not catch you fishin'," a small voice could be heard.

"Hi, who's Bart?" I asked.

"He's the park manager and fishing is not allowed in the park." The voice added. He was a small boy standing astride his bike. "I'm Bob Fischer. Who are you?" He asked.

"I'm Bill Russell. We just moved in across the street."

"Well, that's good but you better look out or you'll get into trouble," Bob added. "Besides there's mostly big carp in the lake and you won't catch them there or with worms. You have to have a heavy line with a big hook and use dried out bread that's rock hard so it'll stay on the hook. Also night is the best time to catch the carp." Bob obviously knew what he was talking about.

Bob laid his bike down and climbed down to the water's edge next to me. "Do you want me to show you how to catch the really big carp? Some are over two feet long." He asked. Well, that was the beginning of a great friendship that would last for many years and really got me started in my love of the outdoors, camping, fishing, especially for trout, wilderness hiking, and river running.

"Sure that would be great." I answered. "Can we do it tonight?"

'No, not tonight. We have to wait until Bart has his day off which is Thursday. Then he can't chase us." Bob warned.

"OK, Bob. Where do you live?" I asked.

"On Burncoat Terrace." Bob answered. "A short walk from your big house. I know the one 'cause I saw you moving in the past couple of days. It's the biggest house in the neighborhood so everyone knows about you."

"Let's meet after dinner on Thursday at my house when it's dark and try to catch some of those big fish," I offered.

"OK. See you then." Bob climbed up the bank, re-mounted his bike and was off.

I helped finish the moving in. Mother gave me the upstairs rear room with a secret stairway down to the kitchen. It must have been the maid's room for the former owners. It was perfect for me. We no longer had a live-in maid for those years which were depression years and money was "tight" as dad said. He was always busy. Just, people didn't pay their bills, but we made do. We always had plenty as dad was a very hard worker.

"Did you find the park fun?" mother asked.

"Oh, yes, and I met a nice kid, Bob Fischer, who'll be over on Thursday evening so you'll meet him. We're going to do some night fishing in the park. Can Bobby have dinner with us?" I asked.

"That would be just fine I would like to meet Bobby" mother replied.

When Bobby appeared at the door on Thursday the family was just about to sit down to dinner, which was always a formal affair with the Russell family. Mother was not only a good cook but liked everything done right. We all appreciated it and learned to eat with manners demanded of all of us.

Dad and mother always liked to use the dinner meal to have a family discussion. It was usually philosophical and dad had many good subjects to introduce. I think this is where I first began to think seriously about religion and its validity. It wasn't the only subject We discussed but it was an important one. We talked a lot about the Nazis in Germany and their oppression of Jews which we all agreed was abominable. There is no doubt that my dad was a freethinker.

"Welcome Bob, we always like to meet Bill's friends. Do you live near here?" Dad asked.

"Yes sir just on the next street Burncoat Terrace." Bob replied.

"Well, come sit down to dinner. Have you lived in Worcester a long time?" Mother asked.

"All my life."

"Bob knows how to catch big Fish," I interrupted. "We are going to try tonight in the park."

"Have you boys been reading much about what's going on in Germany?" Dad asked.

"Well we sure have heard that there's a dictator named Hitler there," Bobby offered. "I've heard a lot about it," Bob added, "since my father is from Poland and we still have a lot of relatives there. They're very afraid that the Germans want to invade his old country and my father is very worried for his relatives—mine too."

"Has your father lived in this country a long time?" Dad asked.

"About 20 years. He came over here as a young man and went to work as a fireman. He's now the fire chief." Bobby added." Many of his friends are Jews and they are really worried about what will happen to them if Hitler takes over."

"It is a terrible problem and it could lead to a war, I'm afraid." Dad added.

"It certainly could but Bob and I want to do some fishing in the park. May we be excused?" I asked.

"The boys are anxious to go, Frank, so let them get at their fishing." Mother said.

We got to the park just about dark. Bob expertly helped me set up my line and we were fishing. We had hardly gotten started when the big carp began to boil the water and we quickly caught three that were between one and 3 feet long, if you can imagine. We threw them back because Bob said they were not very good eating. I had never seen a carp before much less eaten one. I do understand that some people eat them. Jews especially look upon them as delicacies.

"You're dad and mother are so nice," Bob said. "He really understands the world's problems doesn't he?"

"Yeah, I'm lucky, I guess. Does your dad go to all the fires?" I asked.

"He used to but now that he's chief he doesn't go to all of them, just the very big ones." Bob answered. "I guess he spends most of his time in the office working at a desk in these days. What does your dad do?"

"He's a doctor."

"A doctor?" Bob asked incredulously, A Real Doctor?"

"Yeah, a real doctor."

"So you're really lucky in more ways than one." Bobby added, "You must all be taken care real good if you get sick."

"Yeah, I guess so but it would be fun to go to fires, too. Do you ever get a chance to go to fires?" I asked.

"Oh, no, that would never be possible."

"What do you think about Jews?" Bob asked

"I guess I don't think about them very much, if at all. What do you think about Jews?" I asked.

"Well, you know the Jews killed Jesus. That's what it says in the Bible, so we don't like Jews. I'm Catholic." Bob added.

"Do you really believe all that stuff in the Bible? My dad says the Bible is full of a lot of errors and contradictions. He also says all it is really is kind of a history book. Course we don't really believe in the sacredness of the Bible anyway and don't even go to church much, at least I don't. Dad has to he says, because he is a doctor and doctors have to go to church. Mom and grandma usually go with him I suppose for the same reason. Oh maybe I go to Sunday school once in awhile"

"You mean you don't have to go to church?" Bob asked. "That would be sacrilegious in our family and the Priest would really have it in for us. We sure wouldn't go to heaven."

"My dad says that in order to be a good citizen you should love everybody no matter what they believe. Don't you agree with that?" I asked, "I thought Jesus did say that you should love everybody. Didn't he?" I asked.

"Well what are you going to do when the Jews killed Jesus? You just can't love them when they do those kinds of things." Bobby offered.

"It's getting late, Bob, so maybe we better talk about this later. It's a subject I have a lot of interest in and would like to explore it with you thoroughly.

The boys got to be very good friends, both liked camping a lot and spent a good deal of time on their free weekends at a nearby lake Waschakum, which gave them frequent opportunity to sit in front of the fire at night and talk.

Since I went to Sunday school, I learned about the Boy Scouts which met weekly in the family church, Wesley Church, which was Methodist. I got interested in the scouts which really got me started in camping which I have loved all my life. I eventually became a troop leader and started to work on my merit badges.

There were three ranks in scouting, Star, Life, and Eagle. Each was awarded based on the number of merit badges attained. I managed to get to Life Scout and was working on Eagle when I began to think more about religion. Scouting was very religion based and I found myself becoming skeptical of all religion. Eventually my free thinking philosophy took over and I stopped further involvement in scouting.

I was always interested in the subject of religion, even as a small boy and by the time I was entering Prep school at Worcester Academy, it really was dominant in my thinking. So, the opportunity to talk to someone like Bob, who was a Catholic, really was very exciting to me. I had never known a Catholic before.

During my teen years I discovered Darwin when I read his Origin of Species. His theories regarding evolution were very impressive to me and I discussed them frequently with my dad. He was very strongly an evolutionist which I became. I suppose I would describe myself at that point in my life as an agnostic. Since I didn't feel that any theory could prove or disprove the existence of God. I also read Robert Green Ingersoll and Bertrand Russell. They convinced me of the foolishness of all religions. Among other things, I stopped going to scouting meetings because of their religious foundation. I was becoming a free thinker.

I can remember one night in particular, as we sat around a campfire at Lake Waschakum. "Bob, I'd like to ask you a question."

"Sure I'm ready. What is it?" Bob asked

"Well, I've been thinking a lot about your mentioning that you don't like Jews because they killed Jesus. Did we not agree that the Bible was full of inaccuracies? So, if that's where you get your information, can it be dependable?"

"It's my priest, who tells us that really" Bob replied.

"Your priest is teaching you to dislike somebody because of information that may not be dependable? Does that make any sense?" I added.

"Bill, in my Catholic world, we absolutely must follow what our priest says, and that is final. I never heard of anybody going against what the priest says, at least not here, where we live." Bob explained.

"Bob I just don't think it makes any sense to blindly follow someone especially who may be giving you faulty information and with no evidence. Don't you want to think for yourself? I think it is essential for one to think things through by themselves before one draws any conclusions. That's what education is for"

"Bill, you tell me that you don't believe in the Bible. Don't go to church, and I guess don't believe in Jesus. What do you believe then?" Bob asked.

"I believe each person should think for themselves. That means getting an education, studying history and science, thinking it through and then coming up with some logical, reasonable conclusions that make sense in a modern world. This is after all, not the dark ages, and we should be looking to modern science to teach us so we can live better lives. Getting along with each other is important. Religion is too divisive. That's what my dad has taught me and that's what I believe. He says that if God is all powerful and all merciful, then how could he allow for all the horror, murder, and wars that go on in the world? Most of the wars in the world are religion based. It just does not make logical sense. My brain is my god"

The following is a discussion between dad and the family around the dinner table in Worcester.

"I was talking to Bobby Fischer the other day, and he, as you know, is a very religious Catholic. He keeps telling me that religion automatically started when God created man. Well, we all know that that's mythology, but if that is the case where did religions start", I asked.

There are a lot of theories about it, but probably it happened when man first evolved from some lower form into a form that allowed him to be aware of his surroundings and himself and started to think about everyday natural dangers like lightning and floods. It must have been pretty frightening to primitive people when lightning struck and created fire in a forest or when a large wave washed over the land and killed large numbers of people. Or when earthquakes or landslides occurred and swallowed up, whole villages. These things were unexplainable to these early primitive people. So they simply had to invent a cause which they called a God. Over the many eons, these gods have changed. Different civilizations have had different gods, and though the number is not known there have probably been hundreds if not thousands of different gods that humankind has worshiped at different times in man's history. If you were born in ancient Rome, you would have believed in the Roman Gods. If you were born in India, your gods would be the Hindu Gods. Children take the Gods of their parents without reason. It is your reason that should allow you to select or not select a God, not your chance of birth. This is the kind of reasonable information our dad was so good at revealing to us kids.

Primitive people looked to their gods to protect them from unexplainable events. Such an event as lightening could not be explained or controlled. The smarter men of the groups realized that if a God could be created that if they uniquely represented that God they would wield great power over their fellow man and the priesthood was born. These are all defense mechanisms that primitive people turn to protecting them from the unknown terrors of nature.

As priests consolidated their powers, they built elaborate myths about how their God controls everything that happened on earth and in the heavens. They constructed elaborate temples and mosques to impress the ignorant masses and consolidate their powers over ignorant people.

Long before science, there was religion and, of course, humankind searching for ways to answer the difficult questions like what causes lightning and what makes the seas rise and fall and many other simple questions of nature. These all could be answered by saying God controls it all. Science eventually developed and provided scientific answers to so many of these questions. The inquisitive mind of man demanded proofs. Science is delivering those proofs.

Up until the Reformation in the 14th century, the Catholic Church controlled all the power of the Western world, not only did Catholicism become the main religion but it also was the political power in most countries. Then the Reformation came along with the monk, Luther, bringing a philosophy which said that the individual was important and that worshiping idols was wrong and a savage throwback. At about the same time the Gutenberg Bible and the printing press emerged and Luther's word could be brought to the masses.

Henry VIII defied Pope Leo and divorced his wife but idolatry continued to exist in the Catholic Church even though the new religion of Luther considered it an evil. Heretics were burned at the stake and in general the emergence of a new religion did not come easily.

Money lending was said to be evil and yet the lending of money at a rate of interest is fundamental to the growth of industry.

The pilgrims sailed the Mayflower to the new world to escape the religious persecutions of the old world. Much happened in this time. The emergence of the novel the 30 years war the beheading of King's the challenge of authority all served mankind and his need for answers and freedom.

However the Europeans supported slavery which was then imported to the New World and the bible said it was alright. All religions supported slavery.

The world had come to an important turning point. The individual suddenly became important in a country and the New World was formed with religion being strictly relegated to a secondary position and not to be involved with politics in this new country. This was a very important step. It has allowed the country to develop without the restrictions and dogma of religion and science resultantly flourished.

It's only in relatively recent times, that science has emerged to explain the phenomena which before were unexplainable. Such simple ideas, as controlling fire, and using it for a benefit, raising domestic animals for food, building shelter from the elements, and introducing institutions like marriage to protect children. All of these things were generated by early tribes, and ultimately became part of the social norms we can identify today.

Science has largely replaced religion for those with education, and the ability to reason logically and live without blind faith. Someday, surely, science will be able to create life in the laboratory, and very surely explain exactly how the Earth was formed. There are certainly many theories today, like the Big Bang theory and others that attempt explanations to some of these questions.

All these explanations, of course, do not use God in their reasoning, because the mythology surrounding God is without any scientific foundation. In order to believe any of the stories associated with God one must have what is called faith and not depend upon science.

"Why do these religious people believe as they do?" I asked.

"They were carefully indoctrinated as children and have been filled with such fear of the unknown and of death that they are unable to think logically. It is fear that is the father of religion" Dad answered.

We enrolled in the nearby grade school named, Adam Square, which was only about a five-minute walk from our house down Burncoat Street. Classes were small, and I still remember my teacher's name, Mrs. King, in the eighth grade.

One day in September 1938, the principal came into the room and said, everyone has to go home as a very severe storm is coming and it probably will be safer if you are all at home. So school is closed.

Well that was certainly exciting, and as we made our way back home, the sky got darker and darker, and the wind picked up to the highest degree I have ever felt it. When we got in the house, the radio was on and announcing that we are about to be hit by a hurricane. This is very unusual in New England, but here we were. The family was altogether except for dad, who was at the hospital as he usually was. This was the 1938 Hurricane that devastated New England.

We scattered around the yard, picking up anything that could be blown away and that we could carry and brought it into the garage. There was a point where our little sister, Eleanor, could hardly walk against the wind. We knew it was time to get indoors. The house fairly rocked as old houses do squeaking and screaming as the tremendous winds whipped by us. As is the case in most of New England, there are many trees large and ancient in our neighborhood. As we looked out the window they were falling everywhere. It was soon obvious that there was no way for any traffic to move on any road.

Suddenly it was all dark. We had no electricity and the telephone was dead. All we could do was huddle as my grandmother said prayers for us all. She was the one really religious person in the family and I must admit I was comforted by her soothing words.

The storm raged most of the night, but slowly subsided, and by morning. It was quiet. We had a gas stove, so cooking was possible, but there was no electricity. Nor phone service. We had none for weeks. We did have water because we had a well, though there were some parts of the city that even lacked that. Dad was among the missing and mother said he was obviously busy helping others who needed medical attention in the wake of this disastrous 1938 New England hurricane.

Three days later, our father appeared obviously weary. He had to walk or rather climb his way home from the hospital. All of the streets in town were virtually impossible to negotiate as the tangle of downed trees created a jungle. It was many weeks before all the trees were removed. During much of that period, we saw our father infrequently. There was much death in the town and throughout the area affected by the hurricane. It took the region many years to recover from this disaster.

We children finished grade school at Adams Square School and went on to North High School. I went to Worcester Academy prep school which was a private pre-college institution.

One thing my father believed in was that children should be taught early the value of work. It should be a joy to work. All of us had jobs at one time or another. I had a paper route. My brother Frank worked at a local grocery store. Eleanor did babysitting. We all cut lawns in summer and shoveled walks in winter. We learned early that work was fun and earning money was equally gratifying.

I can remember on my paper route one time, I was not feeling very well. So mother drove me around on my route. As a doctor, dad had a Packard. All doctors drove Packard's in those days it seemed, and Dad had a big one with tires mounted on the sides. It was a beauty. I'm sure I was the only paperboy being chauffeured around on his route. I can chuckle about it, even to this day. My mother and dad were always so helpful to us.

CHAPTER 10

Wilderness Camping

I transferred from North High in 1942 to Worcester Academy and graduated in 1944. When I first arrived at Worcester Academy one of my chemistry class mates was one of the tallest boys I've ever met at 6'7". His name, Walter Kistler, became one of my closest friends throughout my life until his recent death following Alzheimer's disease. Walter loved the outdoors especially canoeing and sailing. His father, President of Norton & Co., a large chemical company in Worcester, owned a beautiful 50 foot Herrischoff Yawl, which he kept in Marblehead Harbor. We had many a wonderful sail along the coast of New England from Northern Maine to Martha's Vineyard and Nantucket during the summers of 1940 through 1944.

Walter's greatest love was running whitewater and voyaging by canoe in the Maine wilderness. One place was particularly attractive to him was the north woods of Maine in Piscataquis County. He had been there earlier with his family on a guided trip on the Allagash River in northern Maine. This is a lovely river that ran in northern Maine from Allagash Lake down to Fort Kent joining the St. John River and entering the ocean in Canada.

Walter and I with other good friends, Bob Fischer, Eddie Moser and Bill Malmquist, spent most of the summers in the early 40's canoeing from Greenville to Fort Kent through what has today become the protected

Allagash Wilderness. We did that in a leisurely manner spending time in each of the places where we found good trout fishing, a sport I dearly loved. And the trout fishing in that part of Maine was really spectacular. It was not uncommon to land 15 inch+ brook or rainbow trout.

We took a train from Worcester to Greenville Maine where we rented canoes from Saunders store. This was a wonderful outfitter who sold camping equipment, clothing and rented canoes. We also picked up our food which consisted mainly of dried items like beans, flour, salt, oatmeal, cereal, powdered milk, sugar, powdered eggs, dried potatoes and onions, spaghetti, dried tomatoes and other dried vegetables, coffee, tea, and cocoa, and slabs of salt bacon. We counted on catching a lot of trout to supplement our diet. We could bring no fresh food as we had no way to keep it from spoiling. We also carried a 22 rifle and a pistol which we used to supplement our diet with small game like squirrels, geese, or ducks. So we really ate well for the entire trip. We took turns cooking, but it turned out that I did most of the cooking because the other three managed to burn just about everything they cooked.

Our canoe was a 20 foot guide model made of wood and covered in canvas. These large canoes worked beautifully on the big lakes and rivers even in heavy water. They are flat bottomed without a keel strip so they were very maneuverable on the fast running rivers. We brought along amberoid glue and pieces of canvas to make repairs as needed as we would hit the occasional rock and tear the canvas skin. We found particularly on Moosehead Lake, so large that the wind frequently whipped up waves that could swamp a smaller canoe. We also rigged up a makeshift sail using paddles and a tarp. We could only do it when the wind was favorable which it was frequently. We really enjoyed coasting down the many magnificent lakes resting our paddle arms letting the wind do the work. Sometimes we trolled for trout as the wind carried us along.

I remember on this particular trip we saw practically nobody. Of course, these were the war years when so many were in uniform during World War II. The area was considered unorganized townships. It was before the boom in vacation second houses and I suppose today, many of these wilderness lakes are populated especially since they may be reached easily by floatplane.

The largest lake was Moosehead which started at Greenville in the South and extended up to Northeast Carry. The lake is about 120 mi.² and the distance from Greenville to Northeast Carry about 60 miles on this pristine lake. Every night we camped and the cry of the loon could be heard as we tucked in with the same loons waking us the next morning. The loon song is so characteristic in this wilderness area. I even learned to mimic the cry of the loon and gained that nickname for awhile as a result.

The paddle up Moosehead Lake passes Mount Kineo across from the little logging village of Rockport where the Moose River comes in. This is another river trip we did in later years starting at Jackman down to Rockport and on down Moosehead to Greenville. But that's another story.

Our trip took us up across Northeast Carry to Chesuncook Lake, Chemsiquastibamticook, Long Pond, Round pond, and carrying over the divide where rivers ran northerly into Allagash Lake, the most remote of them all and where the trout fishing was simply unbelievable. We spent most of our time here after which we headed down the Allagash River. The river was at perfect height this year so we enjoyed a wonderful ride. We did have to carry around a few heavy rapids especially Allagash Falls which were spectacular. We passed the little village of St. John on the St John River and finally ended up at Fort Kent where we took a train and shipped our canoes with us on the train back to Greenville.

The memories of this wonderful trip will never fade. I've had the good fortune to do it more than once with Walter and Joanne one time and also in later years with Joanne and the three children we flew by floatplane into Allagash Lake carrying our canoe between the airplane floats. This was a wonderful family adventure and I'm sure that they all treasure the memory.

The Allagash was described by Henry David Thoreau when he canoed this beautiful country in 1846 with two Penobscot Indians Joe Attean and Joel Polis. The trip was well documented in his book, The Maine Woods. The area has been protected by the establishment of Baxter State Park and the Allagash Wilderness. Controlled logging is allowed though the forest grows back quickly. Clear cutting is no longer permitted so the wilderness is not ravaged as in earlier days. We're fortunate that we still have this pristine wilderness area available for camping trips like we took when we were boys.

While living in Worcester, we almost never went to church as most weekends were spent, sailing, camping, and skiing. I did have a good friend named Dean Scott from Worcester Academy who was a member of a youth organization called, DeMolay. This was a social organization for young men with strong religious overtones. It was very active in the social life of the city especially when it sponsored large dances for the public at the city auditorium. Profits went to charity.

I became very interested in DeMolay first becoming Orator, famous for giving the Flower Talk and eventually Master Counselor. My brother also was interested and eventually became State Master Councilor. We both learned a lot about administering a large organization from this experience.

I didn't see much of my close friend Bob Fischer during those years, and the World War II came when we both enlisted in 1944 after graduation. Bob joined the navy and I the army air corps.

CHAPTER 11

Christian Science And Religious Superstition

Dehlia McCoy, my mother's mother, lived with us the last 15 years of her life. She was devoted to her church and was a strong believer in Christian Science. Naturally, living in a doctor's family, we did not discuss this at all, as it was a delicate subject especially as we were non-believers and Grammy was a dedicated believer, not unusual for those of her generation especially as she only went thru the 3rd grade.

She began to develop some symptoms of distress, which seemed to indicate that she was suffering a health problem of some kind, but did not talk about it. It was obvious to the family, and particularly to my dad that there was something seriously wrong. "Dehlia," dad asked, "don't you think you should come down to the hospital for examination?"

"No thank you, Frank, I'm taking care of it."

As it turned out, she said she was consulting with her Christian Science advisors, and felt she was under good care. Suddenly, things turned worse when mother and dad found her in her bedroom unconscious. Dad quickly had an ambulance take her to the hospital where an emergency operation had to be performed. It was a very close call. She nearly did not make it. She needed an appendectomy. Without my father's quick response, she would have died.

When she awakened, and was told the full story. She realized that her Christian Science advisers had nearly caused her death, and she was grateful to my father for his quick action and use of modern science to both define the problem and solve it. She did say that God saved her life. She often referred to it as a miracle. Dad always smiled when she said that but he did not comment.

It was one more story, one of many, that solidified my thinking about how important modern science is and how it serves the world and how useless is religion. The mythology and unverified superstitious beliefs associated with religion and so-called miracles, leaves the unfortunate believer totally unprotected.

It was during these years that my reading choices expanded. My father recommended a look into the writings of Robert Green Ingersoll, a well-known, lecturer, and important freethinker of his time. He spoke importantly about freedom, and how religion restricts freedom. He was a big influence in my thinking regarding religious dogma.

Also, the writings of Lord Bertrand Russell influenced me a good deal. I was especially attracted to the idea because the author had the same last name as mine. But more importantly his logic and clear thinking left me no avenue but atheism.

I also was introduced to the writings of Charles Darwin in his Origin of Species. I came away a firm believer in natural selection, and the concept of evolution.

It seemed ridiculous that the beliefs of a superstitious Bedouin tribe thousands of years ago should be treated on an equal basis with the evidence collected with our most advanced science today. It seemed to me that this completely undermines the entire process of scientific inquiry.

It became clear to me that over the many years there had been many gods and many religions. They all could not be right. Therefore they all must be wrong. Also the concept of an all-powerful and all merciful God was contradictory. How could He be an all merciful God and allow for all of the horrors to which mankind has been subjected down through the millennia? If God is all-powerful, how could he permit it? If He is unable to stop these horrors like wars, murders, disease, and all of the dislocations of the universe, then he is not all-powerful. Finally, since the majority of wars have been religious in nature, religion is a scourge on mankind. It is clear to me that the concept of God and the hereafter was invented by man because of his fear of death.

All of this happened between my years of about 13 and 16. Though I had gone to Sunday school as a young child, my father was an atheist. However he also attended church as is normal for a doctor in a small town especially in Massachusetts. A doctor who does not attend church does not have a practice. All part of the hypocrisy of religion and it's oppressive influence on society.

CHAPTER 12

World War II— Meeting Joanne

One Sunday on December 7th of 1941, Walter Kistler, Bob Fischer, and I went skiing at our favorite mountain, Mt Wauchusetts, about 15 miles north of Worcester. There was one walk-up trail with about 1200 feet vertical drop where we used skins to reach the summit. There was only one ski area with mechanical uphill facilities in New England at the time in North Conway, New Hampshire, which had the skimobile, a sort of little car on tracks that was pulled up the hill by cables as the cars ran on tracks. It was pretty tame skiing, expensive and crowded. We always skied using skins to climb our mountains without crowds. climbing has always been my first love. The challenge of the climb was always rewarded by the wonderful downhill run.

We were driving home from Wauchusetts at about 5 PM and heard over the radio that the Japanese had attacked our naval base, Pearl Harbor, in the Pacific. Later we learned that 2400 Americans were killed and 12 warships were sunk in that sneak attack that started World War II for us. We declared war on Japan and soon after on Germany and Italy. It unalterably changed all of our lives forever.

I joined the US Army Air Corps as a flying cadet when I reached 18 after graduation from Worcester Academy. I wanted to be a fighter pilot but my limited visual acuity kept me from pilot school. I did complete radar flight training at Boca Raton Army airfield in Florida and got my final radar flight training in B-29's.

At the end of basic training in North Carolina, all of us inductees were put on a train and headed off to the next assignment. It was March, 1944. We didn't know where we're going. All we did know was that we had been accepted in the radar training program and were on our way to our next tech school.

We were on the train for several days. The cars were just coaches with no sleeping facilities so we had to do the best we could at night. Meals were served to us in a box and mostly cold. I had a seatmate named Tex Lamason with whom I became good friends and as it turned out for a lifetime. We still visit each other's homes to this day. As we looked out the train window Tex said, "I know where we are. This is Wisconsin; I used to live here in a town named Madison."

Well, Madison was where the train pulled in, to the field where our next electronics tech school was situated. This one was at Truax Army Air Field in Madison, Wisconsin in March 1944 where we attended a basic electronics school in preparation for our subsequent radar flight duties.

Truax field had been the commercial airport for Madison before the war. Now it was turned into an Army Air Corps base and greatly enlarged with a lot of Quonset huts where we both slept and had our classes. It was a 24-hour program with classes day and night. Since I had studied physics in school, I felt pretty comfortable with the basic introduction to electronics. We were told that we were in a highly classified activity and we were to speak to no one about what we were doing. Radar was unknown to the general public at that time. It was very much of a scientific breakthrough which the Allies had and the Germans and the Japanese did not. It gave us a very great advantage in our bombing of their cities. We were able to fly to a target and bomb even in the clouds without being able to see the targets or the ground batteries which were unable to see us.

The school was teaching us electronics and radio. How it worked. How to build one. How to repair one. In later schools, we would go to advanced electronics in Rantoul, Illinois and eventually the more advanced radar school which was in Boca Raton, Florida.

It was a very intensive program in Madison that lasted into the summer. I can remember how excited we all were when June 6 rolled around and we were informed that the invasion of Europe had started on the Normandy beaches. We were all in high spirits and knew this was the beginning of the end for the Nazis.

On our first day off, Tex and I took the camp bus into Madison. Tex had gone to grade school there so he knew the town. We started walking all over town. It was a lovely town with a beautiful main park in the center where the capitol buildings stood. A short walk was to the University of Wisconsin campus which I later attended after the war. We were walking down a street near the campus in a residential section of town when Tex exclaimed, "I know that house. I know the people who live there in 1901 Adams Street. Their name is Jackson. He is a doctor as I remember. Let's see if they remember me, when I lived here and went to grade school with their daughter, Joanne, I believe was her name. We were in the fourth grade together."

We went up to the door of the lovely old English Tudor style house with a large beautiful garden and immaculate lawn. Tex knocked. The door opened and there appeared a distinguished gentleman. Tex said, "Dr. Jackson—I am Fielding Lamason. Do you remember me?"

"I certainly do, how nice to see you, Fielding, please come in."

Dr. Jackson was chief surgeon and President of the Jackson clinic, which was started by his father, Dr James Jackson in 1870 who was born in 1840 and died in 1921. He came from Wolverhampton England in 1852 and married his cousin the daughter of Dr. William Hobbins of Madison. The Jackson clinic developed into one of the most important in the country with the Jackson name becoming well-known throughout the world. Dr. Arnold Jackson served as President of the International College of Surgeons and earned many honors in his lifetime.

We had a good visit, and caught up on the news since Tex with his family moved from Madison to Texas as a young boy. Dr. Jackson was very welcoming of course with the war on, and both of us in uniform. It set a very special stage. Suddenly, we heard high heels on the stairway, and who appeared but the loveliest girl I could imagine.

"Fielding! I have not seen you in years. How have you been?"

I was stunned. Her beauty and every movement charmed me. Her voice seemed musical and her bright blue eyes shown upon me in what I sensed was a special connection at least so I hoped. I had never felt quite the same feeling that came over me at that moment. I know now it was my first true love. Her very presence mesmerized me. Tears come to my eyes as I re-read this.

Well, of course, Fielding started dating Joanne, and she fixed me up with friends. This went on for two or three dates during that spring and summer. When for some strange reason, we switched. I started dating Joanne, and we fixed Fielding up with the friends. It was so natural, almost as if it were destined. It certainly was the most important event of my life. As I look back on it now, I am quite certain that it was the most important single event in my life. I really didn't know it then, as I do now, but Joanne became everything to me and contributed mightily to my success in life.

It was a wonderful summer in Madison, especially since the Jackson's owned a beautiful 29-foot sailboat, which we raced on the lovely Lake Mendota often as we could get time off from camp. I don't think it's necessary to emphasize how I fell in love with Joanne and that was the end of my single bachelor life. We were both 18 years old and the feeling was mutual.

But the war had to go on in spite of everything. Those months in Madison however come back to me so often in my treasured memories.

Tex and I graduated from Truax and attended additional Air Force technical schools at Rantoul, Illinois and Boca Raton, Florida. Tex was assigned to a program in radar in the middle South, I to Victorville,

California B29 school. Tex and I didn't see anything of each other until after the war following discharge from the air corps, he moved home to Philadelphia and attended Princeton where he graduated in 1950. We have maintained a close friendship all these years.

After I completed my training, I was then transferred to on the line training in a B-29 bomber squadron at Victorville Army Air Field in California in preparation for overseas assignment to the Far East. The war was over in Germany, and now all the concentration was on bombing Japan into submission. Our tactical B-29 group was preparing for just that. We were about to ship overseas to Okinawa, as I remember, any day as we were on specific orders.

While at Victorville, I met Dick Bowler, a swimmer who invited me to join the base swim team. I had swum competitively in prep school so it was a natural. Dick was California free-style champion before the war. I swam backstroke. We had a lot of fun competing at other bases along the coast and actually became west coast champions for all the California army air force bases.

Suddenly the news was electric. We had developed what was called an atomic bomb and dropped two of them on Japan which resulted in massive devastation to Hiroshima and Nagasaki. Japan quickly and unconditionally surrendered and the war was over. I choke up even as I say these words. It was such a momentous time in my life and the lives of all GI's and the world. We won the most terrible and devastating war in the history of the world. It was all over and we all hope we would be soon going home to our families and civilian life.

I learned a lot in the Army and really changed from a boy to a man, entering at 18 and discharged at 20. Important growing up years. I was very fortunate to have been in training the whole time and did not have to suffer the terror and horror of combat. Japan unconditionally surrendered in Feb, of 1945 after which Victorville was closed and I was transferred to Williams Army airfield in Phoenix, Arizona. Radar flying specialists were no longer needed.

The army was trying to keep everybody in the service, because the country was anticipating a war with Korea. However, most of us wanted to get out as quickly as possible, and were accumulating what was called discharge points, based on length of service to do so.

When I arrived at Williams Field in Phoenix, there was absolutely nothing to do. My superior, showed me a list of possible jobs. One was volunteering as an MP, which because I was tall, I was pushed into. They fitted me with a side arm, a club, and a very official looking armband and sent me along with a partner in to Phoenix the next night in a jeep and with portable radio telephone that I had never seen before. Since I was a Sgt., I was placed in charge of overseeing GIs playing in Phoenix. Our job was to roam the bars and drag the drunks back to the field. It was a miserable job, and the next day I went back to my superior to see if I could find another job to while away my remaining time in the service which was to be about 6 months as I accumulated discharge points. The soldiers who were in combat got the most discharge points, as they should, so the rest of us had to take our turn.

Because I had some experience on a school newspaper I was offered a job as reporter on Airfax, the camp newspaper. The newspaper had a staff of 6 plus the printing facilities which were in Phoenix at a local newspaper facility.

The editor of the paper, Lt. Ed Ackers, was about to be discharged as he had accumulated enough points as a pilot. I only had a few weeks on the paper with him, but we had gotten to be good friends. He asked me if I'd like to be the editor, and I said, yes.

My boss, a major, told me that my one job was to make the Army look attractive. So that people would stay in. It was really a public relations job. My first to experience this kind of work and I loved it.

As Editor I was immediately provided a private office and a WAC private secretary as well as the availability of my own car with a driver, another WAC. I could come and go as I wanted and all I had to do was make the Army look wonderful. What fun!

Monday I saw in the paper that Phoenix was having its annual grapefruit festival. They had elected a lovely young girl named Sue Amman as grapefruit Queen. I got an idea so I called her and asked if she'd like also to be the grapefruit queen of Williams Field. She said yes. So I went in to Phoenix to interview her. We hit it off immediately. She was movie star beautiful and at my young age I was really dazzled. Thoughts of Joanne temporarily faded into the background but never completely.

Sue and I dated quite a lot, and it almost got serious until I discovered she was a very devoutly religious person and a Catholic at that. That turned me off immediately. I could never get serious about a catholic. Even in those days I had a fairly strong position about freethinking. I had reached the point where I admitted to being an agnostic leaning towards atheism. My family never forced us to go to church, though we did when very young. Father and mother went regularly as he was a doctor and that was expected in that small town of Worcester.

Sue was a wonderful girl in every respect but we really ended up being just good friends. The grapefruit queen promotion was a very important event on the field. The whole thing turned out to be a major promotion with a current movie star named Robert Montgomery, who joined the party at a big celebration we had at the field. Montgomery had been assigned by Hollywood to get involved with the Phoenix promotion, and he came along to the field with Sue. It was just one more thing that made Williams Field look like a country club to the "inmates".

I do admit that that was one of the most fun jobs I've had in my life. It lasted about six months until I accumulated enough points to get discharged. Editor was a position I held until my discharge in July of 1945. My superior, a Major Andrews, said I was the best editor they ever had and I should consider going into newspaper work in civilian life. But I wanted to be a doctor.

CHAPTER 13

Post War Back
To College

Returning to Worcester after discharge, I matriculated at The University of Massachusetts in the pre-med program. Getting back into the routine of school was a rude shock but I was certainly happy to be out of the service and back to a normal civilian life. My program was heavy with biology, chemistry, and comparative anatomy and I loved it. I did well that first year with all A's and B's because I studied. The remainder of my career in college was not that successful as far as marks were concerned.

I did want to be more at home, however, so I made plans and transferred to Clark University in Worcester. This is a great little college and it allowed me to live at home. The months passed quickly with weekends spent skiing and the rest of the time heavily into the books. I did correspond with Joanne and frequently but at that point I was more seriously involved in study than girls. One day the phone rang when I was home on a weekend. "Hello Bill. This is Joanne Jackson."

My heart jumped. We had maintained contact with letters and by telephone during my years in the service and after. We knew we had a very special relationship but managed to control it as I was just a penniless medical student.

"Mother and I are planning a motoring trip to New England. Later this spring, and we thought we would drop by to see you, if that is all right. We'll probably be there about mid April. I'll let you know, the definite date".

"Wonderful, we will get everything ready for you."

Mid April came and Joanne with her mother, Laura, arrived. It was so wonderful to see Jo and her mother who got along with my parents famously. They were able to spend several days with us. We showed them the region and learned a lot about their plans. It was obvious that my heart was completely taken with lovely Joanne. And in fact, I loved her mother, too, like my own.

Much later after we were married, Joanne confided in me that her mother had planned the trip having said to Joanne, "that's the boy for you." Did I have little choice? Nor did I want one?

"You know, I plan to go to summer school this summer." I said. "Why don't you do it in Wisconsin University in Madison? The summer curriculum is excellent. I'll be finishing up my senior year there this coming spring, getting my BS degree and we can do a lot of sailing on Mendota in our boat and take some classes together." Jo answered.

"That is just perfect. I will do it."

I did not realize at the time, how consequential that decision was. I continued my pre-med studies at summer school at the University of Wisconsin to be near Joanne.

Joanne took a couple of courses with me at summer school. One course was Comparative Religion that I found extremely interesting. Wisconsin was known as an atheistic school and the course showed it. At that time I was describing myself as an agnostic non-believer. Joanne had already become a confirmed atheist following her family beliefs. We spent a lot of time that summer discussing the subject. Jo was very convincing and I eventually decided that I could no longer be an agnostic and joined her in her atheism. I have never been sorry. Religions are simply stupid; middle ages thinking designed for people terrified about the unknowns of dying. As the years have gone on in my life, I've developed a very strong position about this whole subject. But that's for later comment and development and maybe a book or two.

In our course in comparative religion we studied many philosophers like Aristotle, Robert Green Ingersoll, John Stuart Mill, Socrates, Bertrand Russell, Jean-Paul Sartre, Ayn Rand, Friedrich Nietzsche to name a few and many others who made me realize that religion is simply man-made and causes far too much divisiveness in the world. It seemed that most of the intellectuals in the world were atheists and I felt I was joining a group dedicated to improving the world and mankind specifically. When you consider the horror that religion has caused throughout history and still does as the source of all the current wars, it is sensible, I feel, to seek a better way.

Joanne and I found we shared most ideas about life, and it was soon obvious to both of us that we were deeply in love. Joanne had graduated with a BS in science with a major in Chemistry and a minor in child psychology. I was only a sophomore pre-med with many years of college and medical training ahead of me. But being young and in love made us not worry about the future.

One evening, we were sailing on Lake Mendota in the Jackson's boat under a full moon. There was not much wind otherwise just two of us could not handle this 29 foot racing craft. In high winds it required a crew of four. It was a romantic evening, and I couldn't resist proposing. To my great joy, she accepted, and we planned to get married as quickly as we could get a license.

Her mother and father were abroad he on a medical society sponsored speaking trip to England so Joanne called a family friend, Judge Procter, and asked if he would marry us. After a thorough talking to us trying to convince us to wait until I graduated, he finally agreed to do the deed. Joanne was a very convincing person. The next day we showed up at the judge's chambers, I in a T-shirt and Joanne in something equally informal. The judge administered the vows and suddenly we were married. What a joyous moment. We borrowed one of the Jackson cars and drove up to their cottage in Door County on northern Lake Michigan for a long week honeymoon in their beautiful isolated lake front cottage. What a wonderful week that was. I learned what true love was. The tiny cottage on the Lakeshore was isolated which was perfect for our honeymoon. It had no electricity or running water. We often cooked on the Lakeshore by fire. Joanne had already learned how to be an excellent cook though in later years she said she really learned most of her cooking skills from my mother.

When both our families learned about it, they were shocked, but gave us their blessings, nonetheless. It was right. We all knew it. And a perfect marriage of over 54 years together has proven it. I could not describe a more perfect marriage. We lived as one and never had any serious differences. She was my best friend, my partner, my lover, my business associate . . . . just everything.

After summer school ended, we moved to Worcester where I continued my pre-med studies at Clark University and lived in my family's home with Joanne. We had a good year but Joanne told me of skiing in Colorado which sounded magical. She had skied there in Aspen years before with her family.

I felt very adventuresome at the time so, I transferred to the University of Colorado summer school in Boulder, Colorado in June 1947 to continue my pre-med studies. Our first child, Bill Jr., was born in 1947 at the Jackson Clinic in Madison where we spent the latter part of that summer.

We lived in campus veterans housing in Boulder which was adequate, and I was on the G.I. Bill, which provided us a minimal monthly income of $120 a month plus tuition, it was a challenge to make ends meet.

Backpacking In The Rockies

CHAPTER 14

The Colorado Mountains

Moving to Colorado was an important milestone in our lives. Before that we were living at home, I with the responsibility of the student and Joanne the responsibility of raising our first young son, Bill jr. Though it was a happy life, Joanne, particularly wanted her own home.

Joanne had skied in Colorado and spoke often of it so without a lot of planning, we decided to go there for summer school at least to see if we liked it.

The University had built married students, accommodations, because a large number of the students were married returning veterans. The buildings were old army Quonset huts so I was right at home.

As a premed student, I had a pretty heavy program, but it slowly became obvious to me that the field of medicine was probably not what I really wanted to do. In fact with a wife and a child and part-time work, my studies suffered. To be expected. Other things in my life became more important than being a doctor.

I did need to bring in extra money so I looked for part-time work. One of the first part time jobs I took was teaching skiing at Arapahoe Basin. One weekend we went to Arapahoe Basin which was one of three ski areas in Colorado at that time. The other two were Aspen and Loveland Pass. Skiing was in its infancy. I got the idea that maybe I could make some extra money as a ski instructor. So I inquired about who was the head of the ski school. It was a famous skier, Willie Schaeffler, champion of the Garmisch, Germany Olympics. He was a wonderful fellow and a superb skier. When I asked him he gave me one look and said "come with me." in a heavy Bavarian accent.

We took the lift to Midway. Willey skated off saying, "follow me."

We headed down the mountain at a pretty good clip, but he was careful to do enough turns so he could evaluate my ability. Then we went over to a flat area and went through some basic routines. He explained the details of how he felt a student should be taught and I listened carefully and followed his lead in every way.

To make a long story short, I was hired. I was the second instructor the Basin hired. The first was Max Dercum a former University of Pennsylvania PHD forestry professor who now lived with wife, Edna, in Dillon. Max had inherited a lot of Colorado mountain land from his family which he wanted to develop so he had moved back to Colorado. As the years went on, he did develop it as it was later called Breckenridge ski area with a friend, Harry Baum. Max died in 2011 at 94.

During the snow seasons, we drove to the basin every weekend on both Saturday and Sunday. I had an old Ford station wagon so carried a few paying riders from Boulder to the Basin each of the days so that was a little income, too.

"Are you ready to go? It's already late and I hate to keep the people waiting."

"Just a minute. I'm still working on these diapers and other things."

"Yes, but my riders won't wait, and they won't come back."

"Okay okay, just a few more minutes. Oh heck, Bill. I think maybe you'd better go without me. There's just too much to get done here today."

"Are you sure? It looks like it's going to be a beautiful day."

"No, you go on, and I'll go next weekend."

So I decided to take her at her word and loaded my ski stuff in the back of the station wagon and went to our meeting place where I picked up my riders. This was something I did on my regular trips to the Basin. I usually got five or six people to ride with us up to Arapahoe and back and at two dollars a head. It paid for my gas and a little extra. Gas was only about 18 cents a gallon then. And I had to go up anyway, because I was teaching skiing there regularly now. And it really did help the exchequer. I arrived at the meeting spot, and there they were with their skis, all ready to go.

"Climb on, Jo's not going to be with us today so we have extra room." Our trip to Arapahoe Basin went without event. When we got there, Larry jump, who was the owner, was already announcing that ski school was getting ready. So I was onstage.

"Okay gather around. Let's get a list of names and we will be off to the meadow." We conducted our classes in Lenawee Meadows, which is a lovely open place near halfway, much like an alpine meadow with usually perfect snow and the ideal spot for teaching skiing to beginners. This day, I only had four, two of whom were father and son Harry Baum and son, Harry Junior. We started off with the usual discussion of equipment. In those days, all the boots were leather, and the bindings were still cable in line, which would be considered antiques, today and totally inadequate for modern skiing.

In those days, a good skier used a modified snow plow and stem turn to get down the hill, while today the stem is rarely used. Watching skiing developed from the snowplow days to today has been very interesting. Equipment has changed radically to suit the new techniques. Today it's a lot more fun and much safer than when I started. In those early days we even used what was called long thongs, which was a long leather strap, about 3 feet in length, that went through a slot in the ski under your instep and wrapped around your boot several times back and forth through the slot so that you were locked to the ski. Falling under those circumstances, almost always resulted in some kind of injury. Then we went to the super diagonals, to keep the heel down, and finally to the modern cable binding, which allows easy entry and exit and the adjustment to permit one to lift the heel for walking. These were not safety bindings with automatic release as the modern bindings of today. As a result in my skiing days I took several serious falls and managed to rupture an Achilles tendon as well as permanently injured both knees. Most of my life I got by but now they give me a lot of trouble. Causing me to walk with a cane and only short distances.

I lined the four students up. First we're going to talk about the most basic maneuver, which is walking on skis. I demonstrated this simple maneuver, and each of them followed quite well. So, it was obvious that this was not their first time on skis. They even used their polls properly and were able to align for the next step in the lesson.

Now are going to do a snowplow let me ask how many have tried this before? All hands went up. Okay, let's do it. I went through the motions, and each person in turn, performed a satisfactory snowplow. This is the basic maneuver that allows us to both turn and stop. It is even an emergency maneuver, though, I hope we will soon get beyond that.

We went through a snowplow, and amazingly, everybody did it satisfactorily after a few tries.

Well that was wonderful. It looks like we can move right into a stem turn, which is a little more advanced way to make a turn. So let's give it a try. First the stem turn requires getting into a snowplow position. And then leaning to place your weight on one or the other ski. The ski on which you place your weight will become what is called the downhill ski. So get in position with a snowplow edging slightly and then release the edging . . . . and again. See how easy it is? You lean on your left ski, and suddenly you turn to the right-do it again. Now lean on your uphill ski, which is your right ski. Notice how quickly you turn to the left. Isn't that simple? We did several of these maneuvers until I felt they had it down.

Now let's try what are called linked turns. That is alternating shifting
your weight from your left ski to your right ski in a rhythmical manner.
Do it. Good, here now, you're skiing and making linked turns. A lot
of people don't get any further than this in their learning to ski, but it
looks to me like you may be ready to try a little more advanced way to
link your turns. Now were going to do linked turns with what is called
follow-through after every turn. You will bring your skis parallel, out of
the stem position.

The important thing here is to develop coordination and a rhythmical
swaying swing momentum using your arms. As you place your weight on
your outside ski, as you traverse, you begin to make a stem turn and then
with your outside arm move it forward in rhythm and lean forward on
what now has become your downhill ski. See how it works?

Now I'm going to demonstrate how you want to be able to do it. I went
ahead with some linked stem turns, and I closed them by swinging my
arms, in coordination and I did this so that my skis were parallel again
as I did this several times. Each of the four students tried to mimic my
action. Two did very well. Harry and his son did not.

Well, that's the end of this lesson. I would advise you to practice these
stem turns and do as much as you can to coordinate the stem turn with a
parallel finish. Using your arms in rhythm. This does require practice. I
advise you to take a day or so before you take a new lesson, which should
be more advanced.

After the lesson Harry came up to me and said, Bill, I would like to book
a private lesson for me and my son Harry Junior. Can we do that?

"Of course, when would you like to set it up?"

"Can we make it this afternoon after lunch, perhaps?"

"Okay I'll check the schedule and if it is alright meet me on the deck of
the warming shack and we will get started at 1 PM."

I left the group at the lift midway and took off down the Molly Hogan Trail named after a former miner looking for gold in these hills in earlier days to the warming shack at the base of the mountain. As I walked in, who was there to my surprise but Joanne?

"I thought you were not coming up? How in the world did you get here?"

"I hitchhiked."

"Hitchhiked? What did you do with Billy?"

"Oh, he's in the backpack."

"Backpack?" And sure enough, there he was happy as a lark. It was obvious he was going to make a good skier.

"The only problem I had was when I got picked up, the driver told me to put my pack in the trunk and when I showed him why I couldn't do this, he was pretty amazed but he went along with it. And here I am."

That was so typical of my wonderful wife. She was the most independent and problem-solving person I've ever met. She never let anything bother her, and I think the years that she raised our three fine children prove it as they all turned out to be outstanding in every way and very good at problem solving.

We had lunch, and I met Harry and his son, where we proceeded to the lift. We were soon at Midway, and went over to Lenawee Meadows to proceed with our lesson. It was very interesting how Harry's son, immediately caught on, but Harry took a lot longer. His problem was the same as so many. He simply didn't have confidence that placing his weight on his outside ski and rotating with the outside arm would make it all work. Leaning forward, putting pressure on the ball of your foot helps make it work. It always does. And if you learn to do it in rhythm, you soon are able to make linked turns, and quickly master the art of parallel skiing.

So much for my skiing career which helped pay the bills and gave the family lots of fun and free skiing. I continued to teach skiing at the basin until graduation, and even did so for the first two or three years after graduation when I worked in Denver. Free skiing was my motivation, but I enjoyed the teaching, too.

Skiing-A Life-Long Love for Joanne and me

CHAPTER 15

I Learn About Sales

I had been teaching skiing on winter weekends at Arapaho Basin but that only provided a spotty seasonal income though I enjoyed it very much and it gave free skiing for the family. One day Joanne came bubbling into the house and said, "I have found the perfect thing for you."

"What's that honey?"

"I just went to a Stanley Home Products Party and I think it's a way for you to make money without spending a lot of time. You are such a good salesman, anyway. You can always sell me anything. So I think you would be a big success doing this."

"Well, I'll give it a try."

"I have the name of the man to talk to. His name is Fred Babiarz. Here is his number."

I called him and was soon set up with Stanley. The company made household products similar to Fuller Brush Company, in door-to-door sales except Stanley used the party system. So now, I had two jobs and we were able to live very comfortably and even save money. I also found out that I liked selling and business in general. Suddenly a new world was opened to me. I had never experienced one like this before. All of my life I thought only about a medical career and now suddenly I began to think about business as being an attractive alternative career. I also got involved in other business activities like selling and installing lawn sprinklers. I did the selling, Al Sisson, my closest school friend did the installing. I discovered I could sell and I liked it. Al was good at installing which I didn't like so we were a perfect team.

In looking back at those years when I was first introduced to selling, I can't help but think about what it takes to be a good salesperson. It makes little difference, what you're selling. How to be good at it is pretty much the same regardless of your product or service. Here's a list of the things that I find have been essential for me to have been successful in selling:

1. Know your product or service.

2. Know your customer.

3. Learn to ask questions especially in the beginning of the interview and be a good listener.

4. Be meticulously honest and sincere in what you say. Don't exaggerate.

5. Be sure, you can deliver what you promise and follow-up.

6. Get people to like you-smile a lot and make eye contact as much as possible.

7. Make a lot of sales calls.

8. Keep good detailed records so you can analyze your performance as you set objectives.

9. Find the fun in your work and know that you're doing something important.

10. Know that nothing happens until somebody sells something.

Being successful in selling also involves learning how to get along with people. Is there anything worse than an overtly aggressive salesperson? There are certainly a lot of books written on how to get along and be likeable. "How to Win Friends and Influence People" By Dale Carnegie, written in 1936 is one good place to start.

The following points he brings out are his recommendation of six ways to make people like you'

1. Become genuinely interested in other people and their interests.

2. Smile.

3. Remember that a man's name is to him the sweetest and most important sound in any language.

4. Be a good listener. Encourage others to talk about themselves.

5. Talk in the terms of the other man's interest.

6. Make the other person feel important and do it sincerely.

Carnegie's book has been enormously successful over many years and following it will help greatly in achieving success no matter what you do.

I graduated from Boulder in June 1950. I was 25 years old and decided business was for me. This was a disappointment for my father but I later learned from mother that he was always proud of my being able to take good care of my family and always make a good income and get top executive positions in major international companies. I've never had regrets and have always enjoyed a wonderful life in every way.

CHAPTER 16

A New Career

U pon graduation in June of 1950, I decided to go into business rather than continue in medical school. The decision made Joanne very happy, as she was very tired of living on a shoestring with a baby. At the end of my senior year, I interviewed a number of companies in the University job placement program. One was Procter & Gamble who offered me an opportunity in a management-training program, which was to start in September in Milwaukee. We decided to accept and packed up, to drive to Joanne's home in Madison for the summer.

When we arrived in Madison in our ancient Ford station wagon there was a letter waiting for me. It was from a friend of mine from Denver, a Harry Baum who took ski lessons from me at Arapaho. He owned a company in Denver named Noreen, a manufacturer and distributor of cosmetic products. The letter stated that he knew of another company in Denver looking for someone with my background and he talked to the president of the company and said he would love to hire me. And in fact, Harry included in the letter the salary that was nearly twice, what I had been offered at Procter & Gamble.

Well Jo and I loved Colorado, anyway and with the larger salary we just couldn't resist. So we turned around and drove back to Denver. I interviewed the president of the company, James Blount, who told me that with my background, I would be a perfect salesman for their products, which were surgical supplies, sold to doctors and hospitals throughout what is known as the Rocky Mountain Empire. The company, Physicians and Surgeons Supply Company was the most prominent in its field in the area. They had an excellent prominent store and offices at the head of 16th St. in Denver. I was very excited.

So, I started work as a salesman with Physicians and Surgeons Supply Company, a medical supply company of Denver, Colorado in September 1950. We bought our first house in Wheatridge for $11,000 and after training on the many medical equipment and instrument products; I was ready to go on the road.

The company provided me with a brand-new Oldsmobile. So I could leave our station wagon at home for Jo's use and I headed out into my territory, which was Wyoming, Montana, Utah, and Colorado. It was quite a challenge, but I did well at it . . . so well that one day, Jimmy Blount, the president, called me into his office. He told me I was the best salesman, and he promoted me to Sales Manager. I managed 6 salesmen. It was my first responsibility in managing others. I have been in management ever since.

That first real full-time job selling surgical supplies was really a challenge. It involved a great deal of travel by car in the four states, which were called the Rocky Mountain Empire. I remember especially the many miles traveled in the state of Wyoming, where, for example, I could drive from Cheyenne to Casper, which was 90 miles without seeing a single house, or even a gas station. To break down on that road would have been pretty serious, especially in the winter when blizzards often brought several feet of snow and total white-out conditions on the roads. I remembered my Boy Scout motto: "Always Be Prepared". I always carried a sleeping bag and emergency food in the car in the event I got stranded in a blizzard. I did one time drive off the road with no visibility, and was stuck there for about six hours and was very happy to have the sleeping bag to keep warm until a snow plow came by, pulled me out and opened up the road. I followed him into Casper and checked into a hotel until the storm passed, which took another two days.

The blacktop roads I traveled in Montana and Wyoming were not there only 70 years before. Then, there were still bison roaming and Indians on the warpath with Custer's last stand.

Working in that territory was surely a challenge and an adventure at the same time. My clients were always very impressed and appreciative that we made the effort to see them regularly as they needed our medical products.

I learned a few things by that whole travel experience.

1. Plan your week carefully so your company and the family always know where you are.

2. Carry emergency equipment in the car like sleeping bag and emergency food.

3. Always have a couple of good books with you for those down times.

I've often thought back about those early years and how, for me, sales was the perfect starting job in my business career. There are number of reasons why I really enjoyed sales so much. First, I had total freedom all day. No boss breathing down my neck. I was completely on my own solving problems as they came up with no help from anyone. My productivity was always immediately evident to management and I didn't get buried in some administrative office. A young person with a good sales job can make more money than most other starting positions. Finally, I was outside, in nature, enjoying the weather and the views in the magnificent expanse of the Rocky Mountain Empire.

In two years I was promoted to Sales Manager. As sales manager my principal responsibility was to recruit train and supervise the six salesmen in our company. I also called on the hospitals in Denver, Cheyenne, and Salt Lake City as they were our largest buyers and these were the largest cities in my territory. The hospital accounts, involves selling everything the hospital uses including medical sutures and syringes and surgical equipment, and all hospital operating room equipment and furniture. I was constantly reading about the technical aspects of the equipment sold so that I could adequately sell them. My medical background helped.

I'll never forget one of my hospital accounts. It was a Denver Seventh-Day Adventist Hospital, and the administrator was a great proselytizer. He tried very hard to convert me to his religion. I did my very best to keep quiet about my philosophical beliefs as I did not want to get into a confrontational situation with him. I did a lot of listening and used the "Uh Huh" technique. That means, I followed practically everything he said with, "Uh-Huh". It worked. He was a good customer and we even became good friends. Sometimes it's better to know when to keep your mouth shut.

We were successful in growing the company, and I became known with many of our suppliers as a successful salesman and manager. Mostly our suppliers were Eastern manufacturers, and I was offered jobs on several occasions one by Becton Dickinson and Ethicon and another by Johnson and Johnson. But at that point I was really happy in Colorado and with my first management job. Of course, being the Sales Manager of the company suited me just fine even though it was a small company with sales around two million.

My life was one of almost constant travel calling on my hospitals and working with my salesmen to train and motivate them. My salesman excepted me very well, except one. His name was Bob Risaker, and I will remember him if I live to a hundred. He always felt the job should have been his and maybe it should have. But it was mine and I did my best and really loved my work. Bob had to quit in disappointment and anger. I never saw him again.

There were other benefits. I had an opportunity to drop in on all friends. Whenever I was in Cheyenne, I stayed with Al Sisson, a classmate from Colorado University. He'd gone into the oil business as a geologist, and he was prospecting for oil in Wyoming. We always had a great time talking about the old college days and skiing days at Arapahoe. Al always enjoyed showing me the sights of the local town.

The first was Cheyenne on the prairies of Wyoming, then Ogallala, Nebraska, a part of the country, though I can never understand anyone wanting to live in. Then Al was moved to Miles city, Montana. That was a much more interesting place, with mountains and a few trees. It always seemed pretty desolate, however, but Al seemed to enjoy looking for oil, no matter where his company sent him. His wife, Carol, didn't like it, though. The back woods was not for her. She was a city gal.

As I drove to villages like Cheyenne, Ogallala, and Miles city. I couldn't help but remember that it was only about 70 years before that this was Indian Territory. Buffaloes in the millions roamed these prairies, and the country was wild and undiscovered. Here I was in 1953 speeding along at 60 miles an hour on blacktop roads. Just 70 years before there were no roads, just wild Indians, and brave settlers, opening the new lands to civilization and with the only transportation on horseback and trains later.

I later discovered that the president of the company, James Blount, was on very bad terms with the owner of the company. That was Harry Baum, my former ski school student when I was teaching at Arapahoe Basin, I later found out.

One day, and when I returned from Cheyenne there was a note on my desk. "Bill, give me a call. I'd like to talk to you." It was signed Harry. I called his office at his main company in his big office. He told me that he and Blount never got along very well. In fact, he was going to discharge Blount. Harry explained to me eventually that he felt I could do a better job running the company than Jimmy Blount so he asked me to take over as president of the surgical supply company in 1953.

I couldn't believe my ears In 3 years to go from salesman to President. I was doubtful but I accepted. We employed twelve people, of which six were salesmen. It was my first important management responsibility. And of course, I had to study hard to find out about basic things in business, that I had never encountered before such as managerial statistics and principles, accounting procedures and numerous other business subjects. I did not even know what a P and L or Financial Statement were. I went to night school at Denver Opportunity School to learn several business subjects like accounting and managerial subjects. I later taught there as a volunteer in their adult night school but that is another story. At last, I was off the road and could spend every night at home and I was involved in general management, which was a terrific new challenge and I loved it. I also ran my daily world entirely myself. My boss was the owner of this Corporation and as president my job was to make it profitable. As long as I did my job nobody bothered me and I did my job very well. Profits were always good. I really loved the level of responsibility and independence that I had reached and knew then that I really wanted to have my own business eventually.

Freedom to me has always been very important. It is synonymous with independence. Running this little company in Denver gave me a wonderful feeling of independence that I have worked to satisfy my whole life. It took me about 20 years to find that out completely when I quit the corporate world and started my own business in 1970.

CHAPTER 17

Noreen

Harry Baum, was owner of Physicians and Surgeons Surgical Supply Company, (the company of which I was now President) and also owned Noreen, a cosmetic manufacturing company and a couple of other smaller companies. Noreen was growing very fast and presented a much bigger opportunity to Harry, than the surgical supply business. So Harry sold the medical supply company and asked me to join him in Noreen as V.P. Marketing Manager which I did. My salary doubled again so Joanne and I decided to do something we had always dreamed about. That was to design and build our dream house and I was only 5 years out of college.

We had been living for several years in our first rather modest house in Lakewood and now with our enlarging family, more space was needed. There was one area about 20 minutes drive south of Denver in the little village of Littleton called Bow Mar, a gated and very elegant community, that was particularly attractive as it had a lovely private lake for swimming, fishing, and sailing. We were fortunate to be able to buy a 2 acre building site on the brow of a hill overlooking the lake and now we had to find an architect. I later learned that the Bow Mar Board was anti-Semitic. Harry was part Jewish and always felt it. It was a problem but he managed to handle it. I was an atheist and felt all religious prejudice was nonsense anyway. Harry really was an atheist, too. The whole subject of religious prejudice has been important to me in my life. I've always felt that religion was so divisive and the worst idea man. There will be more on this later on.

Joanne's family had just built a house in Madison which was designed by their family friend, Frank Lloyd Wright. Both of us loved his style and wanted to do something just like that but of course not nearly as lavish. We located a Denver architect by the name of James Suddler, who had studied under a Wright Fellowship at Taliesin in Spring Green Wisconsin so we hired Suddler.

Wright called his style a Prairie Home and that's what we wanted as this was certainly prairie land. Except for a little fringe of trees around the lake, there were none just endless views from our 2 acre prairie property in all directions with the beautiful snowcapped frontal range of the Rockies off to the west as a final spectacular backdrop. It was a sensational place to build our second house.

It was not easy to come up with the right design but after a few months Suddler produced what seemed to be pretty much what we wanted within the confines of our budget. We had set $20,000 as the limit for the house which in those days was quite a lot for a small house since we had paid only $11,000 total for our first house including the land. We had paid $8,000 for the two acre site on Bow Mar, which meant that the second house was going to be nearly three times as much as we paid for our first house but we felt we had arrived, in all our innocence, and went ahead. We were never sorry.

When we went out to get bids from contractors the lowest bid was $40,000 to build the house. There was just no way we could handle that so we had to cut the house back some to fit the budget. We did so and started building.

The contractor did the tough things like foundation framing, heating, plumbing, and roof. Joanne and I did all the finishing, siding, and decorative interior. In those days I loved woodworking as did Joanne and we had a wonderful time working together to build our dream home. We worked on it nights and weekends for about a year. It dominated our every free waking hour.

There were plenty of compromises but when we finished, we were proud of it and enjoyed the years we spent there in the Bow Mar house on that lovely lake in Littleton. It was there that we first introduced sailing to the children and they thrived on it. We bought a Sunfish sailboat which we used to race on the lake on weekends. It was a family affair and was mighty joyous. There were about 10 boats in the fleet with regular parties after races. It was a perfect life.

Noreen was my big opportunity. Here was an international manufacturer and distributor of a consumer product that was sold throughout the United States and in Europe in the beauty, drug, and variety-department store industries. We had about 20 salesmen, a factory in Denver that employed about 50 and an office staff of about 15. We also waged a national advertising campaign, and it was my responsibility to manage the marketing and advertising as well as a national sales force and I was still in my twenties. It was a very new world to me and gave me the kind of experience that proved very valuable later in life when I moved to New York City and worked with Clairol.

At Noreen, I was introduced for the first time to market research. This was an entirely new world to me and I learned how important a tool it was in managing a national consumer products business. One of the most important kinds of information a marketing manager needs is, what does the consumer think? It's not easy to get unbiased information of this kind. Dr Burt Klass, of Stamford Research Institute, in Palo Alto, California was an expert in this field. Harry hired him and we both worked with him frequently on various research projects.

One of the most important projects was how does the consumer reacts to a hair color product? What do they think about it? Do they have positive or negative attitudes towards the product? Would they buy it? Those were in the days when haircolor was not regarded very highly. Products of this kind were thought to be used by "painted women." Hair color has come a long way since then to today. It is very naturally used by a large majority of women now and the products are much improved.

Another area of interest is media evaluation. What magazines do people read or what television stations do they watch in the targeted demographic group?

Doing research of this kind is expensive and time-consuming but if it is done correctly, management decisions can be depended upon to be more reliable. Of course there is no exact science here. There still is a great deal left to judgment but research of this kind can help management make informed decisions. I learned a great deal about one of the most important elements of marketing a consumer product from Dr Burt Klass formerly head of Stanford Research Institute of Palo Alto, California.

Since I had been a premed major in college, my courses were heavy in science and balanced by liberal arts. I knew nothing about business. Now with this new job particularly I was in the thick of it. I enrolled in a number of training courses in the American Management Association which at that time were conducted in New York. They were usually one or two weeks at a time and covered special subjects like advertising research and theory and general marketing and management. I also took their marketing management course at Rutgers University for one summer which was about two month's duration. It was a struggle to do all of this study as well as do my job but Harry was very supportive. He was like a big brother to me. The brother he said he never had and always wanted. I was very fortunate to have met him. I look back on this now and realize those years constituted my graduate degree in business and really taught me what I needed to know to be a professional marketing manager of an international consumer products company.

I am greatly indebted to Harry Baum for his very important contribution to my early training and development in business. But as we got to know him better, Joanne developed some animosity towards him for one important reason. He had a wandering eye and that was anathema in our family. His wife, Emmy, was a lovely lady and a very good friend. But my career demanded I overlook Harry's personal life and I was able to do so even though Joanne was not. Both Emmy and Harry are no longer living.

Emmy was interested in the theater. She may have been a bit of a frustrated actress. She was active in the local Denver community theater, who put on plays regularly. One was the Ice Man Cometh. And she said they were looking for actors and asked me if I would be interested. I've always had an interest in the theater. So I said yes.

I auditioned and got the part of the Iceman, which thrilled me. I worked hard at it trying to learn my lines and do my best. Eventually, we played and the notices were good. I must admit, I enjoyed it very much. I guess that appealed to the ham and me. However, to my dismay, Joanne felt this was a monstrous waste of my time. She never attended a single rehearsal or showing. I think she just did not want me to be an actor. I did get the message and never tried that again, because I always valued her opinion and support very much. But I am still a bit of a ham.

During my years with Noreen, Joanne and I got to know Harry and Emmy socially and we frequently enjoyed dinners together on the town as well as skiing with them frequently both in Colorado and in Switzerland. One night we went to a wonderful nightclub in Denver at the top of the Park Hotel among the stars, as they said. There was a floorshow on that night between ballroom dancing featuring a comedian named Doodles Weaver who was the headliner. He was a wonderful entertainer with slapstick comedy that we all enjoyed. Harry enjoyed it so much he practically fell off his chair laughing. Harry loved a good show and especially good jokes.

After the show, Doodles came over to our table to thank us and especially Harry who asked him to join us for a drink, which he did. It turns out he was much more than just a comedian. His brother Pat Weaver was president at that time of NBC in New York and Doodles obviously had a good education and seemed to know many in Hollywood show business. He had graduated from Dartmouth. We enjoyed chatting with him. He told us to give him a call when we were ever in Los Angeles and since I traveled there frequently, as we did commercials in the Hollywood studios, which I had to supervise, I took his number down.

On my next trip out there, I called him and learned that he was spending the summer on Catalina Island where he was the town clown in the village of Avalon. He dressed up in a clown costume and wandered around town in the evening as an entertainer telling jokes, bumping into trees, falling down, making the fool, and altogether making the tourists feel happy about the village. He asked me to join him out there and I did the following weekend. I don't know when I have had a more fun couple of days staying at his apartment and just plain enjoying Avalon and Catalina Island which offers wonderful swimming and sailing and plenty of nightlife. It turned out that a well-known actress of the time was Ida Lapino, who also was on the island. She was Doodles' girlfriend at the time so the three of us were together most of the time. They were marvelous company and Doodles and Ida were the center of attraction wherever they went.

One day Harry called me into his office. "Bill, how is your French?"

"Oh, it's pretty rusty, but I guess I could get along as long as I'm talking. It's been a few years since I studied it in college. Why do you ask?" I had two years each of French, Latin, German, and Spanish in school so I could get along anywhere in Western Europe.

"Well, we've been getting a lot of letters from people in the toiletries distribution field in France asking about Noreen and I have decided to go over and see if we could get into that market. Since it's late fall, I might even do a little skiing. How would you like to come along? I'd like to have my favorite instructor with me."

"I think it goes without saying I would love it. How long do you expect to be gone?"

"I guess a couple of weeks or so. Let's play it by ear."

It didn't take long to get packed. The day we left, we had an important sailboat race in Bow Mar Lake. The timing was pretty close so I arranged for a helicopter to land in our yard for the ride to Denver airport and we were soon off to Paris. The neighbors would never get over that incident. We flew by the early gigantic Stratocruisers which were slow, but very luxurious with the entire plane first class. We had beds and excellent meals. There was even a shower. The passage from New York to Paris took 18 hours with re-fueling stops in Nova Scotia, Iceland, Greenland,

and Ireland. It really was the way to go. I did not remember ever being so pampered before or after.

Harry had been corresponding with an agent in Paris by the name of Jean DeSmett, who was a manufacturer's agent in the cosmetic field. So, on landing, we hailed a taxi to the George le Cinq hotel checked in and then to Jean's office. After a long conversation discussing possibilities, Harry made a deal with him to manage our expansion in France. He told Jean that I would be back to train him and his salesmen in the products. That sounded like fun but that's another story. Subsequently I travel to Paris frequently to train this new operation.

"Now, Bill, how about skipping over to the Alps for a little skiing?" Harry asked. And we were off. We landed in Geneva and decided we'd ski in the Chamonix area where Harry had skied before. One of the things that impressed both of us was a new lift that neither of us had ever seen before. It was halfway between a rope tow and a T-bar except instead of the T-bar; there was a little circular platter that you held between your legs. It was very fast, and efficient. We both loved it.

Harry was always a very inquisitive person. So we had to look up the area manager and ask about this unique new lift. We learned that it was manufactured in Grenoble, and that the owner of the company was a man named Jean Pomagowski. Harry called him and made an appointment to see him. After a couple days of beautiful skiing, we headed down to Grenoble and met with Jean who operated a good sized manufacturing company, which made all sorts of uphill facilities widely used throughout Europe. The new lift was something he had recently developed and as luck would have it, he was looking for a USA distributor. Harry and Jean got along very well and after a wonderful French lunch with lots of red wine and escargot, a deal was made and Harry ended up with the North American rights to this new lift which he named the Pomalift. Some called it the Platterpull.

CHAPTER 18

Entrepreneurism— My New Corporate Career

On returning to the states, Harry and I met with Larry Jump, owner and manager of Arapahoe Basin and we made a deal with him to install the first Pomalift at the basin. It was a big success and enjoyed by everyone. Larry went on with my help to develop his distribution franchise. Pomalift since has become a major ski lift supplier and builder in the US and Canada with many installations throughout the country. Larry eventually sold the company and became an instant millionaire and has since died. I miss him as he was always one of my best friends. Marnie, Larry's wife, lived on for many years afterward in Vail. She has since died.

In the beginning people had to learn to use the Pomalift. It was different. One exciting event was when my own son, Bill, who was only about 7 or 8 years old got on the lift and because he was not very heavy it immediately lifted him off the ground over 30 feet at some times. He held on for dear life and being a very brave young boy soon arrived at the top none the worse for the experience. No wonder he became an expert skier. Billy now lives in Beaver Creek, near Vail, and skis daily, as does his sister Lori who has her own business and also lives in the Vail Valley. Both are expert skiers.

Pomalift grew very quickly because it was a fast, easy way to install an uphill facility and far less expensive for ski area operators than any other lift system. Harry eventually sold the company to Larry Jump who spent much of the rest of his life getting Pomalifts sold and installed in many ski areas around the United States and Canada.

One of the things that we were able to do in Colorado was river running. There were no end of beautiful rivers in the Rockies which we ran including the Blue River, the Colorado River, the Green, the Yampa and others. Sometimes we would go with a group and other times we would form our own group. We heard about one of the most famous river outfitters in the West at that time named Buzz Hatch River Expeditions. One of the trips that he regularly did was on the Salmon River in Idaho.

We called him and found Buzz had a trip planned with a group from the east scheduled to do the Salmon the following summer so we signed on. It was a group from the Appalachian Mountain club in Boston. There was also a couple with whom we became very good friends named Ruth and D'Arcy Brown. They were from Aspen and used a 2-person kayak. The river was astonishingly beautiful with excellent trout fishing and numerous black bears. We spent about 10 days on the river and it will always go down with me as one of our most exciting canoe trips we ever took and we took many in our life.

Later when we got back to Denver the following fall, we received a telephone call from Ruth Brown inviting us to join them at their home for a weekend. They owned and lived on a Ranch outside of Aspen.

They were the ideal hosts . . . when I asked D'Arcy how large his ranch was he said in this part of the world that was like asking someone how much money you have in the bank. Naturally, I apologized. He did say that he could walk from Aspen to Salt Lake City without getting off his property so you can get some idea of its immensity. I eventually learned that the Browns had been one of the original pioneer settlers in Colorado. D'Arcy started Aspen Ski Area and owned it at that time. D'Arcy's grandfather built and later sold the Brown Palace Hotel in Denver. The famous Ruthie's run on Ajax Mountain in Aspen was named after Ruth. The "Unsinkable Molly Brown" was D'Arcy's grandmother. It was delightful to know them and over the years we saw and skied with them often. They became close friends and I miss them. They also are no longer living.

We had a very good friend, Bob Probst, who was an inventor and artist. One of the interesting products, he developed, and patented was a wood connector that allowed for the manufacture of knockdown furniture. I took on the management development of this product as a sideline. Harry was providing the financing.

I traveled to a number of furniture shows and saw a lot of the furniture manufacturers in the East where most of them were situated and felt the product, which we named the Fishbone Connector because of its fishbone like appearance, was a commercial winner. And it got to the point where Harry and I were spending more time on the Fishbone than on Noreen, which was really providing all the money and surely the bigger financial opportunity.

Harry's stepmother, Ellen, having inherited the major stock interest in the company when the founding father, her husband, Harry Sr. died, was very worried that her senior executives were not spending enough time on Noreen. Also, the rapid growth of the Noreen Company required an increasing need for operating capital. So, putting money into the fishbone did not make any sense to her. It was obvious that Harry had made a decision. He wanted to sell the company. He did, and offered, it to me and I bought it for $10,000. It was my first venture as an entrepreneur. It was the first time I was really on my own and I loved it. Freedom, to me, has always been of utmost importance. More valuable than money. As I look back on my life, I am happy to report that most of it has been free so I have achieved my most important objective.

Nearly all of my prospects were on the East Coast as was most of the furniture industry so we decided to rent our Bow Mar house and move east at least for the time being.

I put an ad in the Denver Post newspaper and the first reply happened to be my friend, Pete Seibert. I knew Pete when he managed the Loveland

Pass ski area near Arapahoe. We had often skied together. Since he was in the 10th Mountain Ski Troops during the war, we knew a lot of people in common in the ski world. Larry Jump was a Captain in the 10th with Pete as his first sergeant. Pete was the one who introduced me to Mint Dole, Sr. who started the 10th Mountain ski Troops and the National Ski Patrol System. Mint's son has now married Burgess Russell following her divorce from my son, Bill. Some coincidence in our small world!

Pete and his wife, Mary, came to the house and liked it. I wanted $200 a month. Pete told me he was promoting and planned to develop a new ski area he would call, Vail, an area just over Vail Pass. He laid the development maps out on the trunk of my Ford Convertible. It looked impressive. He said he was looking for investors and offered me a downtown acre lot in Vail if I would give him rent-free for one year. That was $2400 that I really could not afford at the time. Besides, it was my feeling that once you were over Vail Pass it was a straight shot to Aspen. I really doubted Vail would make it. I thought Aspen was so much better a mountain area than Vail and the old frontier town was so interesting whereas Vail is mostly a cow pasture. There was no town there at that time.

How wrong could I have been? That $2400 investment then would be worth in the many millions today. Ah, life! Has anyone else ever made a bad decision?

In 1957, I took over ownership of The Fishbone Connector Company. I resigned from Noreen and moved to New York renting a summer house at Lake Kitchewan in Westchester County owned by Don Budge, the tennis player. To make a long story short, the connector project was not successful and I found myself closing the company and moving back into the corporate world. My first big financial loss. Such is entrepreneurism. Now I needed a job.

In my search for a job, I saw an ad in the New York Times that Clairol, a manufacturer of hair care products similar to Noreen was looking for a product manager. I applied for the job and was interviewed by Dick Gelb, the president, who hired me on the first interview. I joined Clairol as a Product Manager in 1958 with offices at 666 5Th Ave in New York City.

Being a product manager is like running your own little company. You have full P&L responsibility and manage all development, production, and marketing activities. I truly loved the job and did well in it.

After the usual introductions, Dick called me into his office and showed me a small bottle, which was a new kind of hair color. Clairol had made their name with a product successfully marketed as Miss Clairol, which was a permanent hair-coloring product. It shot to success, with a very dynamic marketing program, created by the ad agency, Foote Cone & Belding, with copy written by Shirley Poliakoff under the headline of "Does She or Doesn't She, Only Her Hairdresser Knows For Sure". It was clever and catchy, and made headlines all over the world for its double meaning in a day when sex was never or hardly ever mentioned especially in ad copy.

Miss Clairol was a permanent hair color. That is, once it was put into the hair, it could not be removed. However, it did a very excellent job of changing hair color and disguising gray color, which is one of the main motivations for its use. But it's permanence was a negative. Once a woman decided to use this Clairol, she had to live with that color. Although it was a superior product of its kind in the day, hair still did not look natural. It had that "dyed look".

The new hair color product that Dick showed me was a development by their house chief chemist, Dr. Bernard Lustig, which was classified as a temporary hair color product. That meant that the product could be put into the hair for minor change in hair color but could be removed easily. It was a technological breakthrough in the field but importantly, could cover the gray very well without coloring the remainder of the naturally colored hair. It also left the hair with a silken texture that women liked. Permanent hair colors sometimes left the hair with a coarse feeling. The new product did a good job at improving hair feel as well as covering only the gray hair without changing the remaining natural hair color. It would compete with my old Noreen Company. However, this new product by Clairol was a far superior product to Noreen.

Dick assigned me an office, a secretary, and a very smart assistant named Rollin Montillius. I was on top of the world and off on a career that would be very meaningful. I look back on those years now and no that those years spent with Clairol in New York City really established me as a marketing professional.

For any new product introduction, the first step is to describe the product. That had to be done. It was a temporary haircolor product which disguised the gray hair. The next and very important step is to define the market, its needs, its competition, and its expectations of what a new product can do for them.

So research was the first thing that we attacked. We had to design questionnaires and identify our market which was women who are getting gray, meaning that the age group would be in the +50 years segment. The agency, Foote Cone & Belding, with Frank Mayers as account executive did a wonderful job of design and execution for these important research activities. Again, we used my friend, Bert Klass, at Stamford Research Institute to find the answers to the many questions. It was an exciting time for me.

Then we had to design the product. We had defined our market and research had informed us of their need, which was to get rid of the gray without changing our basic haircolor. Now we had to design the package, write the company, design the ads and the various pieces of literature.

I look back on those days as challenging, realizing that the sessions I had with Harry Baum in Noreen attending the Aspen design Inst. and learning what clean, modern design meant had a great influence on my direction and developing Loving Care. The philosophies of leaders like Herbert Bayer and Walter Gropius still dominate my idea of a good design is in this modern age.

Once we had defined the product, the packaging, and the market, we had to test our conclusions so we went to test markets. We used our regular Clairol sales force but that produced an unanticipated difficulty. The sales force had been promoting Clairol as a permanent haircolor product superior to any other products like Noreen for example. Now we had to convince the trade and the consumers that we now had a temporary product which would do the job better than any other. We selected four test markets throughout the United States and varied only one factor and that was the weight of advertising in that particular market all the other elements of our test were standard for each market. Our headline ad proclaimed, "Loving Care, Hate The Gray, Wash It Away".

To make a long story short the product passed the market test with flying colors and the test allowed us to decide that we would introduce the product with a $2 million magazine and TV campaign. At that time, that was a very large expenditure for the introduction of a new product of its kind, so there was a lot riding on the rollout.

It took about a year of hard work, but we managed to name and package the product and classified it as a new classification of hair color, called Hair Color Lotion. We named the product Loving Care, Hair Color Lotion. Our ad headline was, "Hate That Gray? Wash It Away. Loving Care became the most successful product that Clairol ever developed. Rollin and I also later named and managed the development and marketing of Silk and Silver and the basic work development and marketing for Nice and Easy. All were very successful and still lead the haircolor market to this day.

We wanted to make the introduction of Loving Care very spectacular so naturally we contracted for back covers in Life magazine as well as other major publications of the time. The sales executive for Life magazine was Wally Lauder, who became a good friend as he and his wife, Verna lived near us in Westport. We worked out a TV program all around the headline, Hate That Gray? Wash It Away. The idea was that you could use the product without making a drastic change to your hair color as all other permanent products did and still disguise the gray color effectively. We described the product in terms so the consumer did not think of it as a hair dye which had a bad commercial connotation. It actually has something that would condition hair and make it better to the touch at the same time, disguising the gray. It was a very successful marketing strategy.

We rented the main ballroom of the Astor Hotel on Times Square for our introduction to the trade. This was especially nostalgic to me as I was virtually brought up in this hotel as a child. I could remember coming into this ballroom through the back door in our apartment and down the corridors that we children often explored and coming upon this grand ballroom. It was a memory that will be with me forever. The show went over very well and the product was quickly on its way to making a big success. It ultimately became the single most profitable product in the Clairol line. I got a promotion to a VP and Group Product Manager where I managed the other 6 Product Managers along with a healthy raise. Life was treating me just fine. I learned I was secretly being called "The Goy Wonder" as I was the youngest executive around.

During my years working for Clairol in New York City I commuted from Westport. We had moved there, because our closest friends, Eleanor and Ted Waddell, had moved there from Colorado, where we met them and loved the town. Ted was the son of Chauncey Waddell, Founder and owner of Waddell & Reed, a large investment banking firm on Wall Street, where Ted worked as a VP.

In Westport, we lived near the water, enjoying the Cedar Point Yacht Club which at that time was just a shack on Westport harbor. They had a racing program with 30 foot sloops called, Atlantics. These were lovely, vessels designed by Herrischoff, designer of many of the 12 meter boats. I managed to find an Atlantic for sale, and when I talked about it to the Gelb's, they offered to get involved as partners in the boat. So Dick and Bruce Gelb, along with John Mack, the ad manager became partners with me. We each put in $500. Racing with the Atlantic Fleet was our principal summer fun, and it was a family affair.

Clairol wanted to develop a presence in Europe. The founder of the company, Larry Gelb, Dick's father had been trying for two years while living in Paris to get the product line going but had not been successful.

One day Dick called me into his office. "Bill, you may know, we've been trying to get a foothold in Europe for a couple of years unsuccessfully. Dad has done everything he can, and so far, it's not working. I understand you speak some foreign languages, and you obviously are pretty able in the general marketing management area. You've done such a good job with us here in New York. How would you like to try to get us established in that market as CEO of the European operation? It would mean moving to Paris with your family and probably staying over there a couple of years, after which time you would hire and train a European to takeover permanently"

When I left Dick's office, I was walking again on air, I must admit. I now had a new title, President of Clairol Europe, European CEO and Directoir Generale living in Paris. I could not wait to get home to Westport to tell Jo. At last I was President of a major international corporation and I was only in my thirties.

"You'll never guess, what has happened to me, darling. How would you like to move to Paris? I've been promoted to President of Clairol Europe, and should get over there as soon as possible." I said, barely able to suppress my enthusiasm. "I'm supposed to go over in a couple of days to do some preliminary things. And then I'll come back and help you pack and go over with you and the kids on a steamer. How does that sound?" I was nearly breathless.

CHAPTER 19

President of
Clairol Europe

My promotion to European President in 1960 meant moving to Paris as soon as possible. We sold our house in Westport and packed up, boarded the French ocean liner, Liberte, and sailed in a first class 3 room family suite for Europe. it was a fabulous voyage on the Liberte with all the luxuries one could ever imagine. We even had our dog, Bobo, with us. He had a special kennel on the first class deck on board. The kids had him with them all day, as they roamed the many decks of this beautiful ship. There was always a steward following behind the kids and the dog with a broom and pan to clean up after Bobo as required. Can you imagine such service!

It was a six-day voyage, fortunately with perfect weather, that passed very quickly as we were very busy with all sorts of shipboard activities and parties. The French line really knows how to entertain their clients. Though I must say, as far as I am concerned, one time ocean crossing in a luxury liner is enough. I can't relax that much. I need action. I will fly in the future. I have never been on an ocean liner since though I have crossed the ocean many times to Europe but always by air.

We arrived in Le Havre on schedule, boarded the boat train, and headed for Paris. The company had set us up in an elegant hotel, on Avenue

George 5ᵗʰ, The Prince de Galles Hotel, the favorite of Larry Gelb, Clairol founder and Chairman, and just up the block from our offices at No 9 Avenue George 5ᵗʰ. I had lots of work to get started on at the office and Jo had to find an apartment. The kids had to be registered in school, and we all settled down to our new life in the city of light.

Manufacturing in Europe was headed by Tito Saubidet with whom we became good friends. He was the manufacturing head and a Vice-President and managed both the French and English factories under my direction as President.

Jo found an elegant apartment in the 16ᵗʰ arrondisment one block to the Bois de Boulogne park at 19 Avenue Henri Martin owned by a renowned French General named de Guillibon who was a commanding general in WWII under Supreme French General Le Clerc. I spent my time between Paris and London, one week in each place, as I had to oversee the activities in both companies in each country. The local managers in each of the companies oversaw the local factories as well as the sales and marketing. It was a wild round of travel, meetings, and trying to figure out how to make progress in these countries with American products. We were up against local products, like L'Oreal, who dominated the scene almost completely and with Garnier among others.

We did have the best in advertising agencies, the European equivalent of our leading US agency, Foote Cone and Belding, named Publicis with the most lavish offices I have ever seen on the Champs Elysee. They helped to build and execute a heavy ad program that, sadly, made little progress, no matter what we tried.

The major problem was not distribution as our sales department managed to do that pretty well, the problem was influencing French women. Clairol had been a tremendous success in the states with their magazine and TV campaign, Does She or Doesn't She-Only Her Hairdresser Knows For Sure. We tried very hard to find some way to say the same thing in French. The best we could come up with was, Oui Ou Non, Qui Sait? The line failed miserably to get the idea across. It just didn't hit the double entendre that made the line such a success in the USA. Besides sex in Europe was much more open, not hidden as it was in the US at that time. After nearly 2 years of trying many different approaches New York finally decided to give up on France. During this period, Clairol was bought by Bristol Meyers and Dick was made President of that parent company. His brother, Bruce stepped up to President of Clairol, now a division of Bristol.

L'Oreal, so dominated the European market. The company was run by a man named Blaustein Blanchett who had important political influence in the country where that kind of influence meant a lot. The company was also very successful in other countries of Europe and even in the UK even though it was a French company.

Even in the professional field the hairdressers were simply not influenced no matter how much we spent or how many big shows we put on throughout the country. I, of course, was handicapped with my modest command of the language and our French sales force was just not up to the job of getting hairdressers to use the product in any important volume.

CHAPTER 20

The London Operation

The New York office decided that the French operation was really impossible because of L'Oreal, and it was decided that we close it and move to London and concentrate on that country. We thought we had a better chance there. I spent about a year in Paris, and now another year in London, where we rented the most fabulous country estate in Oxshott, about 20 miles south of London in Surrey. It had a swimming pool and a perfectly manicured grass tennis court and four in help that came with the rent. The owner was also an English General who had been moved to command the troops in the Middle East. Life could not be better, but I must admit we were not able to penetrate these foreign markets and suffered operating losses in both France and England.

The family and I did have a fabulous experience, however.

One summer we spent a vacation week in the lovely little village of Arromanches in Normandy where we rented a house overlooking the ocean. We had an opportunity to visit all the D-Day invasion sites. It was a great education for the children, as well as for Jo and me, too. There was the cemetery stretching for acres, with the little white crosses lined up and the battle museum and the many German bunkers that were now empty and decaying. As we wandered the landscape we could almost hear the gunfire, the bombing, and the endless cries of dying brave young men. It was a grim reminder of those terrible days. I could have been among them if I had not been very lucky and selected the air cadet training program which kept me in technical training school most of my service career.

We brought Joanne's mother, Laura. over for a visit so she was able to enjoy the full Normandy experience with us. We drove all over the Normandy Peninsula while we were there. There are many ancient villages and almost no tourists. The restaurants were simple but with fabulous food. I think some of the best French food I've ever had and of course the local wines were out of this world. The Normandy Peninsula is farm country on the sea with no big highways just little winding lanes without any traffic. It was really a delightful experience for that memorable summer.

While in Arromanches, we were on the beach one day for a swim. This was one of the main D-Day beaches. A nun followed by about 10 tiny children climbed down the sandy bluff on a steep pathway. The nun lined the children up on the beach, seated them on a big log and they proceeded to have lunch. The nun pulled out a bottle of red wine, gave each of the little children a cup and filled each with wine. The children averaged about 5 or 6 years old, I would guess. I thought Joanne's mother was going to have a heart attack. We had to restrain her from breaking up the wine party for the tiny French children.

We also brought my mother to England for her first overseas adventure. She lived with us in Oxshott and loved it.

Another trip we took was down through the Pyrenees and over into Spain to the village of Pamplona where we saw our first bullfight. It was quite a spectacle, we felt, right out of the middle ages. The audience was as enthusiastic as our American baseball or football audiences were and the matadors are idolized throughout the country. It is a savage spectacle however and Joanne soon convinced us we should leave after they killed the first bull. We did enjoy Spain, however with the special food and an altogether different feel than one gets in France. The Pyrenees Mountains dividing France and Spain are not as spectacular as the Swiss Alps and have little snow by comparison as they are at lower altitude and further south. They tend to be dry like the Southern Rockies in the United States.

We also had numerous opportunities to ski while we were in Europe and did so often in Switzerland which was our favorite especially Verbier and Wengen. The facilities and the vertical downhill is very impressive compared to anything I know in the US. Some of the runs were miles long and there were lifts just about everywhere. The Europeans at that time were far ahead of us in the development of skiing. They continue to be, in my opinion. With cheap airfare, it really costs less in Europe for a far better skiing experience.

One of Lori's classmates in the French school was Chloe Gavin. Her father, James Gavin, was the US ambassador to France at that time. He was a former US general during World War II and a hero of the Normandy invasion. Lori and Chloe were close friends. Joanne and I were invited to the Gavin home for a party on one occasion and were very pleased to meet the ambassador and his wife. It was a wonderful experience. The American ambassador's home was really the most lavish mansion I have ever been in. We met many French and American dignitaries.

Finally I got a letter from Dick Gelb. He wanted me to come home as he said, "to introduce more profitable products to the American market" and had decided to close Europe down as it was losing too much money. So, Clairol closed its European operations forever. They never were re-opened even to this day.

The family and I will never forget living in France and England which was certainly the highlight of our lives that taught us much about international living and getting along with people who didn't have the same background as we. I would certainly consider doing it over if given the opportunity and I was very sorry that we lost so much money in such a short time. But, Larry Gelb himself couldn't get Clairol going. So I guess I really didn't feel too badly. I was off to my next adventure.

CHAPTER 21

Headhunters' Holiday

I got back to New York and was royally welcomed by all. But, they really didn't have anything for me to do. I sat around for the better part of six months waiting to get into something. I attended a lot of executive board meetings. All the time, Dick and his brother Bruce, promised me that they would soon have something to assign me. But meanwhile, I went a little stir crazy. I was accustomed to action. I had a big office, an assistant, and a secretary and nothing to do except attend executive meetings. I needed an assignment.

In that world, the so-called headhunters are very active. I was getting calls frequently with opportunities for executive positions with a lot of responsibility and an important increase in my salary. Finally I could resist no longer, and I accepted the executive vice presidency of Carol Richards, a cosmetic company headquartered in New York in Rockefeller Center which wanted to get into a broader hair care product line.

When Bruce Gelb heard about this, he called me into his office and spent almost all day trying to talk me out of my decision. But I couldn't be dissuaded. As I look back now on this whole event, I realize that my career with the large corporations would probably have been enhanced if I had been a little more patient. That is hindsight, but I went on for some very exciting things and a wonderful life of independence in general. I sought independence, really with a company of my own.

I decided to take the Carol Richards offer but it was a mistake. I couldn't go along with the president's ideas, so I let the market know I was available. It was a waste of 8 months.

A headhunter attracted me to go to American Cyanamid Company where I was put in charge of the new consumer products division as Director, reporting to Jim Affleck, President. I had an office in the headquarters in Wayne, New Jersey as well as in Rockefeller Center in the City. I spent most of my time in New York as that was where our advertising and PR agencies were so really I only went to Wayne for executive meetings. The research lab and factory was in Stamford, Connecticut. The company was buying smaller companies like Breck from Springfield, Mass. One of my jobs was to try to put Breck into the haircolor business. Cyanamid was a big chemical company, with all sorts of research facilities in Stamford, Connecticut. So we were able to come up with excellent products. Our first was one to copy Loving Care that I had developed for Clairol.

The Breck Company had a fine consumer franchise as a shampoo manufacturer. So we were able to get excellent distribution. But, we were not able to get the typical Breck customer to buy haircolor. Our original research indicated that might be a problem as the typical Breck gal was conservative and haircolor was considered "risky and down-scale", but we all decided to go ahead anyway. So, eventually we had to withdraw the haircolor product from the market suffering substantial losses. We made the ultimate management mistake. We ignored our consumer research and went ahead anyway, against our better judgment, because we were so anxious to get into the market with our new product. Patience is said to be a virtue that we ignored. I suppose patience is one thing I am short on for better or worse. Mostly worse.

I learned something very important from that experience with Breck. We just didn't understand the conservative Breck customer. They tended to be older and more non-cosmetic using than a typical Clairol customer. Also, in those days, haircolor was controversial. It was looked upon by many as downscale and used only by so-called "bleached blondes." One of the big jobs in Clairol was to convince the public that you could still be a lady and use haircolor. We were never able to convince the "Ladies" of Breck in that era to use hair color.

No amount of advertising succeeded in convincing the typical Breck woman that haircolor was right for her. We lost a lot of money trying.

Meanwhile, Cyanamid was going through some very serious financial problems in its chemical divisions. We had to sell off some of our divisions and the future looked rather dim. The rumors were that Cyanamid was in very serious trouble and might not make it. Again, another headhunter appeared on the scene, and the new offering was Director of Marketing of the Gillette Company in Boston reporting to the President, Vincent Ziegler. This meant moving, of course, but also meant living in the Boston area, which was much more attractive to us than New Jersey where we would have had to move eventually from Westport if I had stayed with Cyanamid and it meant a substantial increase in income. So I accepted the position. Soon, thereafter, Cyanamid closed its doors forever, bankrupt. I had made a very good and timely move.

In moving from Westport, we actually sailed up on our boat. Our family of five sailed our Controversy-30 sloop and after packing up the house, we left Cedar Point yacht club behind and headed for Marblehead. On the way we stopped off at numerous interesting places like Martha's Vineyard, Nantucket, and Cape Cod. And finally arrived in Marblehead Harbor, where we moored the boat off the Boston Yacht Club, which I soon joined.

On the way up, we passed the ocean-front house we had bought in Swampscott. The house was right on the ocean, and it was a thrill for the kids who hadn't yet seen it. It was a lovely old Georgian style mansion, and as I think back on it may have been the best house we ever owned. Not as elegant as Ranworth in England, but very impressive and right on the ocean.

Gillette was an old successful company, not exciting but occupying a dominant position in their large international market. One of the first new products I started working on was a heated shaving cream, which I named, Hot Stuff. We got on the market with an extravagant introduction at the Electric Circus in New York City. It was my first introduction to psychedelic music as it was called then, and exotic new-age stagecraft. It was sort of a forerunner of the current rock and roll scene. I must admit

I didn't like it, but our ad agency, J. Walter Thompson, insisted that it was the right way to go in this new market so I went along with it even though it was not my style. But I was the new boy on the block and had to proceed cautiously. Gillette was a very conservative company and I had to work at understanding their modus operandi.

After a year of Gillette, the management, realizing my European experience, wanted me to go back to Europe to be President of their Gillette Corp. in Italy. It amounted to a move up being once again the CEO of a major international corporation. As a career path it carried serious implications. I could get stuck in Europe forever. Was that what I wanted? No, I really wanted the freedoms of my own company.

CHAPTER 22

Entrepreneurism

I came home that night and told Jo the news. I can hear her sigh so well, she and I lying in bed to the wee hours discussing the subject over and over again. It just did not seem right for us to go back to Europe. Our children's education would be disrupted again, and we didn't want to live in Italy, anyway, in a rather unattractive Italian industrial city where Gillette was headquartered. And I did not speak Italian. Also in the 15 years that we had been married, we had moved six times mostly because of the demands of my corporate jobs. Neither of us wanted to move. We both knew we wanted to choose the perfect town to live in and then start our own business where we could always make our own decisions. That's what we really wanted and finally I had reached the point where I could afford to do just that. I have plenty of money in the bank and the urge to go on my own.

Also, I had achieved my life's career objective of becoming the CEO of a major public international corporation. I could stay with this career and have a good life, but there was another objective on the horizon of my dreams-having my own business and the freedoms that could bring. Freedom has always been my prime motivator.

Personal freedom to do as I please has always been foremost in my life's desire. The corporate life had been good to me, but there is never complete freedom. There is always a boss. One must always follow the corporate policies-like it or not. Jo and I decided never for me again. We're going out on our own.

For the first time in my life, I had enough capital so, I could do what I really wanted most in the world and that is to start my own company. I suppose I really could have retired if I had wanted to do so but that was not for me. I was only 45. Too young to retire. Therefore, we decided that I would resign from Gillette and we would move back to Westport, as it was near New York where we knew people and figure out what kind of a business we would start. Westport was in our opinion the perfect town to raise our family. We all loved the town. So that was our first major non-corporate decision and we were always happy we made it. Complete freedom, at last.

The decision was to be an entrepreneur. To embrace the risks and rewards of freedom. After 20 years in the corporate world, that was a pretty serious, yet exciting decision. I was 45 years old. I really did not know the answers-just the questions. I just knew that I wanted to be on my own and be not dictated to by people above me, who have agendas of their own. Looking back on it, I know it took a lot of courage, and maybe a little stupidity. John Wayne is quoted as having said, "Courage is being scared to death but saddling up anyway." The next 40+ year period of my life was certainly the most rewarding and I think the family and I benefited greatly as well. I would not have done anything differently. I think I have had the perfect life enhanced by that decision.

I resigned from Gillette. We sold the Swampscott house for a nice net profit and moved to Westport, which was our favorite town. We found an old farmhouse on S. Compo Road near the Cedar Point Yacht Club where we were still members and kept our boat. It was a good sized property with a large barn that would later come in very handy as a warehouse when we started Peter Storm.

Good friends were Billy Mills and wife, Joan, former neighbors in Westport when we lived on Dogwood Lane. Ailly was a successful entrepreneur as founder and President of Aquacat Corp, a leading multihull sailboat manufacturer and distributor with offices and factory in Norwalk.

"Bill, we're so glad you moved back to Westport. Now, what are you going to do?" Billy asked.

"Well, Billy, I'm not really sure but I guess the thing that I'm best at is sales and marketing." I offered. "I want to start my own business."

"I've got a good idea for you." Mills said. "My dad, Elmer, is a very successful businessman and I'm sure he would be delighted to give you some advice."

"Bill that would be wonderful. Where does your dad live?" I asked.

"In Chicago in Oak Park. Let me give him a call right now and then maybe we'll go out and chat with him." Billy Mills was marvelously supportive and a wonderful friend.

We met Elmer at his lavish home on Lakeshore and had a very instructive time talking about opportunities for young people with energy and imagination. At 45, I still considered myself young.

"Bill," Elmer asked, "how do you like selling?"

"I love it. The first sales job I've ever had was as a Stanley home products salesman part-time while I was going to college. Then after college I started as a salesman in the surgical supply field. I always liked selling and did well at it."

"If you can sell Stanley, you can sell anything particularly if you like selling." Elmer added.

"Have you ever heard of a manufacturer's representative?" Elmer asked.

"Well, yes, we used them at Noreen, a cosmetic company, where I headed Marketing in Denver." I answered.

"Well then you know, it as an independent sales representative who has a number of manufacturing clients at the wholesale level and sells to retail stores in whatever territory you might select." Elmer explained. "I think that would be a perfect start for you especially since the capital requirements are minimal. All you really need is enough money to live and travel until your first checks start to come in." Elmer added.

Elmer then proceeded to explain to me the details of how to get lines and how to set up a territory.

"Elmer, I can't express my true feelings of thankfulness for your very great help. I think it's obvious that the rep business is something I should do. An important idea is I don't have to risk a lot of capital up front, and I know what I have to do, which is travel and sell until the first checks come in. Then I manage the accounts in the territory. I've always liked to sell, and I've been able to do it productively. So this should be a natural," I added.

Billy Mills and I caught a plane home to Westport.

CHAPTER 23

A Manufacturer's Representative

"Honey, Elmer Mills has really put my future in focus for me. I'm going to start a manufacturer's rep business, and do it in the marine field, which I love and know something about and I think I will like it. What do you think?" I asked. As it turned out, most of the product lines I acquired sold also to the sporting goods market as well as to marine stores. So I became established in both industries, marine and sporting goods.

"Darling, it sounds very good to me. I still have plenty of questions, but except for the fact that you will have to travel a lot and be away from home, it seems like the right thing for you to do at this time. I'm all for it." Jo was always so supportive.

Next month, January, was the important New York Boat Show at the Coliseum. It was the most important show of its kind in the country. So naturally, that is where I headed. The show has what they call Dealer Days. The first three days of the show, no consumers are allowed and I was free to go from booth to booth looking for lines. The first line I got was Avon Inflatable Boats from England. This was to prove to be a very fortunate acquisition for me. However, I also picked up a speedboat and sailboat line, a foul weather gear line from England, and a number of smaller marine hardware product lines. I was in business.

I decided I would select New York, New England, and Florida as my territory, because they had the obvious seasonal balance, which was good for the Marine field as well as the sporting goods market. I contracted for booths in all the major marine and sporting goods shows in the Northeast and in Florida for the coming season. Eventually, we exhibited at about 10 tradeshows throughout the country, including Boston, New York and Miami, Chicago, Las Vegas and Los Angeles. The business required a great deal of travel to recruit and establish dealers.

One of my biggest successes was Avon. When I took the line over the company had two dealers, Abercrombie and Fitch in New York City and LL Bean in Freeport, Maine. When I resigned the line three years later, we had over 100 dealers and the company had multiplied its sales many times. Today inflatable boats are a standard marine product with every yachtsman, and Avon was responsible for that important shift in opinion from so-called "Rubber Ducks." Inflatable boats had arrived, and my rep business really benefited by this important success story in fact I was significantly responsible for this change.

The Manufacturers Representatives job was to sell my clients products all over the territory to dealers. I traveled throughout New England, New York, and Florida. It was hard work, but the income was excellent as my lines sold well. Had I stuck with this, I would have become wealthy.

When in Florida, I often flew over to Havana, where my old friend Al Sisson was now a corporate prospector for Mobil looking for oil in the Caribbean. The last time I was there, Batista was about to be overthrown by Castro. It was a pretty wild time. The Cuban revolution was very significant, and I was there right on the eve of it when streets were rioting everywhere. I somehow managed to get out.

I had manufacturers coming to me, with lines. So I could be highly selective. I also found something else; the foul weather gear line that I had acquired was named Peter Storm. It was an English product owned by a man by the name of Noel Bibby. We hit it off right away, and I saw what I considered a big marketing opportunity with that product line throughout North America.

CHAPTER 24

Peter Storm

Since my experience was national marketing of consumer products. I just felt that we could do great things with Peter Storm. I offered to start a corporation with Noel where each of us would own 50% of the company marketing to all of The Americas. I would capitalize it and take all profits. Noel would make his profit on selling the products to me as the North American exclusive distributor. He would do the manufacturing.

Noel agreed and we proceeded to look for inventory/receivables financing. I had gotten to know Bill Anderson slightly as he was a member of the Cedar Point Yacht Club where we had raced our 30 foot Atlantic sloop. Bill was president of the Westport Bank and Trust Company. Noel and I made an appointment at the bank with Bill. We were ushered into his beautiful office in the bank and welcomed warmly after introduction of Noel.

"What can I do for you Bill?"

"Well, Bill, Noel and I have decided to start a new company in the US and in Canada. Noel is a garment manufacturer in Nottingham England of sportswear including foul weather gear. We need a little operating capital."

"How much do you think you need?"

"I think a $100,000 credit line will do it to get going."

"Okay, you have it."

Noel was beside himself. He just couldn't believe that capital was so readily available as he was having great difficulty obtaining capital for his expanding business in England. I had developed a healthy net worth and Bill knew it which helped. He also knew my business background. That line of credit that started out at $100,000 grew eventually to well over $500,000 as Peter Storm developed in the USA.

Operating Capital to fund our company really was eventually our major problem. Peter Storm grew quickly. It was not only a good product but we had excellent distribution eventually with over 2200 dealers and our advertising using the ad headline, "No Sweat," made a good impression on consumers. We had most of the back covers on the major marine and sporting magazines in the industry including YACHTING, SAIL, BOATING, SKI, OUTDOORS and many others. Yachting, especially, became very important as the oldest and most prestigious yachting magazines in America where we had 6 of their back covers. I became good friends with the editor, Bill Robinson, who sponsored me to membership in the New York Yacht Club. As I was frequently in the city, the club was an excellent place to take guests for lunch. In those days, the Americas Cup, which we had held for many years, was on a glassed pedestal in the entry doorway.

Sail Magazine was just started by founder, Bernie Goldhirsch. When he asked if we wanted to be an advertiser, as we had been in his Boat Directory, I said we'd take all back covers. That made us his largest advertiser and largely responsible for his successful start up as he informed me in later years.

I had a large barn in Westport on the property at the back of our house on Compo Road, which we could use as a warehouse which we later moved to a larger place in Bridgeport when we needed more space.

I resigned all my other lines, and really dove into the opportunity making Peter Storm, the leader in its field. This was a family affair. The boys and Lori had graduated from college so we were all together, selling, packing, shipping and managing what became the number one product in its field. I found a sweater manufacturer in England and took it over as well, selling their Oiled Wool Sweaters, something completely new to the American market. We hired a warehouse manager, Bill Spader. Sales zoomed ahead, we eventually sold more sweaters than foul weather gear as, of course, sweaters are worn by more people than foul weather gear and the products complimented each other. We quickly doubled our sales to well over 2 ½ million dollars.

Hello daddy. I'm here, can you pick me up?"

Where are you?"

At the airport?"

The airport, I thought you were coming by bus."

"Well, I wanted to surprise you, so I flew down from college."

"I didn't know there was air service from the Skidmore area."

"There isn't. So I flew myself."

"You flew yourself? What are you talking about?"

"Well, I took flying lessons. I'm a pilot."

"I'll be right out to pick you up, where are you at the gate or where?"

"Private planes come into what they call the fixed base operator. So just come out to the airport and ask for the FBO."

That was the beginning of a whole new era in my life and an exciting one for me. My daughter the pilot really astounded me. But then she has always been a very adventuresome person. So it's not too surprising. I picked her up at the airport, and learned a lot about her experience and vowed that if she can do it. So can I.

In those days I was traveling quite a lot, working with our reps establishing dealers around the country for Peter Storm and it seemed to me that a small private plane might be very efficient. I enrolled in a pilot school first at the FBO in Bridgeport and later at Emery Riddle in Miami and, and in a few days was able to solo. I even got an unlimited instrument rating. I was flying small single-engine Cessna and Piper craft. It really was a thrill. After all these years, I finally won my wings as well as an instrument rating.

I enlisted in the air Corps during World War II, to be a pilot, but that was not to be, because of my visual acuity not being up to military standard. Now, at last, I was a pilot

Flying has always been in my blood. As a young person. I made a lot of flying models, both rubber band powered and with small gas engines. In those days, the popular models for World War I, were airplanes with two and even three wings. I just couldn't get enough of airplanes during those teen years. Actually, it's strange that somehow, I didn't manage earlier to learn to fly. But never got around to it. Lori motivated me.

So I started out using a small rented Cessna in my travels, and it worked out pretty well. I would fly a commercial plane to the local airport and rent a plane and then go off seeing dealers in that contiguous area.

I heard of a very good school outside of Miami, by the name of Emery Riddle so I signed up with them and in about a week I had my unlimited instrument rating. I could fly under most conditions. Normally, the biggest problem is perhaps the 500 or 1000 feet of visual rule flying. And then there's a bank of clouds, which might be another thousand feet above that. It's usually quite sunny. So I was really flying in bright sun light, and only have the problem of going thru the bank of clouds and breaking out usually with another thousand feet or so below, to make a landing. Naturally, it was necessary to use instruments and flying charts. So the navigation skills are required to get from A to B, but it was not complicated. Particularly as even the smaller planes were well instrumented in those days. I can't remember when I had so much fun being on the road selling Peter Storm. I did that for years.

On some occasions, I really did some unusual things. For example I would take a commercial plane to Las Vegas, and then rent a small plane and work in the Nevada area. One time I flew down to the Grand Canyon, and actually went below the rim along the river. In one of the most exciting flights I've ever taken. Another time up in the Northwest. I flew around Mt Rainier outside of Seattle and circled Mt Hood in Oregon completely flying close enough to the mountain so I could see all the features. It was very thrilling. There are many other examples of being able to explore at low altitudes.

Modern aircraft are nearly foolproof I feel it is usually the pilot, who is making errors or flying beyond his skills that create problems. Of course checking everything out is essential before you even get in the aircraft so everything is in perfect working order. All the controls must work exactly right and the engine must sound right. So many questions like small noises when you taxi? One of the biggest problems is weight and balance in a smaller aircraft amount of weight to carry is critical. And weight has to be balanced, so the aircraft will take off and land correctly. And fuel management is critical. You don't have a replacement fuel pump on every corner.

I was able to do this for several years and really enjoyed it immensely. But there came a time when we established our dealers and it was no longer necessary for me to do the initial contacting and our salesman could do the follow-up. My time was required in the office, sadly, as I really missed the open skies that I found so welcoming. But marketing the product took first priority of my time.

We did a lot of advertising in yachting publications. Magazines like Sail, Cruising World, and Yachting, where we actually ended up owning most of their back covers in full color. So we had an opportunity to tell our story with great effectiveness as we were the dominant advertiser in the country in our market. Peter storm had become the best known name in the yachting industry as well, as in sporting goods in general.

I realized how important marketing was so I hired Bill Negron who used to be art director for Clairol. We had always worked well together there. We owned a lot of back covers in the major magazines that are field. Now the job was to fill the space with the kind of advertising that drove people into the stores. That was the kind of challenge I faced many times in the past so I felt right at home.

Bill is not only an excellent art director, but also the photographer of note. We used our family for models as they were all good-looking and we produced some back cover ads that I'm still proud of and have hanging copies of many of them in my home. They struck gold immediately and we became probably one of the more important factors in our industry in both the Marine and sporting goods outlets.

One thing we discovered in both the Marine and sporting goods fields was that all of these stores specialized mainly in hardware items. At that time in the Marine stores we found rope, anchors, winches, nuts and bolts and many items often found in a hardware store except they were of higher quality so they wouldn't corrode in a saltwater atmosphere. In the sporting goods stores there were footballs baseballs hockey sticks and all sorts of assorted sporting hardware.

Son, Bill Modeling Peter Storm Sweater and Trousers

We thought we saw an opportunity to put both of these kinds of outlets into the clothing business so we designed a special spiral clothing rack that we gave to the stores free with their initial order. We also taught the dealers how to sell clothing by letting consumers try on the jackets and sweaters. All the garments therefore were hung up right out front for easy access by the consumer and not tucked away on some shelf. We printed colorful Peter Storm signs for the top of the rack and generally managed to produce our own little point of sale display in each of the stores. We really introduced clothing and in-store clothing merchandising to these industries. It went over very well and we soon became one of the leading lines of its kind in both of these outlets. We also went to both marine and sporting good shows throughout the country so we were all busy going to places like Las Vegas, New York, Chicago and Miami where the major shows are held.

We did well with Peter Storm, so well that I bought a large property and home on Greenfield Hill in Fairfield, Connecticut. There was a pool and tennis court. Life was really treating us very well. This aerial view shows it after we sold it and it had been enlarged by the new owner. We lived there about 12 years. It was really a lovely place. Out in the quiet countryside but only 5 minutes to the Fairfield RR station which was only about an hour into NYC and a little over that to JFK airport. So it was very convenient especially as I was traveling abroad often in those years.

My friend, Bill Mills, owned a large sailing vessel called a brigantine, which was 105 feet long, had six cabins all with private toilet and bath facilities, and required a crew of four. Bill used it to entertain, and for him in the yachting business, it was a complete write-off.

I was looking for something to make our advertising more interesting. We had developed, an advertising campaign, using most of the back covers in the yachting publications. I suggested to Bill that we change the name of the brigantine from Dana to Peter Storm and use it in our ads. Bill liked the idea. So we got started. We inserted a line at the bottom of each ad, The line that "The Brigantine Peter Storm Is Available for Charter to Selected Parties." We began to get plenty of phone calls, which Joanne handled inquiring about the vessel. When they found out that it had six double staterooms they realized it was too large. Joanne offered to find them another vessel, and suddenly we found ourselves in another business, which Joanne ran. We named the new company Russell Yacht Charters and it grew very fast under Jo's able management and soon became a leading charter company.

One day son, Billy came into my office, and I asked him how it's going he replied that he was sick of all the traveling. I asked him what kind job you wanted. He said, "I'd like to have your job."

"Okay, you can become president, and I will be the sales manager. How does that sound?" I answered.

Billy was delighted and did a very good job as president for some time. I also was having a lot of fun flying around the country in my little plane, seeing all the dealers and running the shows. The company continued to grow rapidly.

In fact, it all grew a little too fast. Capital became the problem.

Noel, in England, was having cash flow problems so he couldn't build production to meet sales. He just didn't have the operating cash. As a result, he was heavily back-ordering us so we could not properly service our dealers. It was seriously hurting us—our reputation and our growth.

Bill Anderson, president of the Westport Bank, was unable to keep up with our cash needs and what became increasingly important was our need for additional capital in the company as well. We had found an investor, and I flew over to England to convince Noel, that we should bring in a partner with new operating cash. I also wanted to consolidate the North American operation with England and make it one worldwide company that Noel owned 1/3. Billy had found an investor who was to invest $2 million for a third interest in the company. I would own the other one third.

This is really the first time that Noel, flatly disagreed. I told him that if we didn't get more capital in this business that we would fail. He just did not understand this. We discussed it at great length, but finally I realized he was adamant. Because he was the founder of the name Peter Storm, I felt that he should have preference so though I made him an offer to buy him out he wanted to buy me out and I allowed it. I could have stopped the buy-out, but did not want to. Noel was the originator and I felt I should honor that. Shortly thereafter Noel died and the company went bankrupt.

Russell Yacht Charters which Joanne and I started really almost accidentally when people called to charter the Brigantine Peter Storm, they discovered it was too large for most groups. So they asked if we had smaller vessels for charter. Joanne was interested in the subject. So she picked up the calls and searched for vessels that would meet the need. Slowly the business grew from only Florida and Caribbean charters to a wide variety of charters in the Pacific at Hawaii, the Mediterranean along the coast of France and Italy, as well as the eastern part, near Turkey and Rhodes in Greece.

We always had a number of offers from our charter boat captains to come visit them and take a sail, which we often did as we got airfare first class free and the charters cost us nothing. So we could enjoy an exotic quick yachting trip with virtually no cost. What a wonderful life?

Our favorite place was chartering in Turkey. Joanne had developed a friendship with a booking agent in Marmaris named, Kamal, who set up many of our charters. Though there was every kind of imaginable yacht to charter, we liked the native Gullets best.

Gullets are a traditional Turkish sailing vessel that have been adapted to yacht charter. In the early days, the boats were very basic and provided little in the way of creature comforts. Today that has all changed; with satellite televisions, full air conditioning, Wi-Fi, satellite computer networks, hot showers and a variety of other luxuries; lavishness is now the order of the day. This is one of the most relaxing ways of enjoying a yachting holiday there is. We visited a number of very interesting historical spots.

The Marble Streets of Ephesus—Home to another of the Seven Wonders of the Ancient World is the monumental Temple of Artemis. Ephesus was an incredible center of learning and a city with a fascinating religious history. It was originally founded by Greece in the 11th Century B.C. and was the most important city in Asia Minor for many centuries. It was upon these streets that St. Paul is said to have once preached, and hidden among the overlooking hills, lies a remote chapel built upon the site to be the final home of Mary, the mother of Jesus.

Bodrum, originally known as Halicarnassus, was one of the earliest centers of civilization, settled in the 12th Century B.C. Halicarnassus was home to Herodotus, the "father of history," who traced the city's roots thousands of years back to the Dorians. Later conquering and inhabiting the city were the Carians, Lelegians, Persians, Romans, Byzantines and finally, the Turks, who introduced the name Bodrum.

A gorgeous backdrop of pine-clad mountains looms behind the seaside resort of Marmaris in southwest Turkey. Popular as a cruise ship and yachting port and with the British budget holiday crowd, Marmaris offers an abundance of excellent restaurants, and the restored castle of Suleyman the Magnificent and an appealing cobble stoned old quarter. Bars and restaurants line the marina. Outside the busy town, coves and bays of the Datça Peninsula make lovely daytrip destinations for those traveling by boat. We spent much time there over the years.

Of all the places Joanne I sailed, certainly, the Turkish coast was the most interesting as it offered not only beautiful weather and luxurious Gullets but fabulous ancient sites of great historical significance. It was our favorite place for cruising on a private yacht and we did a lot of it.

CHAPTER 25

Our Children's Marriages

I f you had to indelibly mark the passage of time nothing does it like the marriages of one's children. It was the first time in my life that our firstborn decided to marry that I came to the sudden stark realization that time had really passed and I was growing older.

I don't remember her name or any of the details. Just that Billy was suddenly married. It was very short-lived, and he was suddenly single again. It was a matter of months.

In his further wanderings, he chanced to meet a very lovely girl, Burgess Ahrens of Bronxville. She was from a fine family, educated, and beautiful. Joanne and I could not have wished for a better additional daughter.

Her distinguished father, Dr. Edward Ahrens, known as Pete, was a research scientist involved with the study of whether dietary change could help people avoid arteriosclerosis. He worked at the Rockefeller Institute for medical research, now known as Rockefeller University, studying the effects of dietary fat on blood cholesterol. He eventually headed the Rockefeller Institute and was elected to the National Academy of Sciences. He was awarded honorary degrees at the University of Lund, Sweden and the University of Edinburgh Scotland. His wife of 60 years was the former Bonnie Forbes, also from a distinguished family. They together established the mountaintop arboretum in Tannersville. New York.

Bill's marriage to Burgess produced two fine boys, Peter and Alex, but the marriage ended in divorce after 24 years, unfortunately. Burgess continues to be one of my best loved friends and really continues as a daughter to me, I am very happy to say. She has re-married Minot Dole, a good friend, and now lives in Northern Vermont near the village of Burlington.

Billy has remarried a lovely lady, Janice of Beaver Creek, Colorado where they reside. I know nothing of her background as I have, unfortunately, no contact with them.

Torrey also was briefly first married to a lovely girl, whom Joanne and I loved dearly, but their marriage was also to be brief.

He then met another beautiful girl, Barbara and they married. Barbara is an outstanding contributor. Their daughter Lauren has become an all A's student and graduated from Yale in 2009. Lauren is now executive assistant to one of the presidents of Nike and at the moment living in Africa.

Lori decided to move back to Colorado, where she was born, as she loves skiing, white-water kayaking, and backpacking above everything else. She started her own contracting business and has been very successful building large luxury residences in the Vail Valley. Though she was married briefly, she is no longer married and is living as a single woman in the mountains that she loves.

I was very fortunate in marriage. Though Joanne and I eloped when we were only 21, we were truly in love and maintained that relationship for over 54 years until she died of cancer in 2001. It was the perfect marriage for us both. She was my complete loving partner in everything I did. Going on in life without her is very difficult, If not, almost impossible.

I feel marriage is one of life's most important institutions. When we enter into it, we do so because we are in love. And that is the way it should be. When two intelligent people marry and vow their mutual love, it does not mean there will not be differences. Joanne and I had plenty of differences. However, we had one rule, and that was before going to sleep at night, we would kiss and make up. It worked.

Of course that does not mean the differences went away. It just meant we had to discuss them further and because both of us were reasonable, we were always able to work out our differences to our mutual satisfaction. That seems like such an easy formula. I often wonder why others don't know about it, which could do away with an awful lot of divorce.

CHAPTER 26

RAM Knitting

After reluctantly selling Peter Storm to Noel Bibby, my former partner, I now had plenty of money, a lovely home paid for on Greenfield Hill in Fairfield but no business. I could easily have retired but did not want to especially since I was still in my 50's. Retirement has never been an attractive idea for me. Noel did his best to solve the problems of Peter Storm after he bought me out, but ultimately the company went into bankruptcy, as it couldn't pay its bills, and, sadly, Noel died, a broken man. Peter Storm is no more.

Meanwhile, since I had earned a pilot's license, with instrument certification, I started to fly all over the East looking for companies to buy. I was finally a millionaire and I had a wonderful time in my quest for a new challenging business opportunity.

This was the one time in my life where I was the most independent. We had no debt, owned and lived in a beautiful house on Old Academy Road on Greenfield Hill with a pool and tennis court and had plenty of time to ski and hike. And we still owned Russell Yacht Charters which Joanne had built into a substantial little business and which was fun for us both. Not only was the income nice, but it afforded us frequent use of big yachts world-wide at no cost

On those solitary flights around the Northeast, I had time to think about what I really should do. I could have retired but I did not want to. I know that I never will. Business is too much fun.

Though I had done volunteer community work from time to time in my life, I certainly didn't do as much as I should have. I was a volunteer teacher at the Denver Opportunity School teaching salesmanship and marketing. Later I was a volunteer professor at Bridgeport University teaching inner city kids about sales and marketing. Then I was active for several years with Zero Population Growth and Planned Parenthood working with two Yale professors traveling around New England making speeches to various groups about the problems of overpopulation. This was very interesting work but I got to the point where I was getting threatening letters from those who didn't agree with population control because there was an important religious overtone and in fact I had my mailbox torn down a couple of times receiving nasty threatening letters. From the tone of the letters I received, the writers were obviously religiously motivated. Joanne and I also did a lot of volunteer work for the Appalachian Mountain club on the Major Excursions Committee at Boston headquarters. I was the founder and chairman of the Fairfield AMC Chapter and she and I led many hikes on a volunteer basis. These hikes were in the New England, Colorado, and California Mountains as well as to Switzerland, Italy, and Austria. We also led many ski trips domestically to the Rockies and Alta Wasatch Mountains and to the Alps in Switzerland.

We still had Russell Yacht Charters which Joanne was running and it was profitable but really I still felt the need to buy or start another business. I found several and eventually settled on one manufacturing, children's sweaters with the plant in Deer Park, Long Island employing 99 people. I bought it but that turned out to be a very bad decision.

I had originally planned to move the knitting company to Connecticut and get the state to help in the financing of the move, because we had about a hundred employees. I was unable to do this. I fought the battle for five years, but ultimately lost because contract manufacturing in the knitting industry disappeared from the United States. It went to low-wage countries, like Sri Lanka and China. The company that I had enthusiastically bought and renamed Ram Knitting, failed. I lost my entire working capital. It was a terrific blow. I had really failed disastrously for the first time.

I have often thought about the reasons for this failure. There were many. The most important was that this was a period of transition for the knitting industry. Formerly there were hundreds of knitting manufacturers in the USA. Suddenly they were all going out of business with the work going to Sri Lanka and other countries in the Orient. The reason was the far lower wage scale in these countries for entry level factory labor. American manufacturers could not compete.

There was another reason for me. I found I simply did not like running a factory. I tried diligently during those five years to become accustomed to factory management. It just did not work for me. It became a chore every day just to go to the plant. As I looked out over the factory floor at the 99 workers doing their routine tasks producing knitwear, I could not help but feel that it was all just to make money. There seemed to be no other objective. Just making money has never been a strong motivator for me. I learned that at my factory. There was no fun in my day. Little wonder it failed.

CHAPTER 27

What Do I Do Next?

After I closed the factory with a complete loss of all my working capital, I worked with Joanne in Russell Yacht Charters, answering the phone and surveying yachts, but I must admit the business was not that interesting to me. It was a lot like real estate which I also found uninteresting. Also, it was Joanne's business really. Though I had started it, she really built it, and she liked it. So though it provided a good income, I had to find something else.

With my losses from RAM Knitting, we did not have enough cash flow. So we had to sell our wonderful house on Old Academy Road and move to a lesser property on Hulls Highway, which after fixing it up eventually became a very nice property.

"What in the world am I going to do, darling?" I pleaded with Jo. "I know we still have the yacht charter business, thank goodness, but there's not room for both of us in that. Good gosh, I'm in my 60s without a job or company, and no risk capitol."

"I know you'll figure it out," Jo was always so supportive. She forced me to believe in myself. Her support meant everything.

So, I tried a number of things. First, it was real estate, and then the insurance business then consulting, but I was not happy, and really I failed to get anything started. I was at my wits end. Then we went to dinner one night at son, Billy's house.

"Dad, you know, you and mother have always led hikes for the Appalachian Mountain Club. Have you ever thought of starting a hiking tour business?" Billy asked.

Jo and I had been major excursion leaders for the AMC for many years and have always filled any of the trips that we set up, whether they were in the US or to Switzerland where we got to know the Alps very well. We had developed a good reputation with the AMC for conducting good trips. Maybe it was an idea. Jo and I talked it over with Billy and the more we talked the more sense it made.

Though we both were 65 years old, we were both blessed with a lot of energy and good health. Leading hikes in the Appalachian Mountain club for many years both domestically and abroad kept us in good shape. We were still skiing and hiking regularly and felt up to just about any challenge. When I gave it further investigation I also realized that it required almost no capital.

So, I thought I would give it a try. First I named the company Bill Russell's Mountain Tours and designed some literature. I had a list of names and address of AMC members that Jo and I had led on trips in the past. I set up four trips to Switzerland in areas I knew in the cantons of the Valais, the Bernese Oberland, and the Engadine. I called it The Three Culture Hike and all four trips filled. We booked 80 clients and made a very good income the first summer. We spent all of July and August in Switzerland. I really knew that Billy's suggestion was excellent, and that this was going to be an interesting and profitable business that suited us perfectly. The greatest thing about it was it did not require a lot of operating capital and was fun. I had saved the best for the last.

The Dolomites in The Ticino

Over the years, I added countries, to Switzerland including Norway, England, Ireland, Scotland, France, Italy, Slovenia, Spain, Nepal, and Austria. We started setting up a lot of trips. I began to hire and train guides. I had as many as 11 guides at one time. The business was extremely successful. I was able to pay off the latest mortgage, getting back to where I was before I bought the knitting factory and we were able to put money aside for old age though that was never high on my agenda as I love to work. I am happy to say the Tour business continues to this day as a fun and profitable activity. I really will never retire.

Hiking In The Swiss Alps on The Haute Route-A hike
from Chamonix, France to Zermatt, Switzerland

This period of my life was one of almost constant adventure. Mountain Tours was seasonal with skiing in the winter and hiking in the summer, so Jo and I were able to plan a number of adventures. Additionally Russell Yacht Charters was increasing in activity so we often went to inspect yachts in many parts of the world including the Mediterranean, Turkey, and the Caribbean. Inspecting often led to sailing them. Many were in the 60 foot plus range with experienced crew. We were living the life of the very wealthy. And it all costs us nothing even our air travel first class was free because of my arrangement with Dean Hoffman at his travel Agency.

Joanne in the Alps

One of our greatest adventures was backpacking a portion of the Pacific Crest Trail in California. Located within easy driving distance of San Diego, Los Angeles, San Francisco, Sacramento, Portland, and Seattle, the PCT is both easily accessible and blissfully wild at the same time. It offers the best of the West including the Mojave Desert, the Sierra Nevada and Mt. Whitney, Yosemite National Park, Marble Mountain and the Russian Wilderness in Northern California, the volcanoes of the

Cascades including Mt. Shasta and Mt. Hood, Crater Lake, Columbia River Gorge, Mt. Rainier, and the remote Northern Cascades.

We decided to lead an AMC hike with a group of 20 hikers in the southern section from Lake Tahoe in Nevada to San Bernardino in California, a distance of about 168 miles, which we planned to do in 3 weeks meaning a daily hike average of about 8 miles. We planned 2 miles per hour or 4 hours each day of hiking. With minor adjustments this worked out very well.

Our food and water planning was the most critical as we did not want to carry everything for the full three weeks. Numerous east—west highways cross the trail where we mailed food to the local post offices in our name. We carried only freeze dried foods so spoilage was not a problem and, of course, the trout in the streams supplied fresh and delicious protein. There were numerous streams to cross as well so water was not a problem.

In advance of the trip, we had a couple of prep hikes in the White Mountains of New England to check all participants' abilities and equipment. There were a few we could not accept as their physical condition and experience was not up to the demands of the proposed hike. Our group was only as strong as the weakest among us. We are happy to say all who started were able to complete this memorable hike.

The detailed story of this wonderful hike could be a book by itself. Suffice it to say, this adventure was near the top of our list of adventures.

Then I got a phone call. "This is Al Sisson, how are you, old friend?" Al was a classmate from the University of Colorado. He was like a brother to Joanne and me then and I kept pretty close contact with him over the years. Since he was an oil geologist, he had lived over much of the world. In my travels, I visited him in Cuba, Guatemala, Peru, Mexico, and Canada, and now soon to add Alaska.

"Bill I've got a good friend who has been moved from the Anchorage office to the one in Cordova. He has a great sailboat that he keeps in

Seward and he has offered it to me if I'll deliver it to him in Cordova. He doesn't have time to do it himself right now. The boat is about 40 feet long. A sloop that sleeps four in two cabins with a head and a galley and all the usual equipment. How would you and Joanne like to help me sail it from Seward to Cordova through the Prince William Sound? It would be about 190 miles and we could do it in a week or two but I would like to take three as the place is so beautiful and the salmon and trout fishing absolutely fantastic"

"We would love to do it with you and Carol I presume?"

"Well, I'm delighted you want to do it but sadly Carol will not be with us. She got her PhD last year and has been accepted at the University of Oregon as a professor of history. So she just moved down there and I guess has finally decided she wants to separate. She really doesn't like Alaska. It's a little too primitive for her tastes. You know she is really a city girl"

"I'm certainly sorry to hear about Carol leaving but I think maybe you mentioned a year or so ago that this may be coming."

"Yes, we've had a good marriage and a good family but I'm afraid things have deteriorated and we just have to be practical. I love what I do. The oil business has been good to me and the moving around suited me fine though Carole did not like that."

Joanne and I had been thinking about doing some backpacking in Alaska on the Kenai Peninsula so this invitation from Al was really just perfect. We could spend a few weeks sailing on the Prince William Sound and then go over to the Kenai Peninsula for a week or so of backpacking. When I talked to Joanne about it, as usual she was ready to go as she always was. She could not have been a more perfect mate for me. We both loved the same things—hiking, skiing, sailing, and just generally adventuring. We hadn't taken any time off since the past winter when we did a cross country ski in the Engadine of Switzerland leading a group of about 15 climbing on skins. Summer was coming so we started planning immediately.

We decided to go by way of Japan where we spent 3 week sight-seeing this lovely country. That could be a book, too.

Al sent us pictures of the boat which looked perfect for what we intended to do. I had read a lot about bears in Alaska and in discussing it with Al realized that we had to be careful especially when we moored at night to be far enough off the beach so a bear would not swim out while we were sleeping and board us. The same potential problem was on the backpack that we planned on the Kenai Peninsula. When we arrived in Anchorage one of the first things I did was to buy a 357 magnum revolver and took some lessons at the local firing range. I hadn't fired a pistol in many years but it all came back pretty fast. Having that sidearm available made me comfortable. Fortunately I never had to use it though we did see a lot of big bears up close. They all seemed friendly but we kept our distance just in case. Grizzlies are said to very unpredictable. Anyway, I was ready for them.

Hiking-The Love of Our Life-
Here We Are at 72

I wanted to get a good look at the places we are going to in Alaska, so I rented a four place Cessna, and convinced Joanne and Al to join me in a survey of all the places we planned to go. We took off from a small private airport near Anchorage and headed down for Prince William Sound. It was just beautiful, with very high snow capped mountains all around and many streams and rivers entering the Sound. We flew almost all the way to our sailing destination at Cordova, and then turned around and flew back to the Kenai Peninsula to trace the hike that we planned in that area. Because the trees are relatively sparse in that part of Alaska, we were able to spot our trail in a number of instances as we had our topo maps with us.

On the whole flight, we saw many bears both large and small. Most of them were grizzly bears with some big brown bears. We also saw a lot of game like moose and deer. Our whole flying adventure only took us a few hours. We were back in Anchorage, before dark as the summer days were very long this far north of the equator. And the end of another great adventuresome day.

After getting all of our equipment assembled and buying much of our food we drove down to Seward where the boat was moored in a local marina. It was a very nice yacht about 40 feet in excellent condition with just about any equipment one could need for extended cruising.

The first day we spent getting everything ready and going over our charts. We were not going to hurry because we had heard that the fishing was wonderful throughout the route for salmon. There are also a number of small streams and rivers that entered the sound where we could find excellent trout fishing. We did carry a 22 rifle which allowed us to pick off the occasional grouse or rabbit to supplement our diet. Joanne was such a good cook that we really ate very well for the whole trip. The weather was lovely with only one or two days of heavy rain though in general, skies are cloudy much of the time in Alaska and it rains a little almost every day so our foul weather gear received good use. We did have some sunny days but the temperature even in midsummer never got above about 70°.

Our Itinerary-Seward to Cordova Anchorage, Seward (Kenai Fjord National Park, Fox Island, Rugged Island, Resurrection Bay, Blying Sound, Montague Straight, Green Island, Valdez, Chugach Nat'l Forest, Orca Bay, and finally Cordova about 190 miles on a straight line.

We had a little Avon inflatable dinghy with a small outboard motor so we were able to anchor the sailboat and explore around. We went up some of the small rivers and did a lot of trout fishing there. The salmon were caught in the sound. All of it by flies using a 3 ounce fly rod so you can imagine some of the larger salmon required 20 or 30 minutes to land. We often cooked our fresh salmon over an open fire on the beach. In the dusk we were a little bit nervous about bears but have been told that with the fire blazing, the bears would stay away. That's the way it worked out. But we did have our firearms at ready.

This area is known for its fjords which were not as spectacular as those in Norway, but they were beautiful none-the-less. Most of the mountains we saw off in the distance had plenty of snow on them even though it was midsummer.

Al was just a wonderful sailing companion. He was really like a brother to both Joanne and me. When we got to Cordoba, the boat owner welcomed us and was very thankful to have had us deliver his boat. The next day we took a small seaplane back to Seward where Al parked his car. Our backpack equipment was in the trunk so Al drove us to our trailhead nearby on the Kenai Peninsula. His vacation time was over so he was unable to join us for this portion of the trip but Joanne and I went on for about 10 days and some of the most beautiful backpacking we have ever experienced. I can't remember seeing anyone for the whole time we were in the woods and we did see plenty of game like moose, black and brown bear, grizzlies, deer, and many small animals. It was very exciting and was certainly one of the most interesting adventures that we had ever enjoyed. We had no bear incidents on this trip through we have had them in the past in Yosemite on 2 backpacks, but that, again, is another story.

Skepticism

Life normally brings with it problems. Solving them should be one of life's pleasures and certainly necessary in order to achieve one's goals, the problems must be solved correctly. In order to do that, you need to gather correct related information upon which to make good decisions.

We all seek the truths of life. Unfortunately, the truth is often elusive and difficult to come by. Science seeks to establish truths through examining evidence produced by observing phenomena and then conducting reproducible experiments to confirm the findings. Information gathered by this system is called "the scientific method" and information gathered can be depended upon to be reliable. However, there is a lot of information that is based upon standards of belief that cannot be relied upon to be correct.

There are many examples of information that is believed by many but is not correct. There is a wide body of so-called "reliable information", much of it passed down through the ages, which is simply erroneous. A great deal of it represents hoaxes and a lot finds its source through religious myths. Let's look at the phenomenon of Crop circles in England.

Passersby discovered circles and even more complex pictograms impressed upon fields of wheat and other crops in England in the 1970s. The phenomena grew to worldwide note and were widely believed to be the work of aliens from other worlds. Books were written on the subject. Ghosts were said to be involved. The number of circles grew into the thousands. They were found in many countries. This was supposed to be proof that aliens were visiting our planet.

However, in 1991 two men from Southampton, England finally tired of their clandestine activity and announced that they had been making these crop figures for 15 years as a hoax.

Another is The Shroud of Turin widely accepted by many as proof of the existence of Jesus. The Shroud of Turin (or Turin Shroud) is a linen cloth bearing the image of a bearded man who appears to have been physically traumatized in a manner consistent with crucifixion. It is kept in the royal chapel of the Cathedral of Saint John the Baptist in Turin, Italy. It is believed by many to be the cloth placed on Jesus of Nazareth at the time of his burial.

The striking negative image was first observed on the evening of May 28, 1898 on the reverse photographic plate of amateur photographer Secondo Pia who was allowed to photograph it while it was being exhibited in the Turin Cathedral. The shroud was the subject of intense debate among some scientists, people of faith, historians, and writers regarding where, when, and how the shroud and its images were created. From a religious standpoint, in 1958 Pope Pius XII approved of the image in association with the Roman Catholic devotion to the Holy Face of Jesus, celebrated every year on Shrove Tuesday. Most Catholics have faith that the shroud is the cloth that covered Jesus when he was placed in his tomb and that his image was recorded on its fibers at or near the time of his alleged resurrection. Skeptics, on the other hand, contend the shroud is a medieval forgery; others attribute the forming of the image to chemical reactions or other natural processes.

The Shroud of Turin that shows something too close to a human form to be misapprehended as a natural pattern is now shown through the science of carbon 14 dating to be not the death shroud of Jesus, but a pious hoax from the 14th century—a time when the manufacture of fraudulent religious relics was a thriving and profitable home and handicraft industry. It is still revered, non-the-less, by Catholic religious mythology and yet another example of accepting as fact unsupported myths so importantly supported by religious believers.

Over the centuries we have seen how the masses of humanity can be led astray by faulty information. Whole populations in the middle ages were influenced by various religious appeals to support such pagan acts as the burning of witches and a complete subjugation of all to the dictates and dogma of the church. Science has slowly progressed and educated people have become more aware of the facts of nature and have slowly replaced religious dogma, with the revealed facts of science.

However, even in our modern world, we have seen the power of an individual such as Hitler to influence an entire nation creating an evil empire within the German country. An otherwise intelligent race was led to believe the erroneous so-called fact of race superiority. Even the Pope in Rome supported Hitler in this foolishness. The horrors of the Holocaust resulted.

The current Pope on a trip to Africa said in one of his recent speeches that condoms create aids. How patently ridiculous. This, especially in the region, where aids is rampant, killing thousands. An example of inaccurate information being disseminated under the cloak of religious papal infallibility.

Even in our own country. The attitude towards blacks well into the 20th century was that they were an inferior race. That has changed rapidly as is evidenced by the election of Barack Obama as 44th President of the USA by an important plurality. There are still many who believe in the idiocy of race superiority. The whole idea of slavery and race superiority is supported in the Bible. But then Scripture usually can be counted upon to be wrong as it was written by uneducated Bedouins when the wheelbarrow was high-tech. Innocent, uneducated people, however, continue to believe these myths.

Somewhere over 1.5 billion people are follows of Islam. Called Muslims, they revere the Koran as Christians do the Bible. Sadly, the Koran calls for Jihad, the killing of all infidels (all those other than Muslims), the oppression of women, the cutting off of hands for minor crimes, and many more savage initiatives that should not be a part of any civilized society. Their Sharia Law is dark ages philosophy.

It has always been amazing to me that the masses can be led so easily to believe in blatantly false ideas. It is largely because they do not cultivate a skeptical mindset. Most of them are brainwashed by their parents and their clergy as no one is born religious. "They have to be carefully taught", as the lyrics go in a well-known song.

I recently happened to hear a most interesting yet concerning presentation on television. It was Sunday, June 13, 2009. The program was on PAX channel and affiliated with a website published as inspirationtoday.com.

The proselytizer was someone named Dr. Mike Murdock, using an emotional evangelical camp meeting style, asking the listeners to "send $1000 in seed money to God to receive a harvest of miracles."

He claimed that something supernatural will happen to all those who send in the money to some organization called Inspirational Ministries. It's the most blatant nonsense I have ever heard. I can't imagine taking money from very simple people, and promising them something that will never happen in their lives.

The following is copied from their published website www.inspirationtoday.com.

Give seed money to receive a miracle. Scripture is full of God's promises to His people who choose to walk in a Covenant Relationship with Him. When we release the Seed in our hand, God releases the Harvest in His hand!

As viewers commit to Sowing an Uncommon Seed into the ministry outreaches of Inspiration Ministries, we have seen miracle after miracle in their finances, health, and relationships.

Do you need a miracle in your life? Then join us for this month's airing of "Live the Life You've Always Dreamed," because God has a miracle in store for you!"

Outright thievery is being perpetrated under a religious mantel? This thievery continues on to this day and is perpetrated by many religions, if not all.

Slowly, however, I believe some are beginning to reveal the truths and science is slowly replacing religious myth with scientific facts in the minds of many educated people. I do believe that education is our salvation in the long run. We have to maintain a very strict public school system that does not allow any religion of any kind in the classroom. Prayer must continue to be banned, as well as all reference to religion with children. The curriculum should increasingly include books on science. Freethinking must be encouraged.

Amazingly, there are still towns in our country that do not permit the teaching of evolution in their public school rooms. It is hard to believe and tragic. It is child abuse.

Be careful not to instinctively trust, what is intuitively obvious. A flat earth was once obvious. It was once obvious that heavy body's fall faster than light ones. The earth was once considered obviously the center of the universe with the sun rotating around it. Science has proven all of these intuitively "obvious facts" erroneous.

So the skeptical mind is one that must be nurtured, separating the fallacious from the factual. So the decisions in life can lead us to a better, more productive life based upon reliable scientific truths.

We must use judgment, however, when expressing skepticism. There is a tendency to belittle or condescend when speaking to supporters of religion, superstition, and pseudoscience. They have feelings, too. There are limits to skepticism. Whether we should speak out or be silent when faced by mythology requires the balance of wisdom.

One of the most important fallacies is the so-called "miracle". Recently a damaged aircraft was crash landed in the Hudson River. All 152 passengers managed to get out alive. It is regularly referred to as the miracle of the Hudson. However, as the pilot so carefully explained, the successful water landing was due to a very well-trained crew performing their well-trained duties. Without the years of experience and training, there would have been no "miracle."

In my parents' general view, new things were better than old, and the very fact that some ritual had been performed in the past was a good reason for abandoning it now. Because what was the past, as our forebears knew it? Nothing but poverty, superstition and grief. 'Think for yourself,' Dad used to say. 'Always ask why.' Be skeptical.

CHAPTER 29

Faith and Prayer

" **F**aith is believing what you know ain't so", Mark Twain.

There has been much written about faith especially as our country appears to be turning into some kind of theocracy, a state in which religion and government are not divided. At least, we do know that the percentages of our citizenry who profess a belief in a divine power and a heaven have grown in recent years. We are informed that a majority of our citizenry believe in a divine power, prayer, and a heaven and an earth that is 10,000 years old.

It really should not be so surprising. It requires a lot of courage to admit to being an atheist or even an agnostic. These could be among Americas most oppressed minorities. To admit membership invites scorn and even attack by religious believers. It is doubtful that an admitted atheist could ever be seriously considered a contender for the Presidency or any important government office.

It is my belief that we could help this problem by making a simple law that stated that it was unlawful to ask any candidate running for any office of his faith. It should also be against the law for a candidate to reveal his faith. This matter, a candidate's faith, should never be an issue as his qualification for office. Also it should be illegal to say, "God bless you and God bless the United States."

For many centuries faith that a god existed was required under threat of death. Though the death sentence no longer threatens disbelievers at least in our country, atheists are still ostracized by the majority even though the entire world population is really atheistic today as regards the belief in Thor, Poseidon, Apollo, Athena, or Zeus, to name just a few of the many hundreds of gods that no longer are looked upon as existent or holy. Over the millennia man has created and discarded gods as the current fashion dictated. When will we finally discard all gods as figments of man's imagination?

When we say faith we almost automatically refer to those with a belief in a mystical power that controls our entire universe with a hereafter of eternal joy and happiness open only to believers. Each religion has its own God and presumably its own hereafter.

Faith generally applies to all those unknown regions for which there is no current scientific or empirical proof. If science has not a provable answer then it falls to Faith to explain the phenomena.

Most are willing to accept this rather than search for proofs. In fact, the mere admission that a search is required brands the investigator negatively and casts him out from the accepted society of believers. Is this detrimental? Is this a negative and harmful development in our national philosophy?

To answer these questions, we need to look at the direction that religion leads believers.

History tells us that most of the world's wars have been fought over differing religious beliefs right up to the present. The current war we wage with factions of Islamists is a religious war because they have stated the wish to take over the world and control it by the philosophies supported by Islam and no other. These aims can hardly be connoted with peaceful co-existence with the rest of the world.

I have tried to help my children in a better understanding of the problem and just how I feel on the subject as is noted by the following note I sent:

Here was my Dad's advice about education. "Learn to speak publicly and learn to write. Add one more . . . study history and philosophy of all civilizations. Don't be taken in by unsupported non-scientific mystical beliefs or myths. Be Skeptical. The rest is all mechanics."

I am not against people of faith. I only pity them. It is the mis-use of the power wielded by those leaders of the innocent faithful. It is the Popes and Preachers hereinafter referred to as PP, of which I am critical.

Just think of the PP power to wage war and influence opinion down through history. I will re-state some of the reasons why I am critical of the PP. I am sure you can think of many more.

1. Their philosophies encourage a divisive world, creating most of the wars.

2. They have always stood in the way of scientific progress and continue to do so today.

3. They take money from poor people under false pretenses.

4. They weaken humankinds' resolve, thus their ability to solve their own problems.

5. They fill the world with false information about the state of the universe.

6. They set themselves up as the final arbiter of what is good and bad.

7. They capture the minds of children before they can reason and thus perpetuate the irrelevancy of their unsupportable "mystical beliefs".

8. They create and sustain a world of false idols, which they worship, as did primitive man worship their idols before the emergence of science.

I could go on, but I think that is enough for now.

The use of condoms to control disease and population is opposed by many religions as is stem cell research, population control, and abortion. Many religious leaders would outlaw all these modern scientific practices if given the opportunity. We cannot allow this to be perpetrated on our modern society. To do so would allow us to slip back into the dark ages.

We have been preached at ad nauseum about religion producing better citizens. It is really the contrary. If we examine mankind over the centuries, we find that there are "good" people and "bad" people. There is little evidence that religious belief changes this natural balance. Religion only allows the "bad" among us to continue to be bad yet gain eventual forgiveness in their minds.

A good example of how religion has little to do with changing people. Currently, there is a great scandal regarding the pedophilia of Catholic priests. Not only that, but the top administration of the church, possibly to the Pope himself, have a record of hiding and protecting these pedophiliac priests. The Pope has recently issued an apology for the church for this neglect which is really a criminal act and should be prosecuted. But the act continues.

We see many priests that have been prosecuted for stealing money from their parishes. Many others have been caught in child and sex abuse. These so-called holy people are just bad and religion does not change them one bit.

We certainly see vast outrages against humankind supported by religion. The many years of the Spanish Inquisition, burnings at the stake in reformation England, the Salem witch-hunts, and slavery of humankind itself are only a few of many such evils supported by the religious thinking of the day. There are countless examples down through history.

It is the belief of many that the concept of a God and a hereafter only developed in primitive minds because of the fear of death and events of nature like earthquakes and tidal waves. It was soon found by the leaders that it provided a tool to control the masses and the stories of miracles were invented depending on faith for their perpetuation. This tool to control the masses has become the most powerful tool ever created and has been used very effectively by religious leaders down through the millennia to mis-lead and control the uneducated masses and take their money under false premises.

What could give more comfort than the promise of an eternity of joy in a heaven with all our loved ones without tears to all those who believe especially as these promises are made to children long before they have developed the ability to rationalize. It is a powerful promise without peer, but false and un-supportable nonetheless. It is brainwashing and child abuse.

Though there were many ancient philosophers who were able to see and tell the truth, it was not until Darwin came in mid nineteenth century with his Origin of Species that science could finally point to empirical proofs that revealed many of the so-called truths of religion as imaginary and not based on scientific fact. Modern science through DNA has supported these findings, so today, the ramblings of unscientific writings, as in the Bible and Koran, are revealed for their incredulousness.

The growth of the acceptance of religious belief is testament to the failure of our education system which is daily under attack by those who would merge religion and state instead of maintaining a strict separation of these two. Our laws are continually weakened by those who would allow prayer in public schools and on the playing field and in the military and in our political institutions.

Prayer has been shown through numerous studies to have no affect on any outcome. Here is the scientific evidence regarding the efficacy of prayer. It's among many similar studies done over many years.

In a long-awaited comprehensive scientific study on the effects of intercessory prayer on the health and recovery of 1,802 patients undergoing coronary bypass surgery in six different hospitals, prayers offered by strangers had no effect. In fact, contrary to common belief, patients who knew they were being prayed for had a higher rate of post-operative complications such as abnormal heart rhythms, possibly the result of anxiety caused by learning that they were being prayed for and thus their condition was more serious than anticipated.

The study, which cost $2.4 million (mostly coming from the John Templeton Foundation), was begun almost a decade ago and was directed by Harvard University Medical School cardiologist Dr. Herbert Benson and published in The American Heart Journal, was by far the most rigorous and comprehensive study on the effects of intercessory prayer on the health and recovery of patients ever conducted.

The 1,802 patients were divided into three groups, two of which were prayed for by members of three congregations: St. Paul's Monastery in St. Paul, Minnesota; the Community of Teresian Carmelites in Worcester, Massachusetts; and Silent Unity, a Missouri prayer ministry near Kansas City. The prayers were allowed to pray in their own manner, but they were instructed to include the following phrase in their prayers: "for a successful surgery with a quick, healthy recovery and no complications". Prayers began the night before the surgery and continued daily for two weeks after. Half the prayer-recipient patients were told that they were being prayed for while the other half were told that they might or might not receive prayers. The researchers monitored the patients for 30 days after the operations.

Results showed no statistically significant differences between the prayed-for and non-prayed-for groups. Although the following findings were not statistically significant, 59% of patients who knew that they were being prayed for suffered complications, compared with 51% of those who were uncertain whether they were being prayed for or not; and 18% in the uninformed prayer group suffered major complications such as heart attack or stroke, compared with 13% in the group that received no prayers.

The gods can either take away evil from the world and will not, or, being willing to do so cannot; or they neither can nor will, or, lastly, they are able and willing.

"If they have the will to remove evil and cannot, then they are not benevolent. If they can but will not, then they are not omnipotent. If they are neither able nor willing, they are neither omnipotent nor benevolent.

"Lastly, if they are both able and willing to annihilate evil, why do they exist?"

—Greek philosopher Epicurus

Another quote

"Is God willing to prevent evil, but not able?
Then he is not omnipotent.
Is he able, but not willing?
Then he is malevolent.
Is he both able and willing?
Then whence cometh evil?
Is he neither able nor willing?
Then why call him God?"

—Epicurus

The recent terrible events brought on by the earthquake in Haiti, serve to illustrate how religion does not aid the people. In the first place, how could a merciful and all powerful God allow earthquakes to happen? It is simply not logical. Then following the event, the newspapers were full of pictures with Haitians praying. It was said that "all they had left was their faith." Could any thoughtful person believe that spending time praying, especially under those circumstances, was anywhere near as useful as getting out and helping to clean up the mess and rescue buried neighbors and loved ones? Just another example of the waste that is perpetrated under the heading of religion. It was faith standing in the way of productive action and a complete waste of the people's energies. Faith and prayer occupy no useful purpose in a civilized, educated society.

It is in many seemingly innocent ways that religious philosophies have been imposed upon us. The recent inclusion and designated by congress in 1956 of "In God we Trust" on our money is a typical example of the many small intrusions religions have made to what should be our modern secular world and a country where state and religion should be separate.

It was placed there because the supporters said we are a Christian nation which, of course, is not true.

Our country is often referred to as a "Christian Nation". What about the remainder of our citizens who are not Christians? Are they to be excluded?

Following are some quotations from our founding fathers regarding our so-called "Christian Nation."

From "The Great Quotations" compiled by George Seldes, Citadel Press, / 1993 ISBN 0-8065-1418-3
Laura Darlene Lansberry

> *"The United States of America was in no manner founded on Christian or Jewish principles; quite the contrary the founding fathers found organized religion, particularly Christianity, Catholicism or Protestantism, to be the bloodiest religions in the history of the human race. The Christians, in their religious fanaticism, have created lies twisting and contorting, in order to hide, disguise, and defuse. Thomas Paine did not recant on his death bed, Thomas Jefferson despised Christianity, and the lies about Albert Einstein were started while he was still alive to refute them. In order to redress the wrongs done these distinguished gentleman by a barbaric, bloody, and lying religion we offer their actual quotes in their own words."*

George Washington (1732-1799)
1st Elected President of the United States
"The United States is in no manner founded on Christian principle."

John Adams (1735-1826)
2nd President of the United States
"As the government of the United States of America is not in any sense founded on the Christian religion . . . ."

Thomas Jefferson (1801-1809)
3rd President of the United States
"I do not find in orthodox Christianity one redeeming feature."—

James Madison (1751-1836)
4th President of the United States
"Who does not see that the same authority which can establish Christianity in exclusion of all other religions may establish, with the same ease, any particular sect of Christians in exclusion to all other sects?"

"In the Papal System, Government and religion are in a manner consolidated, and that is found to be the worst of Government."

It is clear that our founding fathers did not consider our country a "Christian Nation". On the contrary, they were very actively opposed to such language. Today many of our representatives in Washington insist upon referring to the country as a "Christian Nation". They must be informed of the facts, which reveal the contrary.

The Christian Nation Myth

John Farrell Till, (born on April 26, 1933) and known commonly as Farrell Till, was the editor of the formerly published Skeptical Review and is a prominent debater against Christianity and Biblical inerrancy in particular, having published several critical articles of the inerrancy subject as well as skeptical examinations of other Biblical interpretations.

He is a member of People for the Ethical Treatment of Animals, the National Center for Science Education, and the Council for Secular Humanism. Mr Till attained a B.A. English and M.A. English from Harvard University. Following are some of his observations

Whenever the Supreme Court makes a decision that in any way restricts the intrusion of religion into the affairs of government, a flood of editorials, articles, and letters protesting the ruling is sure to appear in the newspapers. Many protesters decry these decisions on the grounds that they conflict with the wishes and intents of the "founding fathers."

Such a view of American history is completely contrary to well known facts. The primary leaders the founding fathers of our nation were not Bible-believing Christians; they were Deists. Deism is a philosophical belief that was widely accepted by the colonial intelligentsia at the time of the American Revolution. Its major tenets included belief in human reason as a reliable means of solving social and political problems and belief in a supreme deity who created the universe to operate solely by natural laws. The supreme God of the Deists removed himself entirely from the universe after creating it. They believed that he assumed no control over it, exerted no influence on natural phenomena, and gave no supernatural revelation to man. A necessary consequence of these beliefs was a rejection of many doctrines central to the Christian religion. Deists did not believe in the virgin birth, divinity, or resurrection of Jesus, the efficacy of prayer, the miracles of the Bible, or even the divine inspiration of the Bible.

These beliefs were forcefully articulated by Thomas Paine in _Age of Reason_, a book that so outraged his contemporaries that he died rejected and despised by the nation that had once revered him as "the father of the American Revolution." To this day, many mistakenly consider him an atheist, even though he was an out spoken defender of the Deistic view of the universe. Other important founding fathers who espoused Deism were George Washington, Thomas Jefferson, Benjamin Franklin, Ethan Allen, James Madison, and James Monroe.

Fundamentalist Christians are currently working overtime to convince the American public that the founding fathers intended to establish this country on "biblical principles," but history simply does not support their view. The men mentioned above and others who were instrumental in the founding of our nation were in no sense Bible-believing Christians. Thomas Jefferson, in fact, was fiercely anti-religious. In a letter to Horatio Spafford in 1814, Jefferson said, "In every country and every age, the priest has been hostile to liberty. He is always in alliance with the despot, abetting his abuses in return for protection to his own. It is easier to acquire wealth and power by this combination than by deserving them, and to effect this, they have perverted the purest religion ever preached to man into mystery and jargon, unintelligible to all mankind, and therefore the safer for their purposes"

(George Seldes, The Great Quotations, Secaucus, New Jersey Citadel Press, 1983, p. 371). In a letter to Mrs. Harrison Smith, he wrote, "It is in our lives, and not from our words, that our religion must be read. By the same test the world must judge me. But this does not satisfy the priesthood. They must have a positive, a declared assent to all their interested absurdities. My opinion is that there would never have been an infidel, if there had never been a priest" (August 6, 1816).

Jefferson was just as suspicious of the traditional belief that the Bible is "the inspired word of God." He rewrote the story of Jesus as told in the New Testament and compiled his own gospel version known as The Jefferson Bible, which eliminated all miracles attributed to Jesus and ended with his burial. The Jeffersonian gospel account contained no resurrection, a twist to the life of Jesus that was considered scandalous to Christians of the day but perfectly sensible to Jefferson's Deistic mind. In a letter to John Adams, he wrote, "To talk of immaterial existences is to talk of nothings. To say that the human soul, angels, God, is immaterial is to say they are nothings, or that there is no God, no angels, no soul. I cannot reason otherwise" (August 15, 1820). In saying this, Jefferson was merely expressing the widely held Deistic view of his time, which rejected the mysticism of the Bible and relied on natural law and human reason to explain why the world is as it is. Writing to Adams again, Jefferson said, "And the day will come when the mystical generation of Jesus, by the supreme being as his father in the womb of a virgin, will be classed with the fable of the generation of Minerva in the brain of Jupiter" (April 11, 1823). These were hardly the words of a devout Bible-believer.

Jefferson didn't just reject the Christian belief that the Bible was "the inspired word of God"; he rejected the Christian system too. In Notes on the State of Virginia, he said of this religion, "There is not one redeeming feature in our superstition of Christianity. It has made one half the world fools, and the other half hypocrites" (quoted by newspaper columnist William Edelen, "Politics and Religious Illiteracy," Truth Seeker, Vol.

121, No. 3, p. 33). Anyone today who would make a statement like this or others we have quoted from Jefferson's writings would be instantly branded an infidel, yet modern Bible fundamentalists are frantically trying to cast Jefferson in the mold of a Bible believing Christian. They do so, of course, because Jefferson was just too important in the formation of our nation to leave him out if Bible fundamentalists hope to sell their "Christian-nation" claim to the public. Hence, they try to rewrite history to make it appear that men like Thomas Jefferson had intended to build our nation on "biblical principles." The irony of this situation is that the Christian leaders of Jefferson's time knew where he stood on "biblical principles," and they fought desperately, but unsuccessfully, to prevent his election to the presidency. Saul K. Padover's biography related the bitterness of the opposition that the clergy mounted against Jefferson in the campaign of 1800.

The religious issue was dragged out, and stirred up flames of hatred and intolerance. Clergymen, mobilizing their heaviest artillery of thunder and brimstone, threatened Christians with all manner of dire consequences if they should vote for the "infidel" from Virginia. This was particularly true in New England, where the clergy stood like Gibraltar against Jefferson (*Jefferson A Great American's Life and Ideas*, Mentor Books, 1964, p.116).

William Linn, a Dutch Reformed minister in New York City, made perhaps the most violent of all attacks on Jefferson's character, all of it based on religious matters. In a pamphlet entitled *Serious Considerations on the Election of a President*, Linn "accused Jefferson of the heinous crimes of not believing in divine revelation and of a design to destroy religion and `introduce immorality'" (Padover, p. 116). He referred to Jefferson as a "true infidel" and insisted that "(an infidel like Jefferson could not, should not, be elected" (Padover, p. 117). He concluded the pamphlet with this appeal for "Christians to defeat the `infidel' from Virginia"

"Will you, then, my fellow-citizens, with all this evidence . . . vote for Mr. Jefferson? As to myself, were Mr. Jefferson connected with me by the nearest ties of blood, and did I owe him a thousand obligations, I would not, and could not vote for him. No; sooner than stretch forth my hand to place him at the head of the nation "Let mine arms fall from my shoulder blade, and mine arm be broken from the bone" (quoted by Padover, p. 117).

Why would contemporary clergymen have so vigorously opposed Jefferson's election if he were as devoutly Christian as modern preachers claim? The answer is that Jefferson was not a Christian, and the preachers of his day knew that he wasn't.

In the heat of the campaign Jefferson wrote a letter to Benjamin Rush in which he angrily commented on the clerical efforts to assassinate his personal character "I have sworn upon the altar of God eternal hostility against every form of tyranny over the mind of man." That statement has been inscribed on Jefferson's monument in Washington. Most people who read it no doubt think that Jefferson was referring to political tyrants like the King of England, but in reality, he was referring to the fundamentalist clergymen of his day.

After Jefferson became president, he did not compromise his beliefs. As president, he refused to issue Thanksgiving proclamations, a fact that Justice Souter referred to in his concurring opinion with the majority in *Lee vs. Weisman*, the recent supreme-court decision that ruled prayers at graduation ceremonies unconstitutional. Early in his first presidential term, Jefferson declared his firm belief in the separation of church and state in a letter to the Danbury (Connecticut) Baptists "Believing with you that religion is a matter which lies solely between man and his God, that he owes account to none other for his faith or his worship, that the legislative powers of government reach actions only and not opinions, I contemplate with sovereign reverence that act of the whole American people which declared that their legislature should `make no law respecting an establishment of religion, or prohibiting the free exercise thereof,' thus building a wall of separation between church and state."

Before sending the letter to Danbury, Jefferson asked his attorney general, Levi Lincoln, to review it. Jefferson told Lincoln that he considered the letter a means of "sowing useful truths and principles among the people, which might germinate and become rooted among their political tenets" (quoted by Rob Boston in "Myths and Mischief," *Church and State*, March 1992). If this was indeed Jefferson's wish, he certainly succeeded.

Twice, in *Reynolds vs. the United States* (1879) and *Everson vs. Board of Education* (1947), the Supreme Court cited Jefferson's letter as "an authoritative declaration of the scope of the [First] Amendment" and agreed that the intention of the First Amendment was "to erect 'a wall of separation between church and state.'" Confronted with evidence like this, some fundamentalists will admit that Thomas Jefferson was not a Bible-believer but will insist that most of the other "founding fathers"—men like Washington, Madison, and Franklin—were Christians whose intention during the formative years of our country was to establish a "Christian nation." Again, however, history does not support their claim.

James Madison, Jefferson's close friend and political ally, was just as vigorously opposed to religious intrusions into civil affairs as Jefferson was. In 1785, when the Commonwealth of Virginia was considering passage of a bill "establishing a provision for Teachers of the Christian Religion," Madison wrote his famous "Memorial and Remonstrance Against Religious Assessments" in which he presented fifteen reasons why government should not become involved in the support of any religion. This paper, long considered a landmark document in political philosophy, was also cited in the majority opinion in Lee vs. Weisman. The views of Madison and Jefferson prevailed in the Virginia Assembly, and in 1786, the Assembly adopted the statute of religious freedom of which Jefferson and Madison were the principal architects. The preamble to this bill said that "to compel a man to furnish contributions of money for the propagation of opinions which he disbelieves is sinful and tyrannical." The statute itself was much more specific than the establishment clause of the U. S. Constitution "Be it therefore enacted by the General Assembly, that no man shall be compelled to frequent or support any religious worship, place or ministry whatsoever, nor shall be enforced, restrained, molested, or burdened in his body or goods, nor shall otherwise suffer on account of his religious opinions or belief; but that all men shall be free to profess, and by argument to maintain, their opinions in matters of religion, and that the same shall in nowise diminish, enlarge, or affect their civil capacities".

Realizing that whatever legislation an elected assembly passed can be later repealed, Jefferson ended the statute with a statement of contempt for any legislative body that would be so presumptuous "And though we well know this assembly, elected by the people for the ordinary purposes of legislation only, have no power to restrain the acts of succeeding assemblies, constituted with the powers equal to our own, and that therefore to declare this act irrevocable, would be of no effect in law, yet we are free to declare, *and do declare*, that the rights hereby asserted are of the natural rights of mankind, and that if any act shall be hereafter passed to repeal the present or to narrow its operation, such act will be an infringement of natural right".

After George Washington's death, Christians made an intense effort to claim him as one of their own. This effort was based largely on the grounds that Washington had regularly attended services with his wife at an Episcopal Church and had served as a vestryman in the church. On August 13, 1835, a Colonel Mercer, involved in the effort, wrote to Bishop William White, who had been one of the rectors at the church Washington had attended. In the letter, Mercer asked if "Washington was a communicant of the Protestant Episcopal Church, or whether he occasionally went to the communion only, or if ever he did so at all . . ." (John Remsberg, *Six Historic Americans*, p. 103). On August 15, 1835, White sent Mercer this reply:

> "In regard to the subject of your inquiry, truth requires me
> to say that Gen. Washington never received the communion
> in the churches of which I am the parochial minister. Mrs.
> Washington was an habitual communicant . . . . I have been
> written to by many on that point, and have been obliged to
> answer them as I now do you." (Remsberg, p. 104).

In his *Annals of the American Pulpit*, The Reverend William B. Sprague, D.D., wrote a biographical sketch of the Reverend James Abercrombie, the other pastor of the congregation Washington attended. In this work, Sprague quoted Abercrombie in confirmation of what White had written to Mercer

One incident in Dr. Abercrombie's experience as a clergyman, in connection with the Father of his Country, is especially worthy of record; and the following account of it was given by the Doctor himself, in a letter to a friend, in 1831 shortly after there had been some public allusion to it "With respect to the inquiry you make I can only state the following facts; that, as pastor of the Episcopal church, observing that, on sacramental Sundays, Gen. Washington, immediately after the desk and pulpit services, went out with the greater part of the congregation—always leaving Mrs. Washington with the other communicants—she invariably being one—I considered it my duty in a sermon on Public Worship, to state the unhappy tendency of example, particularly of those in elevated stations who uniformly turned their backs upon the celebration of the Lord's Supper. I acknowledge the remark was intended for the President; and as such he received it" (From *Annals of the American Pulpit*, Vol. 5, p. 394, quoted by Remsberg, pp. 104-105).

Abercrombie went on to explain that he had heard through a senator that Washington had discussed the reprimand with others and had told them that "as he had never been a communicant, were he to become a one then it would be imputed to an ostentatious display of religious zeal, arising altogether from his elevated station" (Ibid.). Abercrombie then said that Washington "never afterwards came on the morning of sacramental Sunday" (Ibid.).

Here is firsthand testimony from the rectors of the church that Washington attended with his wife, and they both claimed that he never participated in the communion service. Writing in the *Episcopal Recorder*, the Reverend E. D. Neill said that Washington "was not a communicant, notwithstanding all the pretty stories to the contrary, and after the close of the sermon on sacramental Sundays, he had fallen into the habit of retiring from the church while his wife remained and communed" (Remsberg, p. 107). In this article, Neill also made reference to Abercrombie's reprimand of Washington from the pulpit, so those who knew Washington personally or who knew those who had known him all seem to agree that Washington was never a "communicant." Remsberg continued at length in his chapter on Washington to quote the memoirs and letters of Washington's associates, who all agreed that the president had never once been known to participate in the communion service, a fact that weakens the claim that he was a Christian. Would preachers today consider someone a devout Christian if he just attended services with his wife but never took the communion?

As for Washington's membership in the vestry, for several years he did actively serve as one of the twelve vestrymen of Truro parish, Virginia, as had also his father. This, however, cannot be construed as proof that he was a Christian believer. The vestry at that time was also the county court, so in order to have certain political powers, it was necessary for one to be a vestryman. On this matter, Paul F. Boller made this observation

"Actually, under the Anglican establishment in Virginia before the Revolution, the duties of a parish vestry were as much civil as religious in nature and it is not possible to deduce any exceptional religious zeal from the mere fact of membership." Even Thomas Jefferson was a vestryman for a while. Consisting of the leading gentlemen of the parish in position and influence (many of whom, like Washington, were also at one time or other members of the County Court and of the House of Burgesses), the parish vestry, among other things, levied the parish taxes, handled poor relief, fixed land boundaries in the parish, supervised the construction, furnishing, and repairs of churches, and hired ministers and paid their salaries (*George Washington & Religion*, Dallas Southern Methodist University Press, 1963, p. 26).

A footnote where the asterisk appears cited Meade as proof that avowed unbelievers sometimes served as vestrymen "As Bishop William Meade put it, somewhat nastily, in 1857, 'Even Mr. Jefferson and George Wythe, who did not conceal their disbelief in Christianity, took their parts in the duties of vestrymen, the one at Williamsburg, the other at Albemarle; for they wished to be men of influence'" (William Meade, *Old Churches, Ministers and Families of Virginia*, 2 vols., Philadelphia, 1857, I, p. 191).

Clearly, then, one cannot assume from Washington's presence at church services and his membership in the Truro parish vestry that he was a Christian believer. Is there any other evidence to suggest that he was a Christian? The Reverend Bird Wilson, an Episcopal minister in Albany, New York, preached a sermon in October 1831 in which he stated that "among all our presidents from Washington downward, not one was a professor of religion, at least not of more than Unitarianism" (Paul F. Boller, *George Washington & Religion*, pp. 14-15). He went on to describe Washington as a "great and good man" but "not a professor of religion." Wilson said that he was "really a typical eighteenth century

Deist, not a Christian, in his religious outlook" (Ibid.). Wilson wasn't just speaking about matters that he had not researched, because he had carefully investigated his subject before he preached this sermon. Among others, Wilson had inquired of the Reverend Abercrombie [identified earlier as the rector of the church Washington had attended] concerning Washington's religious views. Abercrombie's response was brief and to the point "Sir, Washington was a Deist" (Remsberg, p. 110). Those, then, who were best, positioned to know Washington's private religious beliefs did not consider him a Christian, and the Reverend Abercrombie, who knew him personally and pastored the church he attended with his wife flatly, said that Washington was a Deist.

The Reverend Bird Wilson, who was just a few years removed from being a contemporary of the so-called founding fathers, said further in the above-mentioned sermon that "the founders of our nation were nearly all Infidels, and that of the presidents who had thus far been elected [George Washington, John Adams, Thomas Jefferson, James Madison, James Monroe, John Quincy Adams, and Andrew Jackson] _not a one had professed a belief in Christianity_" (Remsberg, p. 120, emphasis added).

Dr. Wilson's sermon, which was published in the *Albany Daily Advertiser* the month it was delivered also made an interesting observation that flatly contradicts the frantic efforts of present-day fundamentalists to make the "founding fathers" orthodox Christians.

When the war was over and the victory over our enemies won, and the blessings and happiness of liberty and peace were secured, the Constitution was framed and God was neglected. *He was not merely forgotten. He was absolutely voted out of the Constitution.* The proceedings, as published by Thompson, the secretary, and the history of the day, show that the question was gravely debated whether God should be in the Constitution or not, and after a solemn debate he was deliberately voted out of it . . . . There is not only in the theory of our government no recognition of God's laws and sovereignty, but its practical operation, its administration, has been conformable to its theory. Those who have been called to administer the government have not been men making any public profession of Christianity . . . . Washington was a man of valor and wisdom. He was esteemed by the whole world as a great and good man; but he was not a professing Christian (quoted by Remsberg, pp. 120-121,).

The publication of Wilson's sermon in the *Daily Advertiser* attracted the attention of Robert Owen, who then personally visited Wilson to discuss the matter of Washington's religious views. Owen summarized the results of that visit in a letter to Amos Gilbert dated November 13, 1831

"I called last evening on Dr. Wilson, as I told you I should, and I have seldom derived more pleasure from a short interview with anyone. Unless my discernment of character has been grievously at fault, I met an honest man and sincere Christian. But you shall have the particulars. A gentleman of this city accompanied me to the Doctor's residence. We were very courteously received. I found him a tall, commanding figure, with a countenance of much benevolence, and a brow indicative of deep thought, apparently approaching fifty years of age. I opened the interview by stating that though personally a stranger to him, I had taken the liberty of calling in consequence of having perused an interesting sermon of his, which had been reported in the Daily Advertiser of this city, and regarding which, as he probably knew, a variety of opinions prevailed. In a discussion, in which I had taken a part, some of the facts as there reported had been questioned; and I wished to know from him whether the reporter had fairly given his words or not.... I then read to him from a copy of the Daily Advertiser the paragraph which regards Washington, beginning, "Washington was a man," etc. and ending, "absented himself altogether from the church." "I endorse," said Dr. Wilson, with emphasis, "every word of that. Nay, I do not wish to conceal from you any part of the truth, even what I have not given to the public. Dr. Abercrombie said more than I have repeated. At the close of our conversation on the subject his emphatic expression was—for I well remember the very words—`Sir, Washington was a Deist.'"

In concluding the interview, Dr. Wilson said "I have diligently perused every line that Washington ever gave to the public, and I do not find one expression in which he pledges himself as a believer in Christianity. I think anyone who will candidly do as I have done, will come to the conclusion that he was a Deist and nothing more" (Remsberg, pp. 121-122).

In February 1800, after Washington's death, Thomas Jefferson wrote this statement in his personal journal.

"Dr. Rush told me (he had it from Asa Green) that when the clergy addressed General Washington, on his departure from the government, it was observed in their consultation that he had never, on any occasion, said a word to the public which showed a belief in the Christian religion, and they thought they should so pen their address as to force him at length to disclose publicly whether he was a Christian or not. However, he observed, the old fox was too cunning for them. He answered every article of their address particularly, except that, which he passed over without notice . . . ."

"I know that Governor Morris [principal drafter of the constitution], who claimed to be in his secrets, and believed himself to be so, has often told me that General Washington believed no more in that system [Christianity] than he did" (quoted in Remsberg, p. 123 from Jefferson's Works, Vol. 4, p. 572).

The "Asa" Green referred to by Jefferson was probably the Reverend Ashbel Green, who was chaplain to congress during Washington's administration. If so, he was certainly in a position to know the information that "Asa" Green had passed along to Jefferson. Reverend Ashbel Green became the president of Princeton College after serving eight years as the congressional chaplain. He was also a signer of the Declaration of Independence and a prominent figure in the colonial Presbyterian Church (Remsberg, p. 124). His testimony has to be given more weight than what modern day clerics may think about Washington's religious beliefs.

Dr. Moncure D. Conway, who was once employed to edit a volume of Washington's letters, wrote an article entitled "The Religion of Washington," from which Remsberg quoted the following.

"In editing a volume of Washington's private letters for the Long Island Historical Society, I have been much impressed by indications that this great historic personality represented the Liberal religious tendency of his time. That tendency was to respect religious organizations as part of the social order, which required some minister to visit the sick, bury the dead, and perform marriages. It was considered in nowise inconsistent with disbelief of the clergyman's doctrines to contribute to his support, or even to be a vestryman in his church."

"In his many letters to his adopted nephew and younger relatives, he admonishes them about their manners and morals, but in no case have I been able to discover any suggestion that they should read the Bible, keep the Sabbath, go to church, or any warning against Infidelity."

Washington had in his library the writings of Paine, Priestley, Voltaire, Frederick the Great, and other heretical works (pp. 128-129).

In a separate submission to the New York Times, Conway said that "Washington, like most scholarly Virginians of his time, was a Deist . . . . Contemporary evidence shows that in mature life Washington was a Deist, and did not commune, which is quite consistent with his being a vestryman. In England, where vestries have secular functions, it is not unusual for Unitarians to be vestrymen, there being *no doctrinal subscription required for that office.* Washington's letters during the Revolution occasionally indicate his recognition of the hand of Providence in notable public events, but in the thousands of his letters I have never been able to find the name of Christ or any reference to Him" (quoted by Remsberg, pp. 129-130).

The absence of Christian references in Washington's personal papers and conversation was noted by historian Clinton Rossiter.

The last and least skeptical of these rationalists [Washington] loaded his First Inaugural Address with appeals to the "Great Author," "Almighty Being," "invisible hand," and "benign parent of the human race," but apparently could not bring himself to speak the word "God" ("The United States in 1787," *1787 The Grand Convention,* New York W, W, Norton & Co., 1987, p. 36).

These terms by which Washington referred to "God" in his inaugural address are dead giveaways that he was Deistic in his views. The uninformed see the expression "nature's God" in documents like the Declaration of Independence and wrongly interpret it as evidence of Christian belief in those who wrote and signed it, but in reality it is a sure indication that the document was Deistic in origin. Deists preferred not to use the unqualified term "God" in their conversation and writings because of its Christian connotations. Accordingly, they substituted expressions like those that Washington used in his inaugural address or else they referred to their creator as "nature's God," the deity who had created the world and then left it to operate by natural law.

Moncure Conway also stated that "there is no evidence to show that Washington, even in early life, was a believer in Christianity". Remsberg also noted that Conway stated that Washington's father had been a Deist and that his mother "was not excessively religious". Christians have often claimed that most non-Christians make death-bed professions of faith when they realize that they are dying. These claims almost always turn out to be unverifiable assertions, but Conway made it very clear that Washington, even on his death bed, made no profession of faith.

When the end was near, Washington said to a physician present—an ancestor of the writer of these notes—"I am not afraid to go." With his right fingers on his left wrist he counted his own pulses, which beat his funeral march to the grave. "He bore his distress," so next day wrote one present, "with astonishing fortitude, and conscious, as he declared, several hours before his death, of his approaching dissolution, he resigned his breath with the greatest composure, having the full possession of his reason to the last moment." Mrs. Washington knelt beside his bed, but no word passed on religious matters. With the sublime taciturnity which had marked his life he passed out of existence, leaving no act or word which can be turned to the service of superstition, cant, or bigotry" (quoted by Remsberg, pp. 132-133).

Some Christians were of course involved in the shaping of our nation, but their influence was minor compared to the ideological contributions of the Deists who pressed for the formation of a secular nation. In describing the composition of the delegations to the constitutional convention, the historian Clinton Rossiter said this about their religious views.

Whatever else it might turn out to be, the Convention would not be a ` Barebones Parliament.' Although it had its share of strenuous Christians like Strong and Bassett, ex-preachers like Baldwin and Williamson, and theologians like Johnson and Ellsworth, the gathering at Philadelphia was largely made up of men in whom the old fires were under control or had even flickered out. Most were nominally members of one of the traditional churches in their part of the country—the New Englanders Congregationalists, and Presbyterians, the Southerners Episcopalians, and the men of the Middle States everything from backsliding Quakers to stubborn Catholics—and most were men who could take their religion or leave it alone. Although no one in this sober gathering would have dreamed of invoking the Goddess of Reason, neither would anyone have dared to proclaim that his opinions had the support of the God of Abraham and Paul. The Convention of 1787 was highly rationalist and even secular in spirit" ("The Men of Philadelphia," *1787* The Grand Convention, New York W. W. Norton & Company, 1987, pp. 147-148).

Needless to say, this view of the religious beliefs of the constitutional delegates differs radically from the picture that is often painted by modern fundamentalist leaders.

At the constitutional convention, Luther Martin a Maryland representative urged the inclusion of some kind of recognition of Christianity in the constitution on the grounds that "it would be at least decent to hold out some distinction between the professors of Christianity and downright infidelity or paganism." However, the delegates to the convention rejected this proposal and, as the Reverend Bird Wilson stated in his sermon quoted above, drafted the constitution as a secular document. God was nowhere mentioned in it.

As a matter of fact, the document that was finally approved at the constitutional convention mentioned religion only once, and that was in Article VI, Section 3, which stated that "no religious test shall ever be required as a qualification to any office or public trust under the United

States." Now if the delegates at the convention had truly intended to establish a "Christian nation," why would they have put a statement like this in the constitution and nowhere else even refer to religion? Common sense is enough to convince any reasonable person that if the intention of these men had really been the formation of a "Christian nation," the constitution they wrote would have surely made several references to God, the Bible, Jesus, and other accouterments of the Christian religion, and rather than expressly forbidding any religious test as a condition for holding public office in the new nation, it would have stipulated that allegiance to Christianity was a requirement for public office. After all, when someone today finds a tract left at the front door of his house or on the windshield of his car, he doesn't have to read very far to determine that its obvious intention is to further the Christian religion. Are we to assume, then, that the founding fathers wanted to establish a Christian nation but were so stupid that they couldn't write a constitution that would make their purpose clear to those who read it?

Clearly, the founders of our nation intended government to maintain a neutral posture in matters of religion. Anyone who would still insist that the intention of the founding fathers was to establish a Christian nation should review a document written during the administration of George Washington. Article 11 of the Treaty with Tripoli declared in part that "the government of the United States is not in any sense founded on the Christian religion ..." (*Treaties and Other International Acts of the United States*, ed. Hunter Miller, Vol. 2, U. S. Government Printing Office, 1931, p. 365). This treaty was negotiated by the American diplomat Joel Barlow during the administration of George Washington. Washington read it and approved it, although it was not ratified by the senate until John Adams had become president. When Adams signed it, he added this statement to his signature "Now, be it known, that I, John Adams, President of the United States of America, having seen and considered This said treaty, do, by and within the consent of the Senate, accept, ratify and confirm the same, and every clause and article thereof." This document and the approval that it received from our nation's first and second presidents and the U. S. Senate as constituted in 1797 do very little to support the incorrect notion that the founding fathers established our country as a "Christian nation."

Confronted with evidence like the foregoing, diehard fundamentalists will argue that even if the so-called founding fathers did not purposefully establish a Christian nation our country was founded by people looking for religious liberty, and our population has always been overwhelmingly Christian, but even these points are more dubious than most Christian-nation advocates dare suspect. Admittedly, some colonists did come to America in search of religious freedom, but the majority were driven by monetary motives. They simply wanted to improve their economic status. In New England, where the quest for religious freedom had been a strong motive for leaving the Old World, the colonists quickly established governments that were just as intolerant, if not more so, of religious dissent than what they had fled from in Europe. Quakers were exiled and then executed if they returned, and "witches," condemned on flimsy spectral evidence, were hanged. This is hardly a part of our past that modern fundamentalists can point to as a model to be emulated, although their rhetoric often gives cause to wonder if this isn't exactly what they want today.

As for the religious beliefs of the general population in pre and post revolutionary times, it wasn't nearly as Christian as most people think. Lynn R. Buzzard, executive director of the Christian Legal Society (a national organization of Christian lawyers) has admitted that there is little proof to support the claim that the colonial population was overwhelmingly Christian. "Not only were a good many of the revolutionary leaders more deist than Christian," Buzzard wrote, "but the actual number of church members was rather small. Perhaps as few as five percent of the populace were church members in 1776" (Schools They Haven't Got a Prayer, Elgin, Illinois David C. Cook Publishing, 1982, p. 81). Historian Richard Hofstadter says that "perhaps as many as ninety percent of the Americans were unchurched in 1790" (Anti-Intellectualism in American Life, New York Alfred A. Knopf, 1974, p. 82) and goes on to say that "mid-eighteenth century America had a smaller proportion of church members than any other nation in Christendom," noting that "in 1800 [only] about one of every fifteen Americans was a church member" (p. 89). Historian James MacGregor Burns agrees with these figures, noting that "there had been a 'very wintry season' for religion everywhere in America after the Revolution" (The American Experiment Vineyard of

Liberty, New York Vintage Books, 1983, p. 493). He adds that "ninety percent of the people lay outside the churches."

Historians, who deal with facts rather than wishes, paint an entirely different picture of the religious composition of America during its formative years than the image of a nation founded on "biblical principles" that modern Bible fundamentalists are trying to foist upon us. Our founding fathers established a religiously neutral nation, and a tragedy of our time is that so many people are striving to undo all that was accomplished by the wisdom of the founding fathers who framed for us a constitution that would protect the religious freedom of everyone regardless of personal creed. An even greater tragedy is that they many times hoodwink the public into believing that they are only trying to make our nation what the founding fathers would want it to be. Separation of church and state is what the founding fathers wanted for the nation, and we must never allow anyone to distort history to make it appear otherwise.

Below are some quotes from our founding fathers regarding religion.

One Nation . . . Under God?
The Founding Fathers Speak Out on God, Religion and the First Amendment

"In God We Trust"

According to the U.S. Dept. of Treasury, the motto 'In God We Trust' came about not at the time of the Constitutional Conventions, but due to increased pressures to recognize God on coins and money during the Civil War. In April 22, 1864, Congress passed an Amendment authorizing the motto to be placed on the two-cent coin. It appeared on various coins throughout the years, and appeared on paper money in 1957. The phrase was eventually printed on all paper bills, superseding the motto "E Pluribus Unum" (From Many, One) adopted by the Union in 1782.

As we enter the Independence Day weekend, it seems appropriate to examine some of the freedoms that we in the United States enjoy because of our Constitution and our Bill of Rights. One of these rights is the Freedom of Religion—guaranteed to all Americans in the First Amendment. The wording of the phrase pertaining to religion, "Congress shall make no law respecting an establishment of religion, or prohibiting the free exercise thereof", has been the subject of endless speculation in our country's history. Perhaps these quotes, from the men who wrote, debated and ultimately adopted the Bill of Rights, can shed some light on their view of God, religion in general, and the meaning of the Separation of Church and State.

"As to Jesus ... I have ... some doubts as to his divinity; though it is a question I do not dogmatize upon, having never studied it, and think it needless to busy myself with it now, when I expect soon an opportunity of knowing the truth with less trouble."—Benjamin Franklin (Alice J. Hall, "Philosopher of Dissent: Benj. Franklin," National Geographic, Vol. 148, No. 1, July, 1975, p. 94.)

"Whenever we read the obscene stories, the voluptuous debaucheries, the cruel and torturous executions, the unrelenting vindictiveness, with which more than half the Bible is filled, it would be more consistent that we called it the word of a demon, than the word of God. It is a history of wickedness that has served to corrupt and brutalize mankind."—Thomas Paine (*The Age of Reason*, 1794-1795.)

Every man "ought to be protected in worshipping the Deity according to the dictates of his own conscience."—George Washington (Letter to the United Baptist Churches in Virginia in May, 1789) "Question with boldness even the existence of a god."—Thomas Jefferson (letter to Peter Carr, 10 August 1787)

"When a Religion is good, I conceive it will support itself; and when it does not support itself, and God does not take care to support it so that its Professors are obliged to call for help of the Civil Power, it is a sign, I apprehend, of its being a bad one."—Benjamin Franklin (from a letter to Richard Price, October 9, 1780;)

I do not believe in the creed professed by the Jewish church, by the Roman church, by the Greek church, by the Turkish church, by the Protestant church, nor by any church that I know of … Each of those churches accuse the other of unbelief; and for my own part, I disbelieve them all."—Thomas Paine (The Age of Reason, 1794-1795.)

"Is uniformity attainable? Millions of innocent men, women, and children, since the introduction of Christianity, have been burnt, tortured, fined, imprisoned; yet we have not advanced one inch towards uniformity. What has been the effect of coercion? To make one half the world fools and the other half hypocrites. To support roguery and error all over the earth."—Thomas Jefferson (Notes on Virginia, 1782; from George Seldes, ed., The Great Quotations, Secaucus, New Jersey: Citadel Press, 1983, p. 363.)

"During almost fifteen centuries has the legal establishment of Christianity been on trial. What have been its fruits? More or less in all places, pride and indolence in the Clergy, ignorance and servility in the laity; in both, superstition, bigotry and persecution."—James Madison (*Memorial and Remonstrance against Religious Assessments*, 1785.)

"Where do we find a precept in the Bible for Creeds, Confessions, Doctrines and Oaths, and whole carloads of other trumpery that we find religion encumbered with in these days?"—John Adams

"The civil rights of none shall be abridged on account of religious belief or worship, nor shall any national religion be established, nor shall the full and equal rights of conscience be in any manner, or on any pretence, infringed."—James Madison (Original wording of the First Amendment; Annals of Congress 434 (June 8, 1789).)

"As the Government of the United States of America is not in any sense founded on the Christian religion; as it has in itself no character of enmity against the laws, religion, or tranquility, of Musselmen; and as the said States never have entered into any war or act of hostility against any Mehomitan nation, it is declared by the parties that no pretext arising from religious opinions shall ever produce an interruption of the harmony existing between the two countries."—(Treaty of Tripoli, 1797—signed by President John Adams.)

"As to religion, I hold it to be the indispensable duty of government to protect all conscientious protesters thereof, and I know of no other business government has to do therewith."—Thomas Paine (*Common Sense*, 1776.)

In closing this chapter, I would like to include a few definitions that you may find amusing:

Christian, n. One who believes that the New Testament is a divinely inspired book admirably suited to the spiritual needs of his neighbor. One who follows the teachings of Christ insofar as they are not inconsistent with a life of sin.

Evangelist, n. A bearer of good tidings, particularly (in a religious sense) such as assure us of our own salvation and the damnation of our neighbors.

Faith, n. Belief without evidence in what is told by one who speaks without knowledge, of things without parallel.

Infidel, n. In New York, one who does not believe in the Christian religion; in Constantinople, one who does.

Pray. v. To ask that the laws of the universe be annulled in behalf of a single petitioner, confessedly unworthy.

Religion, n. A daughter of Hope and Fear, explaining to Ignorance the nature of the unknowable.

Reverence, n. The spiritual attitude of a man to a god and a dog to a man.

Saint, n. A dead sinner revised and edited.

—Ambrose Bierce, *The Devil's Dictionary* (1906)

Thomas Paine, as one of the founding fathers, was frequently attacked by the so-called religious leaders during his work in helping to establish the United States. In fact he was essential in the establishment of our country—in fact he named our country, the United States.

The vilification he received by religious pastors was widespread. He answered one as follows "When then (my much esteemed friend, for I do not respect you the less because we differ, and that perhaps not too much into religious sentiments), what, I ask, is this thing called infidelity? If we go back to your ancestors and mine 300 and or 400 years ago, for we must have had fathers and grandfathers or we should not be here, we shall find them praying to Saints and Virgins of their age, and building in purgatory, and transubstantiations, and therefore all of us are infidels. According to our forefathers' belief . . .

The case, my friend, is that the world has been overrun with fable and creeds of human invention, with sectaries of a whole nation's, sectaries in each of them against the other. Every sectary, except the Quakers, had been a prosecutor. Those who fled from persecution persecuted in their turn, and it is this that has filled the world with persecution and diluted it with blood."

Religious Quotes from Freedom For Religion
Compiled by Annie Laurie Gaylor

Literature is full of statements about religion. Following are a compilation of quotations of some of history's free thinkers.

"A few saints and a little charity don't make up for all the harm religion has done over the ages," has said Peter Watson (born 1943) an intellectual historian and journalist, now perhaps best known for his work in the history of ideas (CBC News, May 5, 2007).

When asked about the good that religion has done in the world in an interview by The New York Times Magazine (December 11, 2005), Watson replied: "I lead a perfectly healthy, satisfactory life without being religious. And I think more people should try it." He went on to say, "I do not believe in the inner world. I think that the inner world comes from the exploration of the outer world—reading, traveling, talking. I do not believe that meditation or cogitation leads to wisdom or peace or the truth." Since 1998, Watson has been a research associate at the McDonald Institute for Archaeological Research, at the University of Cambridge. He lives in London, England.

"Religion has kept civilization back for hundreds of years, and the biggest mistake in the history of civilization, is ethical monotheism, the concept of the one God. Let's get rid of it and be rational."

—Peter Watson interview,
CBC News (May 5, 2007)

"I'm not a person who feels very friendly toward organized religion. I think people have been brainwashed through the centuries. The churches, particularly the Catholic Church, are patriarchal organizations that have been invested with power for the sake of the people in power, who happen to be men. It breeds corruption. I found going to church every Sunday and on holy days an exercise in extreme boredom . . . .

I've never felt that anyone who stands up and says 'Look, I have the answers' has the answers . . .

How can people still be superstitious, still believe in nonsense and astrology and grotesque demonic religions of every kind, every fundamentalist religion crowding us on all sides?"

—Joyce Carol Oates (1938-),
interview, Playboy Magazine, November 1993
(Cited in *Who's Who in Hell* by Warren Allen Smith)

"This young fellow, who was possessed of most violent passions, which he with great difficulty can command, and of unbounded ambition, which he conceals perhaps, even to himself, has been seduced into that bigoted, illiberal system of religion, which, by professing vainly to follow purely the dictates of the Testament, in vain contradicts the whole doctrine of the New Testament, and destroys all the boundaries between good and evil, between right and wrong. But, like all the followers of that sect, his practice is at open variance with his theory. When I observe into what inconsistent absurdities those persons run who make speculative, metaphysical religion a matter of importance, I am fully determined never to puzzle myself in the mazes of religious discussion, to content myself with practicing the dictates of God and reason so far as I can judge for myself, . . ."

—John Q. Adams, diary entry,
Life in a New England Town, 1787-1788,
cited by Franklin Steiner,
The Religious Beliefs of our Presidents

"A large proportion of the noblest and most valuable teaching has been the work, not only of men who did not know, but of men who knew and rejected the Christian faith."

—John Stuart Mill, *On Liberty*, 1859

I'm sure there are all sorts of higher powers like electromagnetism and gravity, and things like that. But I don't believe in a deity, no. I see no evidence for that in my life or anywhere else in the universe. Personally, people can believe what they will and they will believe what they want. I find that most deism, and certainly most theisms take a fairly narrow view of the universe, and most people's views of God or gods seem to be rather impoverished. The universe itself, the physical world that we can perceive with our senses and grasp with our minds, seems to be far more wondrous then most people's conceptions of a deity."

—Ron Reagan, PR.com interview, April 13, 2009

OSCAR HAMMERSTEIN II

On this date in 1895, Oscar Hammerstein II was born in New York City. Hammerstein grew up immersed in theater culture. His grandfather and namesake, Oscar Hammerstein I, worked in theatre and opera along with his father and his uncle, Arthur Hammerstein, a well-known producer. While attending Columbia University (1912-1917), Hammerstein joined the Columbia University Players, beginning his prolific career in theater. He wrote the book and lyrics for the noted production "Show Boat" (1927), working with Jerome Kern (also a nonbeliever). An accomplished writer and lyricist, he teamed up with atheist Richard Rodgers to create Broadway classics such as "Oklahoma!" (1943), "South Pacific" (1949), "The King and I" (1951) and "The Sound of Music" (1959). Rodgers and Hammerstein won the 1944 Pulitzer Prize for "Oklahoma!" and the 1950 Pulitzer Prize for "South Pacific."

He married Dorothy Jacobson in 1929 and had three children: William, Alice and James.

Hammerstein was raised in very secular Judaism: his Jewish father did not practice any religious traditions or customs or give Hammerstein any religious education. Although Hammerstein did not specify his religious views, he was nonreligious. He did not attend church or synagogue, wrote no religious music and requested a secular funeral. *D. 1960.*

"Oscar Hammerstein II [was] nonreligious."

—Dan Barker, *The Good Atheist*, 2010

On this date in 1904, Ricardo Eliecer Neftalí Reyes Basoalto was born in Parral, Chile. He grew up in Temuco, Chile. His first poems were published under the pen name Pablo Neruda in 1918, in a Santiago magazine. His first widely-read book, *Twenty Love Poems* and a *Song of Despair* (*Veinte poemas de amor y una canción desesperada*) was published in 1924, when Neruda was twenty years old. In 1927, he was made honorary consul of Chile to Rangoon in honor of his accomplishments in poetry. His work as an official representative of Chile continued, and he was sent to Spain in 1934, where he became involved with the revolutionaries and the republican cause. He was recalled to Chile in 1937, where he became deeply involved in local politics. In 1945, he joined the Communist Party and was elected to the Senate, fleeing the country three years later when the party was banned by the government. Neruda continued to travel the world, first in exile and after he was allowed to return to Chile in 1952. During this period, much of his poetry was political in nature, including the famous Canto general (General Song), an epic of the New World, which connected the Americas' origins and conquest to their current political state.

Neruda was a confirmed communist, and was even awarded the Stalin Peace Prize and Lenin Peace Prize in 1953. He stated some philosophical views in his poetry, for example describing himself in his poem "A Dog Has Died" ("Un perro ha muerto") as "I, the materialist, who never believed / in any promised heaven in the sky / for any human being." He ran for president of Chile in 1969 as the Communist candidate, but withdrew in favor of Salvador Allende, the candidate of the unified left. He was diagnosed with cancer in 1970, but went on to represent Chile as ambassador to France. In 1971, he received the Nobel Prize in Literature. He survived his friend, President Allende, by only twelve days, dying on Sept. 23, 1973. Eight books of his poetry which he had planned on publishing on his seventieth birthday were published posthumously. *D. 1973.*

In 1817, Henry David Thoreau was born in Massachusetts. He graduated from Harvard University in 1837, taught briefly, then turned to writing and lecturing. Becoming a Transcendentalist and good friend of Emerson, Thoreau lived the life of simplicity he advocated in his writings. His two-year experience in a hut in Walden, on land owned by Emerson, resulted in the classic, *Walden: Life in the Woods* (1854). During his sojourn there, Thoreau refused to pay a poll tax in protest of slavery and the Mexican war, for which he was jailed overnight. His activist convictions were expressed in the groundbreaking *On the Duty of Civil Disobedience* (1849). Thoreau liked to quote Ennius: "I say there are gods, but they care not what men do." In a diary he noted his disapproval of attempts to convert the Algonquins "from their own superstitions to new ones." In a journal he noted drily that it is appropriate for a church to be the ugliest building in a village, "because it is the one in which human nature stoops to the lowest and is the most disgraced." (Cited by James A. Haught in *2000 Years of Disbelief.*) When Parker Pillsbury sought to talk about religion with Thoreau as he was dying from tuberculosis, Thoreau replied: "One world at a time." *D. 1862.*

"Your church is a baby-house made of blocks."

—Henry David Thoreau,
On the Duty of Civil Disobedience, 1849

In 1848, the very first woman's rights convention in the world met in Seneca Falls, N.Y. Feminist and freethinker Elizabeth Cady Stanton, with four friends, instigated and convened the Seneca Falls Convention on July 19-20, 1848. Stanton was the first woman to call for "woman suffrage," as part of the "Declaration of Rights and Sentiments" adopted at the convention. Stanton, initially warned that the suffrage plank was almost too shocking to utter and would alienate supporters, prevailed. The suffrage plank won endorsement and galvanized U.S. women for the next 72 years. The 19th Amendment, guaranteeing women's right to vote, was finally passed in 1920, after nearly a century of struggle to overcome religion-rooted objections toward women's civil equality.

"In the early days of woman-suffrage agitation, I saw that the greatest obstacle we had to overcome was the bible. It was hurled at us on every side."

—Elizabeth Cady Stanton,
an Interview with the Chicago Record, June 29, 1897.
For more on Stanton, read *Women Without Superstition*

"Soul is not even that Crackerjack prize that God and Satan scuffle over after the worms have all licked our bones. That's why, when we ponder—as sooner or later each of must—exactly what we ought to be doing about our soul, religion is the wrong, if conventional, place to turn. Religion is little more than a transaction in which troubled people trade their souls for temporary and wholly illusionary psychological comfort—the old give-it-up-in-order-to-save-it routine. Religions lead us to believe that the soul is the ultimate family jewel and that in return for our mindless obedience, they can secure it for us in their vaults, or at least insure it against fire and theft. They are mistaken."

—Character Stubblefield
from *Villa Incognito*, 2004, by Tom Robbins

"A religious person is a dangerous person. He may not become a thief or a murderer, but he is liable to become a nuisance. He carries with him many foolish and harmful superstitions, and he is possessed with the notion that it is his duty to give these superstitions to others. That is what makes trouble. Nothing is so worthless as superstition . . . ."

—Marilla M. Ricker,
"Science Against Creeds," *I Am Not Afraid Are You?* (1917).
Read more about Marilla M. Ricker in *Women Without Superstition: No Gods—No Masters.*

"A state of skepticism and suspense may amuse a few inquisitive minds. But the practice of superstition is so congenial to the multitude that, if they are forcibly awakened, they still regret the loss of their pleasing vision. Their love of the marvelous and supernatural, their curiosity with regard to future events, and their strong propensity to extend their hopes and fears beyond the limits of the visible world, were the principal causes which favored the establishment of Polytheism. So urgent on the vulgar is the necessity of believing, that the fall of any system of mythology will most probably be succeeded by the introduction of some other mode of superstition."

—Edward Gibbon,
The Decline and Fall of the Roman Empire (1776-1788)

". . . although my father had been raised a Muslim, by the time he met my mother he was a confirmed atheist, thinking religion to be so much superstition."

—President Barack Obama
remarking about his father in "My Spiritual Journey,"
TIME Magazine, Oct. 16, 2006)

President Obama is an intelligent man. He is also a politician. He knows that unless he professes a belief in a recognize religion, that he could not be elected. I would suggest that he is really a closet atheist.

"Godless Morality," by Peter Singer and Marc Hauser, January 2006). Singer condemns religious intrusion into politics and scientific research. On religious opposition to stem cell research, Singer wrote: "If anyone ever tries to tell you that, for all its quirks and irrationality, religion is harmless or even beneficial for society, remember those 128 million Americans—and hundreds of millions more citizens of other nations—who might be helped by research that is being restricted by religious beliefs" (Free Inquiry, "The Harm That Religion Does," by Peter Singer, June/July 2004, p. 17). In a letter to the editor appearing in the New York Times (Nov. 8, 2004), Singer wrote: "Paul Krugman says Democrats need to make it clear they value faith. Is everyone caving in to this religious nonsense? What is faith but believing in something without any evidence? Why should Democrats value that? Formidable as the task may seem at present, the long-term need is to persuade Americans that having evidence for your beliefs is a good idea."

"I don't believe in the existence of God, so it makes no sense to me to say that a human being is a creature of God. It's as simple as that."

—Peter Singer in a transcript of a television program appearing in Religion & Ethics online magazine (PBS), Sept. 10, 1999

Underwood became a noted promoter of Darwin and evolution. He was appointed co-editor, with William J. Potter, of the *Index* in 1881, a weekly newspaper founded by a Unitarian. In 1887, the atheist founded *The Open Court* in Chicago, a well-respected journal which published the writings of many freethinkers. Underwood wrote, lectured and debated as a major 19th century advocate for the freethought movement. His books include *The Influence of Christianity on Civilization*

(1871) and *The Crimes and Cruelties of Christianity* (1877). Underwood chaired the "Congress of Evolution" at the World's Fair in Chicago in 1893. Underwood was a supporter of feminism. His wife, Sara Underwood, wrote *Heroines of Freethought* (1876). D. 1914.

"There is no argument worthy of the name that will justify the union of the Christian religion with the State. Every consideration of justice and equality forbids it. Every argument in favor of free Republican institutions is equally an argument in favor of a complete divorce of the State from the Church. History in warning tones tells us there can be no liberty without it. Justice demands it. Public safety requires it. He who opposes it is, whether he realizes it or not, an enemy of freedom."

—Benjamin Underwood,
"The Practical Separation of Church & State,"
an address to the 1876 Centennial Congress of Liberals

"Another important doctrine of the Christian religion, is the atonement supposed to have been made by the death and sufferings of the pretended Saviour of the world; and this is grounded upon principles as regardless of justice as the doctrine of original sin. It exhibits a spectacle truly distressing to the feelings of the benevolent mind, it calls innocence and virtue into a scene of suffering, and reputed guilt, in order to destroy the injurious effects of real vice. It pretends to free the world from the fatal effects of a primary apostasy, by the sacrifice of an innocent being. Evil has already been introduced into the world, and in order to remove it, a fresh accumulation of crimes becomes necessary. In plain terms, to destroy one evil, another must be committed."

—Elihu Palmer, *Principles of Nature; or,*
A Development of the Moral Causes of Happiness and
Misery among the Human Species, 1801

"'Twas only fear first in the world made gods."

—Ben Jonson,
born June 11, 1572 (D. *1637*).
From Jonson's monologue, "Sejanus, His Fall" (1603)

Brahms the Freethinker-Music Was His Religion

How many parents, soothing their children to sleep with "Brahms's Lullaby," know they are singing a melody written by a freethinker?

Johannes Brahms, the great German composer known as the "3rd B" (after Bach and Beethoven), did not believe in a god.

Brahms's works were influenced by philosophy and literature, including Hoffman, Schiller, Robert Burns, Jean Paul, and Friedrich Hölderlin. He had a keen interest in science, and could hold his own debating politics, literature, religion and philosophy.

When Brahms sometimes spoke of immortality, it was metaphorically, jokingly. To his publisher, he once wrote: "Done! What is done? The violin concerto? No . . . . One knows nothing definite; even the most credulous doesn't . . . . And I am credulous. Indeed, I believe in immortality—; I believe that when an immortal dies, people will keep on for 50,000 years and more, talking idiotically and badly about him—thus I believe in immortality, without which beautiful and agreeable attribute I have the honor to be—your J. Br."

"Apart from Frau Schumann I'm not attached to anybody with my whole soul! And truly that is terrible and one should neither think such a thing nor say it. Is that not a lonely life! Yet we can't believe in immortality on the other side. The only true immortality lies in one's children."

Clara Schumann, by the way, the virtuoso pianist and composer who was a true life-long friend of Brahms, also had little use for the church. "Performing was her religion," Swafford observes. "The world saw Clara Schumann as a priestess, something like a saint. If there is such a thing as a secular saint, surely she was one."

Johannes Brahms did not seek immortality, but he got it anyway: not in children, not in heaven, but in the beauty he bequeathed to the world.

Source: Johannes Brahms: A Biography, by Jan Swafford (1997, Alfred A. Knopf, Inc.)

"As a devout believer, [Gen.] Boykin may also wonder why it is impermissible to say that the God you believe in is superior to the God you don't believe in. I wonder this same thing as a nonbeliever: Doesn't one religion's gospel logically preclude the others? (Except, of course, where they overlap with universal precepts, such as not murdering people, that even we nonbelievers can wrap our heads around.)"

—Michael Kinsley,
"The Religious Superiority Complex:
It's OK to think your God's the greatest, but you
don't have to rub it in," *Time Magazine*, Nov. 3, 2003

"Atheism rises above creeds and puts Humanity upon one plane. There can be no 'chosen people' in the Atheist philosophy. There are no bended knees in Atheism;
No supplications, no prayers;
No sacrificial redemptions;
No 'divine' revelations;
No washing in the blood of the lamb;
No crusades, no massacres, no holy wars;
No heaven, no hell, no purgatory;

No silly rewards and no vindictive punishments;
No Christ, and no saviors;
No devils, no ghosts and no gods."

> —Joseph Lewis, "Atheist Rises Above Creeds,"
> part of an address on atheism delivered at a symposium
> at Community Church, New York City, April 20, 1930.
> *Atheism and Other Addresses by Joseph Lewis* (1941)

"[I reject Christianity's anthropomorphic God,] made in our image, silly and malicious, vain and puerile, irritable or tender, after our fashion."

She went through Deistic, spiritualistic and pantheistic stages, but never returned to Christianity. Her most famous liaison was with the composer Chopin, who, while far more orthodox than Sand in his political views, also refused to return to the Roman Catholic Church. Her enduring legacy is as a rebel and role model living life as freely and fully as men. She instructed there should be no religious rites at her funeral, which was presided over by freethinker Victor Hugo. *D. 1876.*

> —George Sand, cited by
> James A. Haught in *2000 Years of Disbelief*

". . . the very fears and guilts imposed by religious training are responsible for some of history's most brutal wars, crusades, pogroms, and persecutions, including five centuries of almost unimaginable terrorism under Europe's Inquisition and the unthinkably sadistic legal murder of nearly nine million women. History doesn't say much very good about God."

> —Barbara G. Walker, "The Skeptical Feminist,"
> acceptance speech for the "1993 Humanist Heroine"
> award by the Feminist Caucus of the American Humanist
> Association, anthologized in *Women Without Superstition*

"If today you can take a thing like evolution and make it a crime to teach it in the public school, tomorrow you can make it a crime to teach it in the private schools, and the next year you can make it a crime to teach it to the hustings or in the church. At the next session you may ban books and the newspapers. Soon you may set Catholic against Protestant and Protestant against Protestant, and try to foist your own religion upon the minds of men. If you can do one you can do the other. Ignorance and fanaticism is ever busy and needs feeding. Always it is feeding and gloating for more. Today it is the public school teachers, tomorrow the private. The next day the preachers and the lectures, the magazines, the books, the newspapers. After a while, your honor, it is the setting of man against man and creed against creed until with flying banners and beating drums we are marching backward to the glorious ages of the sixteenth century when bigots lighted fagots to burn the men who dared to bring any intelligence and enlightenment and culture to the human mind."

—Clarence Darrow, "Scopes Trial"
courtroom speech, July 13, 1925

"I don't believe in God because I don't believe in Mother Goose."

—Clarence Darrow, speech, Toronto, 1930.
Also see excerpt from his "Scopes Trial" courtroom speech.

"Yes, I believe in revelation, but a permanent revelation of man to himself and by himself, a rational revelation that is nothing but the result of the progress of science and of the contemporary conscience, a revelation that is always only partial and relative and that is effectuated by the acquisition of new truths and even more by the elimination of ancient errors. We must also attest that the progress of truth gives us as much to forget as to learn, and we learn to negate and to doubt as often as to affirm."

—Clémence Royer, preface to Charles Darwin,
L'origine des espèces, in Jennifer Michael Hecht,
The End of the Soul

"In Philadelphia, I inadvertently came upon an edition of Robert Ingersoll's Essays and Lectures. This was an exciting discovery; his atheism confirmed my own belief that the horrific cruelty of the Old Testament was degrading to the human spirit."

—Charlie Chaplain, *My Autobiography* (1964),
cited in *Who's Who in Hell* by Warren Allen Smith

"I've never met a healthy person who worried much about his health, or a good person who worried much about his soul."

—John B.S. Haldane, British scientist (1892-1964).
Dictionary of Humorous Quotations,
edited by Evan Esar (1949)

". . . I've come to realize it's time to sound the alarm.

Whether we Brights are a minority or, as I am inclined to believe, a silent majority, our deepest convictions are increasingly dismissed, belittled and condemned by those in power—by politicians who go out of their way to invoke God and to stand, self-righteously preening, on what they call 'the side of the angels.'

. . . Politicians don't think they even have to pay us lip service, and leaders who wouldn't be caught dead making religious or ethnic slurs don't hesitate to disparage the 'godless' among us.

From the White House down, bright-bashing is seen as a low-risk vote-getter. And, of course, the assault isn't only rhetorical: the Bush administration has advocated changes in government rules and policies to increase the role of religious organizations in daily life, a serious subversion of the Constitution. It is time to halt this erosion and to take a stand: the United States is not a religious state, it is a secular state that tolerates all religions and—yes—all manner of nonreligious ethical beliefs as well."

—Daniel C. Dennett, "The Bright Stuff,"
The New York Times, July 12, 2003

"I cannot imagine a God who rewards and punishes the objects of his creation, whose purposes are modeled after our own—a God, in short, who is but a reflection of human frailty. Neither can I believe that the individual survives the death of his body, although feeble souls harbor such thoughts through fear or ridiculous egotism. It is enough for me to contemplate the mystery of conscious life perpetuating itself through all eternity, to reflect upon the marvelous structure of the universe which we can dimly perceive, and to try humbly to comprehend even an infinitesimal part of the intelligence manifested in nature."

—Albert Einstein, column for The New York Times,
Nov. 9, 1930 (reprinted in The New York
Times obituary, April 19, 1955)

Confusion over his beliefs stemmed from such comments as his public statement, reported by United Press in April 25, 1929, that: "I believe in Spinoza's God, who reveals himself in the orderly harmony in being, not in God who deals with the facts and actions of men." Einstein's famous "God does not play dice with the Universe" metaphor—meaning nature conforms to mathematical law—fueled more confusion. At a symposium, he advised: "In their struggle for the ethical good, teachers of religion must have the stature to give up the doctrine of a personal God, that is, give up that source of fear and hope which in the past placed such vast power in the hands of priests. In their labors they will have to avail themselves of those forces which are capable of cultivating the Good, the True, and the Beautiful in humanity itself. This is, to be sure a more difficult but an incomparably more worthy task . . ." ("Science, Philosophy and Religion, A Symposium," published by the Conference on Science, Philosophy and Religion in their Relation to the Democratic Way of Life, Inc., New York, 1941). In a letter to philosopher Eric Gutkind, dated Jan. 3, 1954, Einstein stated: "The word god is for me nothing more than the expression and product of human weaknesses, the Bible a collection of honorable, but still primitive legends which are nevertheless pretty childish. No interpretation no matter how subtle can (for me) change this," (The Guardian, "Childish superstition: Einstein's letter makes view of religion relatively clear," by James Randerson, May 13, 2008). *D. 1955*

"I'm an atheist, and that's it. I believe there's nothing we can know except that we should be kind to each other and do what we can for each other."

—Katharine Hepburn,
Ladies Home Journal, Oct. 1991

He was a favorite of irreverent author Mark Twain, who gave the keynote at a toast for Grant at the Palmer House in Chicago in 1879, as part of an illustrious line-up of speakers that included agnostic Robert G. Ingersoll. Twain was entrusted to publish Grant's *Memoirs*. Grant was not a member of any church, and was never baptized. After receiving eight demerits as a cadet at West Point for failure to attend chapel, he protested in a letter that it was "not republican" to be forced to go to church (Brown's *Life of Grant*, p. 329, cited by Franklin Steiner, *The Religious Beliefs of Our Presidents*). Grant was on record in favor of taxation of church property. In an annual address to Congress in 1875, he warned of "the importance of correcting an evil that if permitted to continue, will probably lead to great trouble in our land . . . It is the acquisition of vast amounts of untaxed Church property ... I would suggest the taxation of all property equally." D. 1885.

"Leave the matter of religion to the family altar, the Church, and the private schools, supported entirely by private contributions. Keep the church and state forever separate."

—Ulysses S, Grant, address delivered in
Des Moines, Iowa, in 1875

"Christ, according to the faith, is the second person in the Trinity, the Father being the first and the Holy Ghost the third. Each of these persons is God. Christ is his own father and his own son. The Holy Ghost is neither father nor son, but both. The son was begotten by the father, but existed before he was begotten—just the same before as after ....

"So, it is declared that the Father is God, and the Son God, and the Holy Ghost God, and that these three Gods make one God.

"According to the celestial multiplication table, once one is three, and three times one is one, and according to heavenly subtraction, if we take two from three, three are left. The addition is equally peculiar, if we add two to one, we have but one ....

"Nothing ever was, nothing ever can be more perfectly idiotic and absurd than the dogma of the Trinity."

—Robert G. Ingersoll (1833-1899), "The Trinity"
(from "The Foundations of Faith," The Works of Ingersoll).

In 1941, evolutionary biologist and freethought champion Richard Dawkins was born in Nairobi. His father had moved to Kenya from England during the Second World War to join the Allied Forces and the family returned to England in 1949. Dawkins graduated from Oxford in 1962, earned his doctorate, became assistant professor of zoology at the University of California at Berkeley 1967-1969 and a fellow of New College in 1970. *The Selfish Gene*, his first book, published in 1976, became an international bestseller. It and the award-winning *Blind Watchmaker* were translated into all major languages. His other books include *The Extended Phenotype* (1982), *River Out of Eden* (1995), *Climbing Mount Improbable* (1996), *Unweaving the Rainbow* (1998) and *A Devil's Chaplain* (2003). His 2006 iconoclastic book, *The God Delusion*, which he wrote with the public hope of turning believing readers into atheists, became a bestseller in both the UK and the U.S. Dawkins has held the Charles Simonyi Chair of Public Understanding of Science since 1995, and was elected a Fellow of the Royal Society of Literature in 1997. He is married to actress and artist Lalla Ward, who illustrated two of his books. Dawkins has advanced the concept of cultural inheritance or "memes," also described as "viruses of the mind," a category into which he places religious belief. He has also advanced the "replicator concept" of evolution. A passionate atheist, Dawkins has coined the memorable term "faith-heads" to describe certain religionists. Since his remarks in *The Guardian* (Feb, 6, 1999): "I'm like a pit bull terrier being released into the ring, as a spectator sport, to attack religious people . . . ," Dawkins is now affectionately known as "Darwin's pit bull." Dawkins, a vice president of the British Humanist Association, was named Humanist of the Year in 1999. He is the 1997 winner of the International Cosmos Prize, and received an Emperor Has No Clothes Award from the Freedom From Religion Foundation in 2001. His column for *The Observer* ("Children Must Choose Their own Beliefs," Dec. 30, 2001) pointed out: "We deliberately set up, and massively subsidizes, segregated faith schools. As if it were not enough that we fasten belief-labels on babies at birth, those badges of mental apartheid are now reinforced and refreshed. In their separate schools, children are separately taught mutually incompatible beliefs." Following the terrorist attacks of Sept. 11, 2001, he eloquently warned in a *Guardian* column, "Religion's Misguided Missiles" (Sept. 15, 2001):

"To fill a world with religion, or religions of the Abrahamic kind, is like littering the streets with loaded guns. Do not be surprised if they are used."

"My respect for the Abrahamic religions went up in the smoke and choking dust of September 11th. The last vestige of respect for the taboo disappeared as I watched the 'Day of Prayer' in Washington Cathedral, where people of mutually incompatible faiths united in homage to the very force that caused the problem in the first place: religion. It is time for people of intellect, as opposed to people of faith, to stand up and say 'Enough!' Let our tribute to the dead be a new resolve: to respect people for what they individually *think*, rather than respect *groups* for what they were collectively brought up to *believe*."

—"Time to Stand Up," written for the Freedom From Religion Foundation, Sept. 2001.
See Dawkins's Emperor Has No Clothes Award.

Thomas Henry Huxley was born in England in 1825. Huxley coined the term "agnostic" (although George Jacob Holyoake also claimed that honor). Huxley defined agnosticism as a method, "the essence of which lies in the rigorous application of a single principle . . . the axiom that every man should be able to give a reason for the faith that is in him." Huxley elaborated: "In matters of the intellect, follow your reason as far as it will take you, without any other consideration. And negatively, in matters of the intellect do not pretend that conclusions are certain which are not demonstrated or demonstrable" (from his essay "Agnosticism").

Huxley received his medical degree from Charring Cross School of Medicine, becoming a physiologist, and was awarded many other honorary degrees. He spent his youth exploring science, especially zoology and anatomy, lecturing on natural history, and writing for scientific publications. He was president of the Royal Society, and was elected to the London School Board in 1870, where he championed a number of common-sense reforms. Huxley earned the nickname "Darwin's Bulldog" when he debated Darwin's *On the Origin of Species* with Bishop Samuel Wilberforce in Oxford in 1860. When Wilberforce asked him which side of his family contained the ape, Huxley famously replied that he would prefer to descend from an ape than a human being who used his intellect "for the mere purpose of introducing ridicule into grave scientific discussion." Thereafter, Huxley devoted his time to the defense of science over religion. His essays included "Agnosticism and Christianity" (1889). His three rationalist grandsons were Sir Julian Huxley, a biologist, novelist Aldous Huxley, and Henry Fielding Huxley, co-winner of a 1963 Nobel Prize. Huxley, appropriately, received the Darwin Medal in 1894. *D. 1895.*

"Skepticism is the highest duty and blind faith the one unpardonable sin."

—Thomas Henry Huxley,
Essays on Controversial Questions (1889)

The best of Emerson's rather wordy writing survives as epigrams, such as the famous: "A foolish consistency is the hobgoblin of little minds, adored by little statesmen and philosophers and divines." Other one—(and two-) liners include: "As men's prayers are a disease of the will, so are their creeds a disease of the intellect" (*Self-Reliance*, 1841). "The most tedious of all discourses are on the subject of the Supreme Being" (*Journal*, 1836). "The word miracle, as pronounced by Christian churches, gives a false impression; it is a monster. It is not one with the blowing clover and the falling rain" (*Address to Harvard Divinity College*, July 15, 1838). He demolished the rightwing hypocrites of his era in his essay "Worship": ". . . the louder he talked of his honor, the faster we counted our spoons" (*Conduct of Life*, 1860). "I hate this shallow Americanism which hopes to get rich by credit, to get knowledge by raps on midnight tables, to learn the economy of the mind by phrenology, or skill without study, or mastery without apprenticeship" (*Self-Reliance*). "The first and last lesson of religion is, 'The things that are seen are temporal; the things that are not seen are eternal.' It puts an affront upon nature" (*English Traits*, 1856). "The god of the cannibals will be a cannibal, of the crusaders a crusader, and of the merchants a merchant." (*Civilization*, 1862). D. 1882.

"The dull pray; the geniuses are light mockers."

—Ralph Waldo Emerson,
Representative Men (1850)

McKellen is open about his personal atheism, but does not often speak on the subject. He has said that he only considers himself an expert in acting and in being a homosexual. McKellen came out as a gay man publicly in 1988, and became active in the gay rights community. He became a founding member of the UK LGBT advocacy group Stonewall, and meets with politicians in order to advocate against discriminatory legislation. McKellen was made a Commander of the Order of the British Empire in 1979, and knighted in 1991 for his contributions to theater. In 2008, he was made a Companion of Honor for his services to drama and equality.

Matt Lauer: There have been calls from some religious groups. They wanted a disclaimer at the beginning of this movie saying it is fiction because, again, one of the themes in the book really knocks Christianity right on its ear . . . . How would you all have felt if there was a disclaimer at the beginning of the movie? Would it have been okay with you?

Well, I've often thought the Bible should have a disclaimer in the front saying this is fiction. I mean, walking on water, it takes an act of faith. And I have faith in this movie. Not that it's true, not that it's factual, but that it's a jolly good story. And I think audiences are clever enough and bright enough to separate out fact and fiction, and discuss the thing after they've seen it.

—Ian McKellen, in an interview with Matt Lauer on "The Today Show" about "The Da Vinci Code," May 17, 2006

"Free People From Superstition"

Prof. Steven Weinberg prefaced his acceptance speech as the first "Emperor Has No Clothes" awardee by saying, "I enjoy being at a meeting that doesn't start with an invocation!"

Weinberg addressed the audience at the 22nd annual Freedom From Religion Foundation convention in San Antonio last November on "insidious" creationist arguments, the Big Bang and its evidences, public misunderstandings of the scientific method, and his rejection of religion.

Weinberg confessed he has almost envied his friends in evolutionary biology for being on the front lines fighting the creationists.

"But these people in Kansas have done me the great service of attacking the standard cosmological theory, the Big Bang theory, so that we cosmologists are now in the thick of it along with our friends in evolutionary biology. I think that's simply wonderful."

"Nothing," he said, "has been more important in the history of science than the work of Darwin and Wallace pointing out that not only the planets but even life could be understood in this naturalistic way." He added:

"I personally feel that the teaching of modern science is corrosive of religious belief, and I'm all for that! One of the things that in fact has driven me in my life, is the feeling that this is one of the great social functions of science—to free people from superstition.

"But I don't think that that attitude of mine should control the high school curriculum," he said, adding "my own personal motivation is irrelevant," just as the motivations of religious people should not affect high school curricula: "Science should be taught not in order to support religion and not in order to destroy religion—science should be taught simply ignoring religion."

While he called creationism "a persistent problem," Weinberg termed more serious the fact that "a large majority of Americans, without believing very much in the teachings of their religion, nevertheless believe strongly in religion." While actual belief is gradually diminishing "there continues to be respect for the moral teaching of religion."

This, he said, raises all sorts of questions, such as: "Why do you think your religion should be respected as a source of moral authority if in fact your religion has nothing to say about the world?"

Weinberg pointed out that two or three hundred years ago, "Most of the world's great religions coexisted very comfortably with slavery."

Part of the general moral improvement of the human race can be credited to "the growth of science—a sense of rationality, a scientific view that we don't really differ that much from one another, that there is no divine right of kings and so on, there is no intrinsic racial difference that should allow us to enslave one race for the benefit of another race."

"People have just gotten less religious and more moral," he explained.

Weinberg expressed some frustration with what Susan Sontag calls "piety without content."

He addressed the current claim that the Ten Commandments are "not religion, just good morality."

"If you read the Ten Commandments, the first four have nothing to do with morality—they're purely descriptions of piety.

"The Ten Commandments portray a deity who is self-centered, selfish, jealous, obsessed with his own importance; this is not a nice kind of person. The traditional teachings of religion are, from the point of view of the morality most people share today, pretty immoral."

Speaking of Abraham being ordered to sacrifice Isaac, he asked: "What kind of leader, if he was a human being, would want that kind of loyalty, demand that kind of loyalty?"

He said there is a perversity in the creator of the universe regarding the crucial test, "determining whether or not you spend an eternity in torment or joy, as whether or not you believe in him, even though he's done a damn good job of hiding evidence of his existence."

Weinberg does not know "whether or not we're headed for another Dark Age when people do start crusades and jihads and pogroms again, or whether the course of rationalism and humanitarianism is going to continue, and religion will gradually dwindle into something much less important.

"From my own point of view, I can hope that this long sad story will come to an end at some time in the future and that this progression of priests and ministers and rabbis and ulamas and imams and bonzes and bodhisattvas will come to an end, that we'll see no more of them. I hope that this is something to which science can contribute and if it is, then I think it may be the most important contribution that we can make."

On the subject of religion, Weinberg told the New York Times: "The whole history of the last thousands of years has been a history of religious persecutions and wars, pogroms, jihads, crusades. I find it all very regrettable, to say the least.

Weinberg is outspoken about his lack of religion and encourages other scientists to be more vocal in their opposition to religious ideas. He has said, in reference to the conflict between religion and science, "As you learn more and more about the universe, you find you can understand more and more without any reference to supernatural intervention, so you lose interest in that possibility. Most scientists I know don't care enough about religion even to call themselves atheists. And that, I think, is one of the great things about science—that it has made it possible for people not to be religious" (quoted in Natalie Angier, "Confessions of a Lonely Atheist," The New York Times, Jan. 14, 2001). In 1999, Steven Weinberg became the first official recipient of FFRF's "Emperor Has No Clothes" award, a golden figurine reserved for public figures who make known their dissent from religion. He began his acceptance speech by saying, "I enjoy being at a meeting that doesn't start with an invocation!" He said, "Nothing has been more important in the history of science than the work of Darwin and Wallace pointing out that not only the planets but even life can be understood in this naturalistic way." More excerpts from his acceptance speech can be found here.

"Religion is an insult to human dignity. With or without it you would have good people doing good things and evil people doing evil things. But for good people to do evil things, that takes religion."

—Steven Weinberg, in an address at the Conference on Cosmic Design, American Association for the Advancement of Science, Washington, D.C., April 1999

"I believe that when I die I shall rot, and nothing of my ego will survive. I am not young, and I love life. But I should scorn to shiver with terror at the thought of annihilation. Happiness is nonetheless true happiness because it must come to an end, nor do thought and love lose their value because they are not everlasting."

—Bertrand Russell, "What I Believe," 1925,
reprinted in *Why I Am Not a Christian* (1957)

"The Church is now more like the Scribes and Pharisees than like Christ ... What are now called the 'essential doctrines' of the Christian religion he does not even mention."

—Florence Nightingale, 1896 letter,
quoted by Sir Edward Cook,
Life of Florence Nightingale (1913)

"Religion has been compelled by science to give up one after another of its dogmas, of those assumed cognitions which it could not substantiate."

—Herbert Spencer, *First Principles*, 1862

Christian, n. One who believes that the New Testament is a divinely inspired book admirably suited to the spiritual needs of his neighbor. One who follows the teachings of Christ insofar as they are not inconsistent with a life of sin.

Eucharist, n. A sacred feast of the religious sect of Theophagi. A dispute once unhappily arose among the members of this sect as to what it was that they ate. In this controversy some five hundred thousand have already been slain, and the question is still unsettled.

Evangelist, n. A bearer of good tidings, particularly (in a religious sense) such as assure us of our own salvation and the damnation of our neighbors.

Faith, n. Belief without evidence in what is told by one who speaks without knowledge, of things without parallel.

Infidel, n. In New York, one who does not believe in the Christian religion; in Constantinople, one who does.

Pray. v. To ask that the laws of the universe be annulled in behalf of a single petitioner, confessedly unworthy.

Religion, n. A daughter of Hope and Fear, explaining to Ignorance the nature of the Unknowable.

Reverence, n. The spiritual attitude of a man to a god and a dog to a man.

Saint, n. A dead sinner revised and edited.

—Ambrose Bierce, *The Devil's Dictionary* (1906)

Mr. Chief Justice, and may it please the Court:

Every school morning in the Elk Grove Unified School District's public schools, government agents, teachers, funded with tax dollars, have their students stand up, including my daughter, face the flag of the United States of America, place their hands over their hearts, and affirm that ours is a nation under some particular religious entity, the appreciation of which is not accepted by numerous people, such as myself. We cannot in good conscience accept the idea that there exists a deity.

I am an atheist. I don't believe in God.

And every school morning my child is asked to stand up, face that flag, put her hand over her heart, and say that her father is wrong.

—Michael Newdow's oral argument to the U.S. Supreme Court, March 24, 2004 (The Oyez Project)

"Does history support a belief in God? If by God we mean not the creative vitality of nature but a supreme being intelligent and benevolent, the answer must be a reluctant negative."

—Will and Ariel Durant,
The Lessons of History (1968).

"Gullibility and credulity are considered undesirable qualities in every department of human life—except religion ... Why are we praised by godly men for surrendering our 'godly gift' of reason when we cross their mental thresholds? ... Atheism strikes me as morally superior, as well as intellectually superior, to religion. Since it is obviously inconceivable that all religions can be right, the most reasonable conclusion is that they are all wrong."

—Christopher Hitchens, "The Lord and the Intellectuals," Harper's (July 1982), cited by James A. Haught in *2,000 Years of Disbelief* (1996)

"I believe in an America where the separation of church and state is absolute—where no Catholic prelate would tell the President (should he be Catholic) how to act, and no Protestant minister would tell his parishioners for whom to vote—where no church or church school is granted any public funds or political preference—and where no man is denied public office merely because his religion differs from the President who might appoint him or the people who might elect him.

"I believe in an America that is officially neither Catholic, Protestant nor Jewish—where no public official either requests or accepts instructions on public policy from the Pope, the National Council of Churches or any other ecclesiastical source—where no religious body seeks to impose its will directly or indirectly upon the general populace or the public acts of its officials—and where religious liberty is so indivisible that an act against one church is treated as an act against all ....

"Finally, I believe in an America where religious intolerance will someday end—where all men and all churches are treated as equal—where every man has the same right to attend or not attend the church of his choice—where there is no Catholic vote, no anti-Catholic vote, no bloc voting of any kind—and where Catholics, Protestants and Jews, at both the lay and pastoral level, will refrain from those attitudes of disdain and division which have so often marred their works in the past, and promote instead the American ideal of brotherhood."

—John F. Kennedy, born on May 29, 1917 (*D. 1963*). Speech to the Greater Houston Ministerial Association, Rice Hotel, Sept. 12, 1960

"We atheists lead happy lives, never concerned with the-dying-and-burn forever-in-hell nonsense. We know better. We enjoy happiness with our friends and neighbors and ignore all the greed and rituals that pay the parasite priests. Let them wallow in their medieval superstition while we enjoy all the wonders of our God-free universe."

—Harry Harrison in "They're Afraid of Us!" on the Harry Harrison Official News Blog, April 23, 2011

"I do not pretend to be able to prove that there is no God. I equally cannot prove that Satan is a fiction. The Christian God may exist; so may the Gods of Olympus, or of ancient Egypt, or of Babylon. But no one of these hypotheses is more probable than any other: they lie outside the region of even probable knowledge, and therefore there is no reason to consider any of them."

—Bertrand Russell (1872-1970), *What I Believe,*1925

In 1743, Thomas Jefferson, who became third president of the United States, was born in Virginia. As a young attorney and member of the Continental Congress, Jefferson drafted the Declaration of Independence. Jefferson became Governor of Virginia in 1779, when the Anglican church was disestablished as the state religion. Jefferson wrote the Statute of Religious Freedom, whose preamble indicted state religion, noting that "false religions over the greatest part of the world and through all time" have been maintained through the church-state. To "compel a man to furnish contributions of money for the propagation of opinions which he disbelieves is sinful and tyrannical." The heart of the Statute guarantees that no citizen "shall be compelled to frequent or support any religious worship, place, or ministry whatsoever." It was adopted in 1786 and is replicated in most other state constitutions. Jefferson spent five years in France as an ambassador, and therefore was out of the country at the time of adoption of the U.S. Constitution. He strenuously urged the addition of a Bill of Rights. Jefferson became the first Secretary of State in 1789, Vice-President in 1796, was elected president in 1800, and re-elected in 1804.

In his *Notes on Virginia* (1781), Jefferson wrote: "Millions of innocent men, women and children since the introduction of Christianity have been burnt, tortured, fined, imprisoned. Yet have we not advanced one inch towards uniformity. What has been the effect of coercion? To make one half the world fools and the other half hypocrites. To support roguery and error all over the earth . . ." The Deist wrote: "The day will come when the mystical generation of Jesus, by the Supreme Being as his father, in the womb of a virgin, will be classed with the fable of the generation of Minerva in the brain of Jupiter." (*Works*, 1829 ed., Vol. IV, p. 365). Jefferson, who contemptuously rejected the trinity concept and regarded Jesus as a human teacher only, made a 46-page extraction of the teachings of Jesus that he accepted, discarding the rest. In an Oct. 12, 1813 letter to a friend, Jefferson explained that he had arranged "the matter which is evidently, his, and which is as easily distinguishable as diamonds from a dunghill." Writing to James Smith on December 8, 1822, Jeggerson said, "Man, once surrendering his reason, has no remaining guard against absurdities the most monstrous, and like a ship without rudder, is the sport of every wind. With such persons, gullibility, which they call faith, takes the helm from the hand of reason and the mind becomes a wreck."

As President, Jefferson issued his famous letter to the Baptists of Danbury, Connecticut on Jan. 1, 1802, explaining that the Establishment Clause of the First Amendment builds "a wall of separation between church and state." He refused to issue any days of prayer or thanksgiving, believing civil powers alone were conferred on public officials. Jefferson instructed that the epitaph on his tombstone read: "'Author of the Declaration of American Independence, of the Statute of Virginia for Religious Freedom & Father of the University of Virginia,' because by these, as testimonials that I have lived I wish most to be remembered." He and John Adams died on the same significant anniversary of July 4, 1826.

"Question with boldness even the existence of a God; because, if there be one, he must more approve of the homage of reason than that of blindfolded fear . . . . Do not be frightened from this inquiry by any fear of its consequences. If it ends in a belief that there is no God, you will find inducements to virtue in the comfort and pleasantness you feel in its exercise, and the love of others which it will procure you."

—Thomas Jefferson's letter to nephew Peter Carr,
written from Paris, Aug. 10, 1787

"... as a scientist, I cannot help feeling that all religions are on a tottering foundation. None is perfect or inspired.

The idea that a good God would send people to a burning hell is utterly damnable to me. I don't want to have anything to do with such a God.

I am an infidel today."

—Luther Burbank,
interview in *San Francisco Bulletin*, Jan. 22, 1926

"In the same way when we dream we draw absurd inferences by association. Even when men are awake, those parts of their mind to which for the moment they are not giving full attention are apt to draw equally unfounded inferences. People in a state of strong religious emotion sometimes become conscious of a throbbing sound in their ears, due to the increased force of their circulation. An organist, by opening the thirty-two foot pipe, can create the same sensation, and can thereby induce in the congregation a vague and half-conscious belief that they are experiencing religious emotion."

—Graham Wallas, *Human Nature in Politics*,
"Non-Rational Inference in Politics," 1908

"I think I could turn and live with animals, they're so placid and self contain'd, ...

They do not sweat and whine about their condition,

They do not lie awake in the dark and weep for their sins,

They do not make me sick discussing their duty to God,

Not one is dissatisfied, not one is demented with the mania of owning things,

Not one kneels to another, nor to his kind that lived thousands of years ago,

Not one is respectable or unhappy over the earth."

—Walt Whitman, *Leaves of Grass*, 1891 edition

"Religion is the sigh of the oppressed creature, the feelings of a heartless world, just as it is the spirit of unspiritual conditions. It is the opium of the people."

"The first requisite of the happiness of the people is the abolition of religion."

—Karl Marx,
A Criticism of the Hegelian Philosophy of Right (1844)

"The gods can either take away evil from the world and will not, or, being willing to do so cannot; or they neither can nor will, or lastly, they are able and willing.

"If they have the will to remove evil and cannot, then they are not omnipotent. If they can but will not, then they are not benevolent. If they are neither able nor willing, they are neither omnipotent nor benevolent.

"Lastly, if they are both able and willing to annihilate evil, why does it exist?"

—Greek philosopher Epicurus
(341-270 B.C.E.), *Aphorisms*

"To talk about a Superior Being is a dip in superstition, and is just as bad as to let in an Inferior Being or a Devil.

When you once attribute effects to the will of a personal God, you have let in a lot of little gods and evils—then sprites, fairies, dryads, naiads, witches, ghosts and goblins, for your imagination is reeling, riotous, drunk, afloat on the flotsam of superstition. What you know then doesn't count. You just believe, and the more you believe the more do you plume yourself that fear and faith are superior to science and seeing."

—Elbert Hubbard section,
from *An American Bible*, edited by Alice Hubbard (1912

"In India, as elsewhere in our darkening world, religion is the poison in the blood. Where religion intervenes, mere innocence is no excuse. Yet we go on skating around this issue, speaking of religion in the fashionable language of 'respect.' What is there to respect in any of this, or in any of the crimes now being committed almost daily around the world in religion's dreaded name?"

—Salman Rushdie, "Slaughter in the Name of God,"
Washington Post, March 8, 2002

"... it was largely to escape religious test oaths and declarations that a great many of the early colonists left Europe and came here hoping to worship in their own way. It soon developed, however, that many of those who had fled to escape religious test oaths turned out to be perfectly willing, when they had the power to do so, to force dissenters from their faith to take test oaths in conformity with the faith . . . .

"There were, however, wise and farseeing men in the Colonies—too many to mention—who spoke out against test oaths and all the philosophy of intolerance behind them . . . .

"We repeat and again reaffirm that neither a State nor the Federal Government can constitutionally force a person 'to profess a belief or disbelief in any religion.' Neither can constitutionally pass laws or impose requirements which aid all religions as against nonbelievers, and neither can aid those religions based on a belief in the existence of God as against those religions founded on different beliefs."

—Justice Black for the U.S. Supreme Court,
Torcaso v. Watkins, 367 U.S. 488, June 19, 1961

"We all ought to understand we're on our own. Believing in Santa Claus doesn't do kids any harm for a few years but it isn't smart for them to continue waiting all their lives for him to come down the chimney with something wonderful. Santa Claus and God are cousins.

Christians talk as though goodness was their idea but good behavior doesn't have any religious origin. Our prisons are filled with the devout.

I'd be more willing to accept religion, even if I didn't believe it, if I thought it made people nicer to each other but I don't think it does."

—Andy Rooney, *Sincerely, Andy Rooney*, 1999

"I don't differentiate much, except in degree, between people who believe in religion from those who believe in astrology, magic or the supernatural."

"We all ought to understand we're on our own. Believing in Santa Claus doesn't do kids any harm for a few years but it isn't smart for them to continue waiting all their lives for him to come down the chimney with something wonderful. Santa Claus and God are cousins."

"I just wish this social institution [religion] wasn't based on what appears to me to be a monumental hoax built on an accumulation of customs and myths directed toward proving something that isn't true."

"*Christians talk as though goodness was their idea but good behavior doesn't have any religious origin. Our prisons are filled with the devout.*"

"*I'd be more willing to accept religion, even if I didn't believe it, if I thought it made people nicer to each other but I don't think it does.*"

"We are lucky enough to be living in a country that not only guarantees the freedom to practice religion as we see fit, but also freedom FROM religious zealots who would persecute and prosecute and even physically harm those of us who do not believe as they do . . . . If you refuse to salute the flag and say God in your pledge, you're actually judged un-American. But that's not the way America is supposed to be. That's the way Iran is . . . . Predicating patriotism on a citizen's belief in God is as anti-American as judging him on the color of his skin. It is wrong. It is useless. It is unconstitutional."

—Harvey Fierstein in the segment "Outtakes,"
from the program "In the Life,"
broadcast by Generation Q, Nov. 2004

"To become a popular religion, it is only necessary for a superstition to enslave a philosophy.

We have enslaved the rest of the animal creation, and have treated our distant cousins in fur and feathers so badly that beyond doubt, if they were able to formulate a religion, they would depict the Devil in human form.

Perhaps the most lasting pleasure in life is the pleasure of not going to church."

—William Ralph Inge, writer and Anglican prelate.
Born June 6, 1860, *D. 1954*. (Internet sources)

"When men have realized that time has upset many fighting faiths, they may come to believe even more than they believe the very foundations of their own conduct that the ultimate good desired is better reached by free trade in ideas—that the best test of truth is the power of the thought to get itself accepted in the competition of the market, and that truth is the only ground upon which their wishes can be carried out. That, at any rate, is the theory of our Constitution. It is an experiment, as all life is an experiment."

—Oliver Wendell Holmes, Jr., quoted in the
obituary run by The New York Times

Quotes Of Mark Twain

Man is a Religious Animal. He is the only Religious Animal. He is the only animal that has the True Religion—several of them. He is the only animal that loves his neighbor as himself and cuts his throat if his theology isn't straight. He has made a graveyard of the globe in trying his honest best to smooth his brother's path to happiness and heaven . . . . The higher animals have no religion. And we are told that they are going to be left out in the Hereafter. I wonder why? It seems questionable taste.

—"The Lowest Animal"

India has two million gods, and worships them all. In religion all other countries are paupers; India is the only millionaire.

—Following the Equator

Monarchies, aristocracies, and religions . . . . there was never a country where the majority of the people were in their secret hearts loyal to any of these institutions.

—The Mysterious Stranger

The easy confidence with which I know another man's religion is folly teaches me to suspect that my own is also. I would not interfere with any one's religion, either to strengthen it or to weaken it. I am not able to believe one's religion can affect his hereafter one way or the other, no matter what that religion may be. But it may easily be a great comfort to him in this life—hence it is a valuable possession to him.

—*Mark Twain, a Biography*

In religion and politics people's beliefs and convictions are in almost every case gotten at second-hand, and without examination, from authorities who have not themselves examined the questions at issue but have taken them at second-hand from other non-examiners, whose opinions about them were not worth a brass farthing.

—*Autobiography of Mark Twain*

I am quite sure now that often, very often, in matters concerning religion and politics a man's reasoning powers are not above the monkey's.

Man is kind enough when he is not excited by religion.

—*A Horse's Tale*

Religion consists in a set of things which the average man thinks he believes, and wishes he was certain. Faith is believing what you know ain't so

—Notebook, 1879

I was educated, I was trained, I was a Presbyterian and I knew how these things are done. I knew that in Biblical times if a man committed a sin the extermination of the whole surrounding nation—cattle and all—was likely to happen. I knew that Providence was not particular about the rest, so that He got somebody connected with the one He was after.

—Autobiography of Mark Twain

The Koran does not permit Mohammedans to drink. Their natural instincts do not permit them to be moral. They say the Sultan has eight hundred wives. This almost amounts to bigamy.

—The Innocents Abroad

I have a religion—but you will call it blasphemy. It is that there is a God for the rich man but none for the poor . . . . Perhaps your religion will sustain you, will feed you—I place no dependence in mine. Our religions are alike, though, in one respect—neither can make a man happy when he is out of luck.

—Letter to Orion Clemens, 10/19-20/1865

". . . now at least, in our immediate day, we hear a Pope saying slave trading is wrong, and see him sending an expedition to Africa to stop it. The texts remain; it is the practice that has changed. Why? Because the world has corrected the Bible. The Church never corrects it; and also never fails to drop in at the tail of the procession—and take the credit of the correction. As she will presently do in this instance."

—Mark Twain (1835-1910), *Europe and Elsewhere*, 1923

Those are just a few quotes. We could easily find many more. The fact is that the intelligentsia of this world are freethinkers. How can we believe otherwise?

CHAPTER 30

My Best Friend

When I first met Joanne, I was in an electronics technical training school studying radar in the Army Air Corps in Madison Wisconsin. She had been a grammar school classmate of my closest air corps bunkmate and friend, Tex Lamason. He introduced me to her and from the first moment I knew she was going to be something special in my life. That was in 1944 and I remember it as if it were yesterday. My life changed from that moment on.

After the war during my sophomore year in summer school at the University of Wisconsin we were constant companions. One of the courses we took together that summer was comparative religion. She was already a confirmed atheist. I described myself as an agnostic but she would have none of it. We discussed the subject at great length all summer. With each discussion I came closer to her position. Eventually it was obvious that she was more honest in her philosophy than I. I joined her and became an atheist and have continued with that philosophy life-long.

Her rationale was so crystal clear. It went something like this. God is supposed to be merciful, and all-powerful, and in complete control of the world. If so, why would he perpetrate such horrors on the world as we have gone through many times? If he is simply all-powerful, then he must be a maniac. No, it's just not logical that God exists. How can I argue with that? Joanne was the most logical person I ever knew.

When we eloped that summer, it was pretty shocking to both of our families as neither of us had a penny in savings and though she had completed her degree, I still had at least three years to go for my undergraduate bachelors degree and then another four for my doctorate and intern training after that. Both of our fathers realized how difficult that was going to be and it turned out that they were both right. However, I wouldn't have changed it for anything. I learned true love from Joanne as well as how to lead a full life. On her dying bed she said, "I have had a wonderful life with no regrets and I am not afraid to die." I learned that from her and certainly fully join her in that feeling after our wonderful 54 years of marriage.

We lived with my family in Worcester, for one year, while I completed my sophomore year at Clark University. I had the G.I. Bill which provided me with a monthly stipend, modest though it was. On weekends we enjoyed skiing, hiking, and whitewater river running in Maine with my closest friend Walter Kistler who later became a physicist and a PHD professor at Worcester Tech University. I found Jo to be the perfect partner in everything we did. She also carried more than her share of every load, no matter where we went or what we did. Walter spoke to me later about how impressed he was with her. I did value his opinion. He certainly was one of the smartest persons I have ever known. He died of Alzheimer's in 1988.

My family was very welcoming but we both wanted our own abode. Since Joanne had skied in Colorado with her family and spoke so highly of it, we decided to transfer to the university in Boulder. That was the first time I really found myself with the full responsibility of life. We had our first child, that first year and though it boosted my G.I. Bill stipend, it did not begin to cover the expenses.

Joanne was the perfect mother, giving full attention, lovingly to Billy, our first child. It was up to me to figure out the rest of it. And I did, first with a job teaching skiing at Arapahoe Basin, which was quickly followed by additional part-time jobs selling. In addition to an academic education,

I learned a lot about the facts of life especially meeting responsibilities that always stood me in good stead for the rest of my life. I always made my own way financially and received no inheritance as mother used up what was remaining after dad died. I never depended on anyone to give me money. Nor did I ever receive any from anyone.

Joanne and I were inseparable. We did everything together; she did not let the baby stand in the way of joining in. We often slept in the very cold warming hut at Arapahoe Basin Ski area where I taught skiing but no complaints from either Joanne or Billy, though sometimes his diapers were frozen in the morning. It's not surprising that he became an excellent skier as did all our children.

After college, Jo was the perfect mother and help mate, and especially when I started out on my own, she was very important to me in organizing the numerous businesses I started. I could always depend upon her to give me the best of advice, support, and assistance. I attribute to her, most of the success I've had in life.

Jo and I Hiking In The Sierra's—1980's

I've often thought about those characteristics of Joanne's that were so perfect for me as my life's mate. Certainly her intelligence and natural beauty were important, but there were much more important attributes than those. She was my partner in everything we did. She sailed, skied, backpacked, ran whitewater rivers by canoe, you name it. She didn't criticize. She only made intelligent suggestions on how to improve things. And she was usually right. She was not superficial. Her use of cosmetics and jewelry was minimal. She just didn't need those things to make her beautiful. And she was a real beauty. When she died, a few items of that kind could have been held in one cupped hand. She was simply my idea of the perfect woman. My brother, Frank, has called her "a saint"

Her last year, she said, "I have had a wonderful life. I have no regrets and I am not afraid to die" I certainly join her completely in that statement. Following our wonderful married life together of 54 years she died of pancreatic cancer. She was always my best friend and closest companion and partner, in everything I did. I shall never forget her.

CHAPTER 31

Identity

Who are we? What is our identity?

As children, our parents establish our Identity. No one is born a Catholic or a Republican or anything else. We are carefully taught by our elders. About the only thing that we're sure of is that we are children and life spreads out before us with all of its challenges of excitement, opportunity and adventure.

Then we become students and our identity begins to change as our school environment, as well as our home environment begins to mold us into whom we are becoming. We build our identity as we mature, from student to worker and to many choices in different environments. We develop skills and put those skills to work to make a living. And so we identify ourselves with our chosen professions. We join organizations, social, religious, political, and many more. And we begin to crowd into our lives, identities, which follow us through the years. We find out who we are.

Identity is so important to living a full life. As we age, and reduce our activities one by one, we risk losing our identities. Perhaps one definition of a successful life is having a meaningful identity. Losing identity as you age means too often suffering an unhappy and unfulfilling old age.

As I have reached the final years of my life. I find it increasingly important to maintain my identity. We all need to be somebody. Unfortunately, many old people so often lose the identity that comes with retirement. They forget who they are. I am fortunate that I still am managing my hiking tour business and will continue to do so to the end. It gives me identity.

During the last 20 years, starting at age 65, I've developed a small retirement business, which matches my lifelong interests in mountaineering, both hiking and skiing. Though it becomes increasingly difficult to operate this mountaineering business due to my own physical limitations, I know that I need this business very much to maintain my identity. It's not only fun for me to operate my business but it allows me to know who I am. Oftimes people call me to ask for information and when they hear my name, they sometimes respond with, "Is this the real Bill Russell?" I know then that I have a meaningful identity and it pleases me. If you put "Bill Russell" into the internet, I come up, often on the first page. The only other Bill Russell that comes up is the basketball player. I'll settle for that.

I have had people interested in buying this business, but I don't want to sell it because it is "my baby." But more importantly, it is my identity. It took me a while to learn this. It is a lesson that I am grateful to have learned. Others, in their old age, join organizations or are active in their churches. This works for many. It does not for me. As an additional alternative to operating my business, I have been trying in recent years to develop my writing skills. I am finding this very difficult, even though I've taken creative writing courses at college level. It still is not easy. This is my first book. I hope that when the family reads it, they will enjoy it and get something out of it. I want to go on with other books, which I have in my head. But so far have been unable to get them down in the computer. Slowly one important theme continues to impress me and that is the foolishness and irrelevancy of religion in our modern world. My second book will address that subject.

Writing this book has forced me to look back on the history of the family and my history. I hope it does not sound like just bragging, but I must say, I have enjoyed a most successful life and still do. It has been "the good life."

Why is that? How come life is treated me so well?

1   I started off with good genes and wonderful, intelligent parents

2   I have had a lifetime of near perfect health maintaining bodily physical ability.

3   I was smart enough to have picked loving intelligent parents and followed their wise guidance.

4   I married the perfect woman.

I was always taught as a kid that self-determination is very important. I never depended upon superstition, prayer, or any other mystical guidance. I understood early in life from my father that it was all up to me and I must take responsibility for my actions. I determined my life's success through study and applied determination and work.

Then, dad advised me to set my goals and prepare myself by study and hard work. Oh, yes, one more .... spend less than you earn.

That does not sound very complicated. But I did follow simple rules, and managed always to love what I do.

I can remember in my senior year at college when I decided not to be a medical doctor and felt that business would be more interesting for me as a career, I found with Stanley Home Products that I was able to be productive as a salesman, so that is the job I started at. I was a salesman for a couple of years until I was promoted to sales manager and then for the first time, I was put in charge of other people, that was very new to me and I liked it. Management suited me because I found I was able to make consequential decisions and take responsibility for them. But I did not know anything.

I did not really understand the word, "marketing" At that time in my life, that meant going to the grocery store to buy your food. That is how little I knew, but slowly, I learned that marketing was a profession, and it involved not only sales, but how to sell what to whom and why. I began to read books on marketing, and finally went back to night school and concentrated on the subject. I attended many courses, both in Denver at the University of Colorado graduate school and in New York with the American Management Association and at Rutgers University and at New York University. I became a "Marketing Manager" professional and followed that profession all of my life. I am within 6 hours of a Master's degree in marketing which my move to Europe interrupted. When I returned to the USA, I did not finish the MBA as I just did not have the time.

I did get into general management early in my life, and liked that even more as it was not just marketing but all the other functions of the company, including planning, finance, production, and general organization. I spent most of my life at that level of responsibility.

CHAPTER 32

Ecumenism

The term "ecumenism", according to the Webster dictionary has to do with the getting together of the various Christian cults. I would like to use the word ecumenism in a broader sense referring to all religions getting together.

Recently, the pope was in the holy land on a mission which was described as peacemaking. He planned to meet with the two heads of the other leading religions, namely Judaism and Islam.

As I understand it this is the first time in the history of the world that the heads of the three leading Western religions were going to meet to talk about how they can get along. That, after all these years a meeting of the three leaders seemed finally imminent, is regretful.

In our age old struggle from savagery to civilization the countries of the world finally seem to have learned the importance of getting along. That is something very new. Even in my lifetime the animosity between nations has been monumental leading to two world wars and many minor wars in the past 100 years.

The struggles between Fascism, Communism, and Democracy threatened to destroy the Earth. Somehow or other, our politicians are learning that in a civilized society countries must get along and to do so a dialog must be encouraged. Now we have Islam disrupting the peace.

In the Middle Ages, wars frequently arose between city-states. They were often religious in nature but more often they pitted one petty ruler against another. We've moved from that level of confrontation through world wars to today when all the nations of the world are maintaining a dialogue. It's because of communications among other things but mostly it's out of necessity. The existence of atomic weapons makes it essential that we talk to each other. Our political leaders recognize that dialogue between nations is essential for the peace and future existence of the world.

I think it's tragic that the three leading religions of the Western world are just now for the first time in history deciding if they will talk to each other.

I don't know what will come of it and I'm not too optimistic that on the first go around anything will be accomplished. The principal reason is that the basis for religion in the first place is to allow for those who die to meet their god in heaven. Each religion, of the three, have their own gods and dogma has always dictated that each of the gods were unique. Each religion did not recognize the validity of the other gods. How can, now, these religious leaders actually find "ecumenism" when their fundamental god identities fail to recognize the others?

When three different religions say that theirs is the only true religion, then two of them must be wrong. The fact is that all three are wrong. There is such thing as true religion.

There is another big problem. At one time, 80% of the population in the holy land was Christian. Today it is a fraction of that. Throughout the Muslim world Christians have fled, because they are terrified of the new aggressive Muslim policies. Now, with the pope in the holy land, is his objective to try to build Christianity in that region? If so, it would result in massive unrest and retribution by the Muslim majority. Hardly a peaceful result to the Pope's visit

This is a subject of great importance second only in my opinion to the importance of the rise of the black race in our society but nonetheless today's most important subject.

Unfortunately the pope's visit did not result in the three heads meeting. An important opportunity was lost. Not surprising.

For many centuries mankind was ruled by monarchies. It was the accepted form of political organization. Then our founding fathers established the United States as the dominant secular Democratic country it has become. Slowly throughout the world we have seen monarchies disappear to be replaced by democracy. And maintaining separation of church and state. It is a trend that is altogether healthy for mankind.

I feel that those of us who understand the folly of religion, will speak out and find substitutions for some people's philosophical needs. So that eventually religion can be replaced in the minds of the masses by a healthier philosophy of self-determination not dependent upon the non-science of superstition and myth. Certainly this will not happen in my lifetime, but this book along with others I hope will aim to support that objective.

It is interesting to note that our current war in Afghanistan and Pakistan are religious in nature. The Islamists say they want to kill all infidels, rid the world of all Jews, and rule the world. Does that sound like sanity? It sounds like Hitler speaking all over again. The free world cannot permit this.

The fanatics behind this war are said to be "Extremists." They should be described as "Religious Extremists" so the world will know that we are not just fighting some obscure political idea, but a serious philosophical, evil idea called religion. An idea that will bring the world to ruin if allowed to continue to develop. Fortunately our country is dedicated to putting a stop to it for once and for all. More power to the great United States of America.

CHAPTER 33

Frank and Eleanor

As the younger brother Frank was always in Bill's shadow: Bill left for the U.S. Army air Corps in February 1944 so it was now Frank's position to take over. Many of the initiatives started by Bill were taken over by Frank. Such things as running DeMolay were important. Bill had been Master Counselor of the Worcester chapter. Frank not only became that but went on to become state Master Counselor of Massachusetts, a great honor which demonstrated his early leadership abilities.

Though Frank struggled in his early academic career, he soon learned the value of education and as he rose through high school he found important mentors like Roscoe W. Fletcher in physics whom he admired and gained a wide knowledge. Frank was an outstanding student in physics he says because he loved the "reasonableness" of it. Physics presented the facts of how things work and opened up a world of mechanical invention that he found fascinating. While in high school he assisted with dad in the autopsy of Nan Masters. He was so impressed that he decided that he was going to be a doctor and a surgeon. Most of Frank's studies in high school support his interest in becoming a doctor. Therefore there was a strong emphasis on science courses. However, Frank recognized the need for more classical type courses like philosophy and psychology which he added as soon as he could.

In April 1947, during his last year in high school, Frank obtained a leave of absence for six weeks to drive our father and his cousin Henry Peers through the South. On the way they stopped in Washington DC to visit with Jackie and Nestor Foley. Jackie was Henry's daughter. Nestor was a government lawyer. Their son, Bobby, also practiced law in Washington. They then went to the Carolinas where they visited a cotton plantation owned by a friend of Henry's. Henry was a cotton broker on Wall Street as he had a seat on the cotton exchange.

They went to Pensacola to see Hamilton, dad's brother who was away in Warm Springs Arkansas in a medical facility as he was terminally ill.

Then down to Tampa, where they stayed with Ernest Berger in Ybor city. They also spent some time at Berger's Kilcare Lodge on a Lake north of Tampa.

They ran into friends of dads when he was young and played violin in an orchestra. One in particular, had an accent like Gomer Pyle, the comedian. Dad said he worked very hard to get rid of that accent. He always spoke perfectly with very little accent. He was successful in that effort. He emphasized using good diction for all his family.

Hamilton, Keys, and June were dad's siblings but little is known of their lives. It is known that Hamilton was owner and President of the Russell Drug Company, a wholesale drug distributor in Pensacola. Dad was the oldest. His friends said that Dad always had the fastest horse in town back in the days when horses were the only way to get around.

After graduating from North high school in 1944, Frank, Jr. matriculated at the University of Tennessee in a premed course. As our dad did, he specialized in surgery wherever he could. In his sophomore year he married Harriet Pendleton of Knoxville Tennessee daughter of John Pendleton VP of Southern Railroad. Frank's studies at Tennessee included a major in philosophy and a minor in psychology. Here again he was trying to emphasize classical education even though pre-med requires heavy emphasis on science-based studies. He graduated from Tennessee in 1951. Frank has said that philosophy offers the finest in under graduate education especially if supported by history as a minor.

Frank often refers to the self-education of his father who didn't go to college and didn't even finish high school but did go through medical school and became a successful surgeon. Why? The answer is reading. Dad always kept books nearby and was a voluminous reader. If he was waiting for someone he would have something in his pocket worthwhile to read. Reading was very important to him. He educated himself. Reading was always dad's main activity after surgery. He had no other hobbies.

Frank applied to medical school and was turned down several times. Meanwhile the draft was breathing down his neck and rather than get drafted into the ground forces he enlisted in the Navy. He passed the qualifying exams for officer training school and came home one night announcing to Harriet "I'm in the navy, I've been accepted, I leave tomorrow at 5 AM for California."

When he arrived in California for the 11 week basic training he was faced with the various additional tests to allow him to move on to officer training. One was a serious problem he had with his draining ears. He had trouble with his ears most of his life and when the doctor discovered the problem Frank begged him not to report it. The examining doctor went along with Frank's request and Frank was suddenly on his way to officer training school in Newport, Rhode Island.

Frank has spent years in the South in school and then in basic training in the California desert. When he was transferred to officer training school in Rhode Island he says he nearly froze to death in the New England weather.

Frank says going to officer training school was rather serendipitous. Frank took the exam with a friend Jack Zimmermann from Waukesha Wisconsin in April of 1951. The exams were in Macon Georgia. Frank was finishing up college in Knoxville. After the exams, Frank went back to Knoxville and graduated. He was about to be drafted as he was waiting to get a medical school acceptance. Frank worked in a construction job in Knoxville for that summer. Frank then went to California for boot camp. He then got orders for officer's candidate school in Newport

Rhode Island. At that time he got a two-week leave, which he spent in Worcester.

Frank moved to Newport with Harriet. She got a job there in the Navy Department, while Frank attended officer's candidate school. They lived in an apartment on Bellevue Avenue.

Frank was at school for four months finishing in April when he got his commission. He was valedictorian of his class and gave the class speech. After a two-week leave Frank reported to Washington DC. They stayed in Washington with Harriet's brother Johnny, who was working for the FBI. Frank stayed in Washington until he was assigned to the cruiser, Pittsburgh, which he picked up in Istanbul, Turkey. The Pittsburgh was famous because during the war off of Okinawa a storm tore 102 feet off the bow. It had to back all the way to the naval repair station in the Solomon Islands where the bow was replaced.

Frank was the assistant signal officer on the bridge of the Pittsburgh. He shared a cabin with a full lieutenant who was a career naval officer. Usually officers of that rank have their own private cabin; A full lieutenant in the Navy is equal to a captain in the Army. On board ship, Frank had the run of the entire ship. He says that his favorite spot was on the bridge and when he was later on the Randolph aircraft carrier a favorite spot was on the flying bridge at the very top where he could watch airplanes landing and taking off in great elegance enjoying his sunbathing royally seated in the captain's chair.

His salary as an ensign was $137 a month from which he paid $33 for his meals in the ward room.

His ship, operated mostly in the Mediterranean and the Indian Ocean. Some of the ports he visited were Marseille, Istanbul on the Bosporus, Naples, and several ports on the North African coast. Frank was operating in war games with the sixth Fleet. The Korean War was going on at the time.

Frank was operating in these Mediterranean ports in the early 50s which still were showing the results of the heavy bombing during the world war. The ports were leveled by heavy allied bombing. Additional ports visited were in Nice, Cannes, and Gibraltar.

The ship then returned to Norfolk Virginia. He then went down to Guantánamo, Cuba for another shakedown cruise. Then went back to Europe for another six-month cruise. Harriet came over to Palma, Majorca, where they spent a couple of weeks together before Frank went off to India on another cruise. In India he visited Bombay and Calcutta.

One of the top-secret missions during this period that Frank was involved in was the establishment of missile bases surrounding Russia. As this was the time of the Cold War.

Frank felt as he visited some of these cities in India and Afghanistan as if he has stepped back into the 12th century. There was tremendous poverty to be seen everywhere. People were dying in the streets and corpses were everywhere. The smell was monstrous. In India, Madras, there was a famine. People were being cremated in the streets. Pakistan smelled like an outhouse. No sewage disposal. The poverty was unbelievable.

The battles between the Muslims and Hindus continued daily with killings everywhere. The vultures and the dogs in the neighborhoods were all very fat as they had plenty to eat from the corpses lying all over.

Frank was on the Pittsburgh for fourteen months. At the end of this duty on the Pittsburg, he was promoted to assistant radio officer.

The Randolph, an Essex class carrier was commissioned and Frank was sent aboard the Randolph as cryptographic officer. The Randolph then went down to Guantánamo, Cuba for a shakedown cruise. The Randolph was more exciting because it was an aircraft carrier. So, a lot was going on, compared to the life on the Pittsburgh. Some of Frank's friends were fighter pilots. They then took a cruise to the Mediterranean. He was on the aircraft carrier for over two years.

Doing Franks time in the Navy, he frequently applied to medical school, but was turned down repeatedly. He applied for flight training and was accepted, and just as he was about to go to Pensacola for pilot training, he was accepted to medical school.

Frank had learned to like the Navy. After a few months, he managed to fit in very well and says that he came close to thinking about the Navy as a career.

Frank says that Harriet went to Knoxville for the pre-acceptance interview at the Tennessee University medical school. He thinks he was accepted because Harriet made such a good impression on the interviewer. She was a very beautiful and intelligent person.

When Frank was coming home from Europe, he did so on a Constellation aircraft. This was state of the art aircraft at that time. They flew to England and on the way one engine went out leaving three engines. So they continued on. When they were in the process of landing in a blinding snowstorm at Heathrow, another engine went out. So it got to be very tense. They did make the landing, however, safely. They repaired the problem and re-fueled, and then were unable to take off, because they were unable to de-ice the plane. The passengers were transferred to a B-24. It arrived in New York, without further event. However, the plane that Frank had left shortly thereafter, crashed in Newfoundland with all lost. That was in 1955.

Frank went back to Knoxville to revalidate some of his credits in chemistry, physics, and biology before starting medical school.

Frank's experience in medical school he describes as routine. He wanted to be a surgeon from the very beginning so whenever he had time he interviewed a doctor-who interestingly enough had interviewed our father in 1913 when dad rode to Memphis on a bicycle and applied for medical school at that time and also since dad was a pharmacist he worked to supplement his income while in school.

Having completed his four-year studies he received his M.D. and applied to a number of hospitals for internship. He was accepted at Bellevue Hospital in New York City in the same division as our father which was Cornell division L2.u Bellevue.

Because Frank wanted to be a surgeon, he did not take the normal rotating internship but rather did a straight surgical internship there.

Frank was her much interested in trauma and the hospital that offered the most opportunities in this field was Beekman Downtown New York where he applied and was accepted for residency specializing in trauma rather than ob-gyn.

Frank did his second third and final fourth-year residency at Beekman during which time in his fourth year he was chief resident. During his tenure Frank worked under Dr. Robert Kennedy who was the organizer and chief of the American College of surgeons division of trauma which he founded.

Frank was trained in over 1000 procedures so was well-trained not only in general surgery and trauma specifically but also in orthopedic surgery. Frank completed his training at Beekman in June of 1963. Having completed his training, he took over the job of running the emergency room. While completing his training, Frank had done some moonlighting in Harlem where he got a lot of firsthand experience with real-life patients who were in need of help.

Frank's experience in Harlem taught him a lot about how black people lived and how they are just like anybody else trying to figure out how to live life and share the many life challenges and opportunities. He learned that blacks were just like whites except for color.

At this time Frank met a doctor Jesse Mahoney who was the head surgeon at Mathur and St. Charles in Port Jefferson Long Island. They found much in common immediately and Frank decided to start his new practice working in that service under Dr. Mahoney. Dr. Mahoney, interestingly, remembered our father from training as they were in the same class. Dr. Mahoney at that time was a resident whereas dad was an attending physician.

At the end of Frank's residency at Beekman Harriet moved back to Knoxville with her family and Frank went on to start a practice in Port Jefferson. They divorced about that time.

During Frank's residency at North Shore Hospital on Long Island in Manhasset he met Bunny Reedholm. She was also in the process of getting a divorce. Later they married. She was the daughter of Capt. Bill Reedholm executive vice Pres. of American Airlines. They lived in Port Washington.

During the ensuing years Frank and Bunny had five children Frank, James, John, Christine, and William.

Besides his professional career Frank has had interest in art and architecture, sail handling and building in his workshop. Specifically he likes to build boats, planes, and restore old cars.

He retired in 1996 and bought 13 acres on Lake Champlain. He built a large beautiful home pretty much with his own hands having designed it exactly the way he wanted it and has enjoyed life with his numerous hobbies building an important relationship with the people of Bridport Vermont especially with his interest in the cleanup of beautiful Lake Champlain. Frank was one of the organizers and founders of the Lake Champlain Restoration Association.

He invented and built an effective weed harvester. This has been useful in developing a program to clean up the Lake.

Over the years Frank has had a number of interests including the development maintenance and running of a tennis club in Florida where he was partners with Tom Falkenberg brother of Jinks Falkenberg the actress. The club was in Stuart Florida operating for 12 years after which it closed.

Frank was also interested sailing and had a 38 foot racing catamaran built for him by Rudy Choy in California in 1969. The cat was named IPO KAI and Frank sailed it actively on Long Island sound for 25 years. This interest in catamaran sailing got him a berth on Jim Arness's big cat, Sea Smoke. Other members in the crew and cruise Warren Seaman, David Capahuahua, Bruce Russell, and Joel Cochran

Frank also raced in the Ensenada race on Sea Smoke which was a shakedown race for the Transpac race. Buddy Epsen was also crew on this race.

Prior to retirement, Frank and Bunny divorced in 1986. He met Elizabeth Kaalund, who had been a surgical nurse for Frank at the hospital. She was from Denmark spoke several languages and was well-traveled and well-educated. Her father also was a surgeon in Denmark living in Copenhagen. They married in 1994 and together developed Frank's property in Vermont. They divorced in 2004.

Frank has seven children, Leslie 1, Kevin, Frank Jr, Leslie, John, James, and Christine.

Eleanor, our young sister, married early, to high school classmate, Don Lyons. Don was an officer in the service so they traveled widely for a number of years living in many parts of the country. Following Don's premature death, Eleanor settled in Long Island where she worked for brother Frank as office manager. She has raised an exceptional daughter, Leslie, who is a very successful executive in New York in the public relations field.

CHAPTER 34

Time Marches On

When Joanne died on April 14 of 2001, I was devastated. Even now, 11 years later, I can barely speak when I think of her. She was such a part of me as I was of her. After those wonderful 54 years of marriage, it could be expected to be easy to take a relationship for granted but we never took each other for granted. I know now at this moment that life will never be the same and that I shall have to continue to try to lead a new life without her. I hope I can do it. I try every day. Some days with modest success. If it weren't for my hiking business, my reading, research, and writing, and my piano and guitar, and boating on the Connecticut River, I would be lost.

We held no funeral. Both of us believed that a funeral is a silly waste of money and otherwise useful real estate perpetuated by foolish religions and that a more sensible alternative is cremation. I distributed her ashes on one of our favorite hiking trails on a bluff overlooking a beautiful valley in northwestern Connecticut where we often hiked. Our three children were with me. I've asked them to do the same with my ashes hopefully in the same place.

I held a memorial service for her at one of our favorite hiking places in the woods nearby Fairfield and announced it in the Fairfield newspaper. There were too many sad faces to count. And of course it had to rain, as we stood there talking about our dear departed friend. I said a few words interrupted by sobs. We then went home to our house for refreshments, and we sang some old songs as I played the harmonica that Joanne loved. It certainly was one of the saddest days of my life.

Later at the Newport Boat Show, the Yacht Charter Brokers Association, of which she was an active member, held a memorial in Joanne's honor. There attended over 400 speaking of her humanity and humility. It was a tremendous tribute to her which brought great joy to me.

I buried myself in my work. Year 2001 was my biggest year for Mountain Tours taking over 180 people to Europe. I spent much of the summer working with my guides throughout Europe, Norway, and the British Isles helping leading groups. It did not help my sorrow, however, as life will never be the same without Joanne.

I hiked in Switzerland in the summer with some of my guided groups. In the fall, I had pretty much decided to sell out and move to Switzerland. The Fairfield and Westport areas held too many sad memories for me. I have always loved those gorgeous Swiss Alps and the Swiss people are so delightful. I especially love the French area of Lake Geneva with the marvelous food and excellent wines. Living in Switzerland would probably be affordable as I had again, for a second time, accumulated cash of over a million dollars. I had nothing in Fairfield to keep me. Lori and Torrey had moved west and Billy to Essex. Therefore, I had no family nearby. Skiing and hiking in Switzerland is the best I can imagine anywhere. I had more than enough money again to retire and I felt I needed a new start in life in Switzerland. I thought I would move to Montreux near skiing, and hiking in Verbier, and sailing on Lake Geneva.

Billy became concerned and convinced me that I should move to Essex instead. It is a lovely town, and now that I have lived here for over 10 years, I have come to realize that this move was a wise decision and a good suggestion from Billy. I sold the Fairfield house, so the next big decision was what kind of house to buy in Essex.

As I was now in my mid 70s, I realized that I needed a house with minimum upkeep; one I could grow old in, and within walking distance of stores and services so I concentrated on houses in the village center.

There were two of them available, and one in particular, seemed just right at 3 Pratt St. I bought it. I still had a reasonably good income from Mountain Tours and other sources. My cash balance I subsequently lost, through unwisely investing with, son, Billy. It was money I had planned to give to all three of the children. Anyway, I will make it all back when Mountain Tours recovers from the current economic slump. I do not worry about such things. Having a lot of money has never been a major goal of mine. I have all the income I need to live well and no debt with a good income from Mountain Tours. I am very fortunate.

Sorcery—a 30 foot Etchells one of the several
racing yachts we owned and raced

I joined the Essex Yacht Club and bought an Etchells 30 foot sloop, which was an active racing class at the club. Billy and I with a crew recruited from the club campaigned the boat for several years and enjoyed it very much. However, when Burgess divorced Billy, he moved to Vail, so part of my motivation to own such a racing machine dissolved and I sold it. I thought perhaps a small cruising boat might be interesting. So I bought a Catalina 30 with four bunks, head, and galley. However, I used it so little, that I decided to sell it as I found cruising alone not very interesting, so now I just sail the club sloops on the river when I feel like getting out on the water. Even now, I sail infrequently as I am beginning to recognize my balance problems, especially when working the foredeck. Advanced age brings with it limitations that must be recognized and accommodated. I have now bought a power boat for exploring the beautiful Connecticut river.

I have always loved music. Since mother was an opera singer, classical music was around our house a great deal. It seemed like she was always giving parties, and everyone sang in their turn or played the piano or dad on the violin. Many were professionals; I even remember sitting in Carnegie Hall and listening to mother perform as the featured concert soloist. She had a wonderful contralto voice, which is very rare. The famed Marion Anderson was a contralto. Many thought mother's voice was as good as or better than Anderson's. Mother was trained at the Boston Conservatory and Julliard in New York. Her voice coach was Frank LaForge and her accompanist in Hollywood was Sid Grauman of Chinese Theatre fame. Mother sang in the Hollywood Bowl and was in the movies, making a movie with Douglas Fairbanks.

I took piano lessons as a child, but soon other things seemed more important like skiing, camping, mountaineering and girls. So my piano lessons were neglected. But I always loved music.

Then when we were living in Denver, I took lessons again and started to play a little. But I found that my guitar was more useful on skiing trips. In fact in Dillon, we had a little band. It met at Max Dercum's house weekly, which was known as Ski Tip Inn in Dillon, Colorado near Arapahoe Basin. A party each Saturday night after skiing featured our little musical group including Max on the clarinet, Dick Ryman on the drums, Jackie Gorsuch on the base, and Edna Dercum on the piano and at that time I had an electric guitar. At least we were noisy but we had fun. We sang a lot, too. I just learned that Edna died. She was 95 years old. The others are gone, too.

We gave our Steinway to Billy that we inherited from Jo's mother and then when Joanne was in her last months; I bought an electronic piano and started practicing again. I was able to get back to playing simple tunes. She enjoyed it. But then I gave it up again when I moved to Essex. Now I've started practicing again, and am enjoying it very much. It has become an important part of my daily routine. I know I'll never be a great pianist, but it gives me great personal pleasure.

I still have a problem with what today is currently called pop music. It just doesn't make any sense to me at all. Why can't this generation produce people like Richard Rogers, Oscar Hammerstein, George Gershwin, Cole Porter, Hoagie Carmichael, among many others who produced the kind of music that was so lyrical? Their music like Summertime, I'm in The Mood For Love, or Stardust have more than three cords and screaming was not required. The contemporary crop of so-called musicians performing today are simply not well trained. I guess the audiences are not demanding enough. The standards have changed so radically. About the only singer from my generation still around is Tony Bennett. Who will replace him? Where are the Sinatra's, the Nat King Cole's, the Glenn Miller's, the Benny Goodman's and the Tommy Dorsey's? It's a different world of popular music today and I am not part of it. Nor do I want to be. Thank goodness for the great symphony orchestras which are not influenced by the current junk musical culture. My preference is classical music.

Time marches on, and I am now 86. I cannot keep up the pace of leading hikes and doing slideshows all around the country. Therefore, my hiking business has suffered accordingly. Also, the poor economy has contributed to the reduction in tours. After all it is a luxury business. I am running it at a low level to keep it alive and I love it mostly as a hobby. Lauren said she wanted to take it over when she graduated from Yale, but she is now off to a much more exciting opportunity with Nike. She has such an excellent brain, and with her background, education, and her unusual ability, she could do much more than spend her time running a hiking tour company. I think national politics would be an excellent career for her eventually. Now, Lori has expressed interest in taking over the business when I am unable to run it.

Success came to me early in life. After graduation from college, in three years I was the president of the wholesale surgical supply company in Denver where I had started as a salesman. I was quickly offered opportunities in marketing management in Noreen, an international manufacturer and marketer of hair care products far beyond what my training was at that point. My subsequent work at Clairol in New York had resulted in several very successful international products, which made my reputation in marketing nationally. In my 30s I had reached the position of President of Clairol Europe and was President and CEO of all the Clairol European operations living in both France and then England. On returning to the States, I became Director and CEO of the Consumer Division in American Cyanamid, one of the country's largest industrial chemical companies, and ultimately reached the position of VP and Director of all marketing operations for Gillette in Boston reporting to the President, Vin Ziegler.

At this point, I had reached a level in the corporate world next to the president of a major international public company. And I was still in my early 40's. When Gillette wanted me to return to Europe to be President and CEO of their company in Italy, I had to make a decision that was very consequential.

Joanne and I decided that this was the wrong time for us to return to Europe for a second tour because our children would have had their studies disrupted again. We decided it was time for me to leave the corporate world behind and do what I had always wanted to do most of all, which was to run my own business and make all my own decisions. I left the big opportunities and vast power of the big corporation behind me with all of its promises of wealth and power for the future for the challenge of entrepreneurism and its rewards of independence. Independence and freedom to me is of the greatest importance, and I have enjoyed it all of my adult life, I am happy to say.

It was a tremendously important decision, one that I look back upon now and know that it was the right one for me. My ventures into my own businesses have been successful, but they did not deliver the riches for reasons, I think I know. Maybe I was not ruthless enough in some of my decisions. That's what Billy has frequently said. Most importantly, I spent much time adventuring with my darling wife as we traveled extensively throughout the Western world skiing, sailing, river running, backpacking, and hiking. Personal wealth was never a top priority in our lives though I always made enough to do anything we wanted and live as well as anyone could ever want to live. Life style, travel, and independence were more important than money to us both. We never considered wealth to be important in itself. I had always made my own way and only had to thank my parents for the positive can do philosophy and self-confidence they instilled in me and with Joanne's unwavering support that has so contributed to my wonderful life.

The most important factor of it all to me is that I spent over 40 years in my own business making all my own decisions and not having to answer to anyone while earning an excellent living. And I am still doing it. Being able to do what I want and go where and when I want was worth everything to me and to Joanne; in addition, I also enjoyed her devoted partnership and a loving marriage through it all. We did everything together which included not only raising a successful family but enjoying the many recreational activities that we shared and the several businesses we ran together. We were complete partners in everything that probably was the most important factor in my life.

Every young person really needs to know how to grow up being successful. Everyone wants to give advice, and a lot of it is not good. The best advice I had from my father on the subject was to be the best that you can be and be critical and questioning of all of the so-called "facts of life". Live up to your skills and training and define your objectives. Don't fear failure.

Probably, the most important element in achieving success is wanting to. I've known a lot of people who say they don't care. Maybe they really don't feel like working very diligently or studying something in achieving their level of skill. But for those who want success, they have to decide if they're willing to do what it takes. It can be very demanding. I can remember long days traveling when I missed my home and family but knew it had to be done.

Training is so important, whether it be communicating properly with the written word, or the spoken word or achieving athletic ability or skills in specialized areas like some of the professions, business, medicine, or law.

Training is important. I was fortunate to have had good training, both academically and with top corporations during my early years.

I feel, what is more important is recognizing that you have to find out what people are looking for. Most of us have needs, but we keep them primarily to ourselves. It takes a little investigation to find out what these needs are. You have to ask questions and be a good listener. Are you up to supplying the needs of others? I would like to ask you a question. Do you think you're up to really doing the job? I think you have to answer that positively with the word. Yes. Even if you're not sure, you still have to say yes. It's a matter of confidence in recognizing, if you're going to achieve what you set out to achieve.

I've been in the business of managing businesses most of my life. I have found that many others in the same organizations were unwilling to step forward and voice their opinions and are afraid to be wrong or take responsibility. Don't be afraid to be wrong. Don't be afraid to voice your opinion. I think that's one place where it starts. Having now expressed yourself to those in a position to make decisions affecting performance, you now have to deliver. That's when it becomes a little frightening. Can you deliver? Again, the answer should be yes.

It's a matter of confidence, remember, attacking any one job really is a function, when it comes to succeeding, of whether you have the time to take the necessary steps to get that job done. If someone says, can you fry an egg you say yes and you can do it in a matter of minutes or someone says, can you build a house. And you say yes, that could take months. It's the same with all activities, and all skills. We must first decide that you can do it and then be willing to spend the time to get it done.

Then there is the issue of personal comfort. Some people say that they don't like to travel. Others say they have to live in some special place and not just in any place. Some say they hate the crowds in big cities. Some say they would never consider working seven days a week. And on and on. However, if your personal comfort comes first, then achieving high goals will have to come second. What's the result? Maybe you have to reduce your goals in order to provide for your personal comfort. That's a decision we all must make and it is very consequential. We have to live with the consequences of our decisions and take responsibility.

It is easy to discard monetary rewards as a measure of success. But, it certainly is nice to be able to pay for the good things of life like nice houses, cars, education for your children, interesting travel, etc and that means having enough money. How do you get it? First, you have to train yourself so that you have the necessary skills to do what you plan to do. Then you have to devote the time to getting where you want to go using those skills to be productive and putting your personal comfort second.

If you waste your time idly in a bar, watching television, playing mindless games, or recreating, you're not being productive. And I might add another waste of time. If you spend your time in churches praying, you certainly are not productive. Church going is a monumental waste of time. So, quit envying other people's success. Quit wasting your time. Get properly trained. Maximize your time working on your objectives and find fun in your work. In order to achieve success, you must be productive. That takes training and skills and time and dedicated focus. It really is that simple.

Over the years I was often impressed with the difference of our two families, Joanne's and mine, when we first met. It seemed to me that her family was identical to mine. Both were headed by a strong, highly intelligent man, who was head of his own medical hospital and successfully practiced surgery. Both were prosperous. In the Jackson family there was a loving mother and a beautiful family of five children. They occupied a place in their community of respect and service. Indeed, it was the kind of family that was so much like mine that it was easy for me to find myself identifying with them completely. My dad and Dr Jackson even both drove similar Packard cars. Big ones, I might add.

As it turned out, I discovered how really different two families can be and still seem to be so similar. It starts with the father. He sets the stage, demands the performance, sets the goals, rewards the achievements, and establishes patterns of living. Then the mother, the home keeper, provides the nurture, the tender love the looking after the little details of the growing family that make her the caretaker extraordinaire.

In the Russell family, the father performed perfectly. In the Jackson family, the father did not. As a result, the Jackson family was, as I would describe it, dysfunctional. Tragically, two of their beautiful daughter's, Eleanor and Virginia both took their own lives, for reasons we can only speculate. Unhappiness, unloved, and insecurity that they felt certainly were important elements.

One daughter Marjorie, who was killed in a motor accident, was still a young girl. Pepper was a prep school headmaster, but he didn't like it and changed to a life of farming. Joanne fulfilled her role as my wife and partner in a most exemplary manner, doing everything the perfect wife, partner, and mother should do to raise a family and have a very happy married life.

Dr. Jackson did achieve great heights, in his profession. He was the president of the International College of surgeons, among many honors. In his travels abroad, in one case, he had a private audience with the Pope, even though he was an atheist. But when it came to giving his family the kind of love and support they hungered for that Dr. Russell was able to provide, he fell far behind.

Does fame, which Dr. Jackson had, make it more difficult to raise a family properly? It's a question I've often thought about. Even Joanne was puzzled by the difference, but appreciative to be a part of the Russell family.

Dr. Jackson was a classmate and friend of Frank Lloyd Wright. Wright built a house for the Jackson's at their large property named Skyview in Madison. It was a wonderful structure, which today is in a Wisconsin museum.

Skyview

Wright made several attempts at designing and commercializing residential properties, but they were never cost effective and though they were very beautiful they never became an important contribution of his. His main contributions were larger commercial buildings like the Johnson Wax Building in Racine, Wisconsin, the Imperial Hotel in Tokyo, and the Guggenheim Museum in New York. These spectacular structures contributed to his recognition as a genius and the most important of all American architects in history.

In those years the Bauhaus in Germany occupied worldwide importance with such contributors as Corbusier and Mies van der Rohe. The leading American would be Philip Johnson as a member of that school. But Wright felt it was cold and impersonal and led to "window box buildings" with no style or character throughout the major cities of the world. Wright called his style organic and probably one of the most famous buildings to illustrate this would be one he built for Philadelphia department store owner, Edgar Kaufman named Falling Waters. This lavish residence will surely go down in history as one of the most significant architectural examples of Wright's residential work. I met Kaufman, incidentally, at the Aspen Design Institute of which we were members. We (Harry Baum and I) were there on a design conference and also a meeting with Bert Klass of Stamford Research Institute. Bert was running a series of motivational research projects for Noreen to learn more about women's attitudes on cosmetics in general and hair color in specifics.

One visit, that Joanne and I made to Madison; we were invited to join her mother, Laura on a visit to Taliesin, Wright's home in Spring Green, Wisconsin, and had lunch with Frank and Olgovana, his third wife. At the time I was very much interested in architecture, and I asked Mr. Wright about his tenure in Japan where he built the Imperial Hotel. It always seemed to me that his style of architecture had a certain Oriental influence to it. I asked him if in fact he didn't feel he was influenced in his architectural styling by his experience in Japan. In his usual modest manner, he replied, "Mr. Russell I influenced the Japanese."

Dr. Jackson knew Frank Lloyd Wright well not only from their mutual university experience but also Jackson was Wright's doctor. Joanne's sister, Virginia, had also taken part in the Fellowship program at Taliesin East where she actually lived for about a year

It was a real thrill to see Taliesin with a personal tour by Wright, himself. Taliesin means Shinning Brow of the Hill as the impressive building was built on the side of a hill rather than at the top which Wright felt was the correct way to use the landscape in the most effective manner. It certainly was a wonderful house in every way and Wright and Olgovana were wonderful charming hosts.

Though we often visited Madison after Joanne and I were married, we never stayed too long as the house was not warm compared to our family's house in Worcester. By "warm", I mean there was little of the kind of love there was always present in our house. The Jackson's were fine people in every way but they were not easy to know.

One of my most important philosophical interests during my life has been religion. I am constantly amazed that such large numbers of people, well over the majority of citizens, continue to believe in these religious myths created by man. It is obvious and well proven in my opinion that prayer has absolutely no effectiveness, and that there is no God or hereafter. Numerous double blind experiments have been conducted on the efficacy of prayer. Here is a typical report on one of them.

Southern Medical Journal. 81(7):826-829, July 1988.
BYRD, RANDOLPH C. MD

Abstract:

"The therapeutic effects of intercessory prayer (IP) to the
Judeo-Christian God, one of the oldest forms of therapy,
has had little attention in the medical literature. To evaluate
the effects of IP in a coronary care unit (CCU) population,
a prospective randomized double-blind protocol was
followed. Over ten months, 393 patients admitted to the
CCU were randomized, after signing informed consent, to an
intercessory prayer group (192 patients) or to a control group
(201 patients). While hospitalized, the first group received
IP by participating Christians praying outside the hospital;
the control group did not. At entry, chi-square and stepwise
logistic analysis revealed no statistical difference between the
groups."

There have been other similar studies done all with the same results.

In simpler terms, prayer has no effect on the outcome of anything. It is
simply talking to yourself. If that helps you, so be it.

It is interesting that half the tested group had knowledge of the test
prayers and half did not yet the group that had knowledge of the prayers
being said for them had a poorer recovery experience.

All of this seems so clear to me after having thought about it a good
deal and read much on the subject. Joanne joined me completely on this
subject. I also believe that the idea of religion has not served mankind
well. It provides people a false security, which can never be realized.
It takes away man's drive to solve his own problems and relegates the
development of solutions to a fictitious God. Thus followers lose control
and abdicate responsibility for their actions. The religions were created
and maintained by the rabbis, popes, priests, and pastors over the centuries
as a way to control the brain-washed and less educated masses and take
money from susceptible people who are afraid to die and are looking for

everlasting life, falsely promised to them by these self-appointed so-called religious leaders. These religious leaders continue to build ever larger cathedrals to impress their following masses with the foolish, fictional "glory of God". Fear is the father of religion.

Most of the wars of history, as well as the current wars in which we are involved are religious wars. Religion is a divisive element in our lives, which has always created most of the misery in the world and steals from man his self-determination so essential for the good life.

Today we are involved in war in Afghanistan and Pakistan. These two countries are considered to be the most dangerous in the world today as they have stockpiles of atomic weapons and religious fanatics who could gain control of these lethal weapons with world destructive potential.

Here is purely a religious war, threatening the world and oppressing people everywhere with their radical and idiotic religious mythical beliefs.

Religious wars have dominated civilization from the earliest times, and created misery, seemingly without end. When will all civilized people realize that the whole idea of religion is without any basis in fact? And only serves the priests, rabbis, and pastors who wish to control the ignorant masses. Not a single so-called miracle has ever been proven nor will one ever be. There is just no such thing as a miracle that solves problems, there is only training, hard work, and tenacity that solves problems. Oh yes, and the belief that the problem can be solved.

In June 2008, the Pew Forum on Religion and Public Life published a controversial survey in which 70 percent of Americans said that they believed religions other than theirs could lead to eternal life. This threw evangelicals into a tizzy. After all, the Bible makes it clear that heaven is a velvet-roped V.I.P. area reserved for Christians. Jesus said so: "I am the way, the truth and the life: no man cometh unto the Father, but by me." The evangelicals believe theirs is the only way. There are no second opinions in their philosophy. It is all so divisive.

It is this kind of divisiveness that has created so much misery and war in history. One terrible modern day example of how religion mis-guides the innocent is the development of the modern-day so-called People's Temple cult, headed by the monomaniacal Jim Jones that resulted in the murder-suicide of 918 innocent followers in Jonestown, Guyana in 1978. There are countless other examples of religion mis-leading its innocent followers. The world has a long history of being victimized by these cults. Of course, Christianity started as just another cult of the countless cults that have come and gone throughout the many millennia of man's existence. Christianity will fade eventually, as have all the other cults.

It is revealing that the highly religious Muslim and Hindu countries are those with the most poverty and misery down through the centuries. They also have a long history of excessive violence which continues to this day as well as the unacceptable oppression of women.

A serious objective of religion is their opposition to population control which if it is allowed to continue, will result in the extinction of the human race.

I think the following quote from Einstein effectively sums for me what one of the world's greatest minds felt about the subject:

This is a quote from Albert Einstein, in his book, The World as I See It.

> "I cannot conceive of a God who rewards and punishes his creatures, or has a will of the type of which we are conscious in ourselves. An individual who should survive his physical death is also beyond my comprehension, nor do I wish it otherwise; such notions are for the fears of absurd egoism of feeble souls. Enough for me the mystery of the eternity of life, and the inkling of the marvelous structure of reality, together with a single hearted endeavor to comprehend a portion, be it ever so tiny, of the reason that manifests itself in nature."

I would like to add that God is said to be all powerful and all merciful. If so, how could he permit the suffering of His multitudinous peoples down through history? Why would He not answer the prayer of the amputee praying for the return of his lost leg? No, it is simply not logical that there is a God.

The answer, of course, is education to bring the facts of science to the peoples of this world, which will eventually show them the preposterous falsity of religion and allow them to lead their lives unhampered by the handicapping burden and totally unnecessary and wasted costs of religion which so limits mankind's development and intellectually enslaves him.

The education of the public must of necessity be a slow process. Most religious believers depend upon their religion almost as sustenance. To take it away without a meaningful replacement could cause serious sociological upheaval. A new intellectual independence must be instilled in those who now need religion for their very lives to exist. This can only be done through education starting with the youngest children. Secular education can replace religion if only given a chance and the time.

I would like to see a course at least in all state universities which is entitled, "Atheism in a Modern World." There are certainly courses in universities today in the philosophy department that discusses basic atheism. But we must go further to establish it more firmly. That will be a monumental social battle.

President Obama gave a speech at Notre Dame University, a Catholic institution, at graduation ceremonies for the class of 2009. There were a large number of protesters, which had to be restrained. They were demonstrating against the fact that the president was pro-choice, believing that a woman should be able to choose abortion. Catholicism opposes abortion. They insisted that Obama should not be permitted a public platform in light of his philosophy.

It is interesting to note that neither one of the students, nor one of the faculty members of the University took part in the demonstration. The group, including at least one priest, were obviously extremists and radical and demonstrated the oppressive tendency of some Catholics to impose their philosophy on others.

One of the professors at the University was quoted as having said that a university is a place of learning, where opposing thoughts should be examined in the light of science. It is refreshing to find a Catholic university supporting this open and reasonable philosophy.

For many years, public education was only provided in the first eight grades. Then a high school education finally was offered free to everyone. I think the next step is for a secular college education to be offered free to all. This would give to the great poor masses an opportunity to really be exposed to science in a secular atmosphere. I believe it would revolutionize our society. Today the relatively privileged go to college, now it would be open to all the masses. With free college, no one would have an excuse to remain ignorant.

Naturally, this secular advanced education will be fought at every turning by religious leaders who will recognize it as a threat to their control over the masses. It will not be easy but the continual emergence of new science that answers the unknown questions of the universe will continue to bring the light of understanding to the uninformed masses.

I have always believed in science. If an idea cannot pass scientific scrutiny and the scientific method, than there must be something wrong with it. We also must keep an open mind and be prepared to accept new ideas in order to move ahead to a better world.

Paradigm shifts tend to be most dramatic in sciences that appear to be stable and mature, as in physics at the end of the 19th century. At that time, physics seemed to be a discipline filling in the last few details of a largely worked-out system. In 1900, Lord Kelvin famously stated, "There is nothing new to be discovered in physics now. All that remains is more and more precise measurement." Five years later, Albert Einstein published his paper on special relativity, which challenged the very simple set of rules laid down by Newtonian mechanics, which had been used to describe force and motion for over two hundred years. In this case, the new paradigm reduces the old to a special case in the sense that Newtonian mechanics is still a good model for approximation for speeds that are slow compared to the speed of light. Einstein's revelations have changed the world.

To allow oneself to follow the dictates of the mythology of the dark ages is the formula for disaster.

My feelings about religion are well known but I continue to be subjected to religious pressure wherever I go. Recently granddaughter, Lauren graduated from Yale in what was the most impressive ceremony. I have never liked in the past to be involved in ceremonial affairs but this one got me to recognize their value.

There was one thing, however, that disturbed me. At times during the ceremony I felt I was in church. Numerous prayers were said and the entire audience was invited, ne forced, to participate in this nonsense.

I believe that a university should be involved in science not myth except perhaps in their divinity school but certainly not at a secular commencement. To force prayers, which science shows do not work and have no effect on anything, on an secular audience is simply not acceptable. It is also against US law for all public institutions.

At least 15% of the audience do not believe in God and certainly not in prayer but the religious establishment keeps pressuring all of us to follow their dark ages myths.

I know that Yale was founded as a religious school as is the case with many universities, but I must admit that I was happy to have graduated from a state university where I do not remember any prayers ever being said as it is against the law and rightly so.

Now, well into my 80s, though I still manage a business in the travel industry, my main effort is to develop my writing career. I am finding it very difficult, but at the same time challenging. I may never get published, but I do not think I should make that my main objective which should be to produce works, of which I can be proud. This is my first book. I hope the family enjoys finding out about our history and philosophies and benefits from it. My continuing challenge is to watch my health through careful diet and exercise so I may continue to live the good life that I have been privileged to enjoy for all of my life.

I find myself frequently thinking about my current relationship with our three children. They're growing up years could not have been more perfect. I have always felt that Joanne and I provided an excellent home and the right atmosphere for the children's development. We lived abroad in France and England and have traveled extensively all together throughout Europe. And we did give them a lot of love.

The children have always supported the idea of being raised in a wonderful loving home and I have never for a moment felt that Joanne and I ever did anything but provide the best home we could.

I have the perfect relationship with Lori but Billy and Torrey are different. Torrey often is difficult to talk to because of his extensive criticism of me in my interest in religion and especially Islam and its negative effects on a civilized society. I do not know why he has taken this position. He seems to have no interest in what I am doing. That is too bad, but I am not going to change what I am doing because of his lack of intellectual curiosity.

I have recently written several letters to both Lori and Frank, which refer to this problem. I have reprinted some of these letters below:

Date: 6/24/09

> Dear Lori:
>
> I have thought of almost nothing else since hearing your comment that is if Billy does not contribute to my book that I should write his history anyway, telling the total truth.
>
> When I said what I did on that open telephone line, I think I made a mistake. I should not have said what I did. I have apologized to Billy by telephone and by mail for what I said.
>
> For a father to say such a thing about a son is certainly terrible even though true. For me to write about it in my book for the world to read compounds a felony. I don't think I should do it. I do not think the lives of my readers will be enhanced

by hearing that kind of information about a member of our family.

That does not mean that my book will not tell the truth. It simply means that I will leave out some elements of our family history that I feel better forgiven and forgotten. That is an author's privilege. I know you do not agree, but I just do not see it any other way.

I feel similarly about Torrey. I will only print what Torrey brings up about himself and try not to editorialize.

The same with you. Mother and I did not approve of your leaving in that truck that sad day with John. We were wrong and you were right. You saw in him, what we did not. He is obviously an unusual person, and I have respect for him. Also your lifestyle suits you though, it may not suit me. But that makes no difference. You're having a great life, and you've been very successful in your chosen route in life. I want to write about that and tell as much of your story as you think is important.

I just returned home from the club, where I had a wonderful lunch and chanced to meet my old friend, Wally Lauder's daughter, Joanie. She looks wonderful and sends her love to all the family. As I believe, you know, she and her husband, Doug Paul, own the Griswold Inn. She's a lovely gal and looks so much like her mother, Verna, that it is haunting.

Incidentally, my intent with my second book (which I have started), is to use my first book as a rough scenario but changing all the names. That's what I'm thinking at least as of the moment.

July 27, 2012

Dear Frank:

Your wish to have Mark stay here for a few days is fine as I would like to help him if I can. I think he needs help. Why would he not want to go home? Has he been expelled? We are all different, as you say, and you and I differ on how to raise children. You are more permissive in setting standards.

I mentioned to you that there was no educational second option in our family. Everyone graduated from college, and that was that. They all did. Lori and Billy had no problem with this. Torrey was thrown out of just about every school he attended. He was a tremendous challenge for us to get him educated but he finally made it successfully and even with a Masters degree.

Weight control was important in our family. We had rules about over-eating. Only Torrey was not able to control his eating habits and has been obese and non athletic most of his life unlike the other two children who always have been excellent athletes and trim.

Then there were certain standards in our house about language and dress. Vulgarity, bad grammar, and slang were not permitted and sloppy dress and long hair were also not permitted. Again, Lori and Billy had no problems with this standard. Torrey had a tremendous problem with it. I remember one time Torrey came home from college with long hair. He was not permitted to sit at the dinner table until he had it cut to an acceptable length.

Drugs were not acceptable in our house. No problem for Lori and Billy. Torrey used drugs.

All three children, worked for Peter Storm after college. Guess who I came close to firing many times? Yet he was a very good and productive salesman.

Torrey has had an early disastrous business career. He has had so many jobs that I have lost count. This has not been the case with Lori and Billy. Though Torrey is smart, reliable, and hard working, his entrepreneurial computer software business, he tells me, is about to turn around, happily.

I tell you all this because I want to reaffirm that there were rules in our house and that continues to this day. If my children are not willing to comply with my standards, I would rather have them live elsewhere.

Now back to Mark. He is very sweet, and I would like to help him but his appearance is not acceptable. I certainly would not take him anywhere like the club for lunch where I eat frequently. I just do not associate with people who look like that. I hesitate to set a sartorial or personal grooming standard for him, but I find myself on the horn of a dilemma. Your wise counsel is invited.

July 27, 2012

Dear Frank:

The recent recurring problems with Torrey have me philosophizing.

I lead about the most perfect interesting and secure life in the most perfect place that anyone my age could desire with my delightful yacht club for yachting and meals. My little tour business provides me with a profitable commercial interest that requires just enough of my time, is fun, and offers me first class travel abroad whenever I feel like going. Then I have my daily exercise, writing, my boat and my piano to take up a little time. Most of my time, however, is devoted to researching and writing.

When I started this program, I wasn't sure of my direction. But as I get into it and begin to see where I am going, my direction begins to take shape. My first book is clear. It's about the family. The second book, well I've been equivocating a lot on that subject, but I finally have firmed up my thinking. My second book is going to be aimed at revealing Islam for what it is, an evil to mankind.

You may ask why that for a subject?

I believe that religion is so divisive in the world that those of us who do not need it should speak up about the problems it creates. One religious group hates another religious group, and that's been going on since the beginning of religion. It has created most of the wars in history. Our current costly war is a religious war where we were attacked first because of our secular philosophy.

The second problem is that religious groups believe that they know what's right for mankind because God told them what is right. "He "led them in the path of righteousness." So, they impose on mankind such idiocy as opposition to stem cell research, abortion, population control, and many other important initiatives that are designed as advances for civilization.

These are just a few of the reasons why more voices are needed to point out the problems of religion. And that's what I'm ready to do at least for the near future. Not only is it important to do, but it gives me an opportunity to do something for mankind that's needed.

I live alone. It has not been easy to learn how to do that after 54 years of successfully living with another person. But I have learned.

Living alone has its benefits and its negatives. The benefit is you don't have to compromise any of your positions or activities to suit your partner. The negative is you don't have anyone to talk to. It is lonely.

That's why I call you and the rest of the family frequently. It's a shame now that my two boys have a problem with that. One will not talk to me; the other finds it difficult to talk to me on a vast number of subjects. You know the reasons very well. Maybe I earned that, I don't know. Whether I'll ever be able to solve that or not is questionable. I'll keep trying, but meanwhile I'm mature enough to know that my life is satisfying and goes on, productively, as it is. And we do have to learn to live happily in our world as it is when we recognize that we are unable to change it.

Just thought you'd like to know.

Whenever I mention the word, "religion" Torrey dissolves into paroxysms of abuse. It has occurred to me that Torrey really only wants to talk about his subject. He does not want to talk about my subject. He frequently says of me that I "hate religion and hate religious people." Of course I do not. I only love freedom and science. I love a world free of divisiveness. Another love is a world that allows science to operate without religious restriction. I try to get that simple idea across to Torrey but he is not interested.

What will happen? Well first, I have recently suffered a couple of bad falls breaking an arm, a leg, and my back and have suffered serious gastro-intestinal maladies, which hospitalized me recently for several weeks and made me a virtual cripple though, I hope, temporarily. I am recovering though I am discouraged about my physical incapacity even though I exercise daily first with a daily swimming program and now on my treadmill and indoor gym, and walking and now riding my bike, have joined a health club and have a positive mental attitude. I am making progress but doubt if I will ever return to my physical ability of only a few years ago.

I am not able to run Mountain Tours the way it should be run but I keep doing it because it is fun and provides me a small income and first class travel internationally as I wish. However, my interest in travel has largely diminished as I love Essex and what I am doing and I have been to just about every place I have ever wanted to go.

My very good and dear friend, Jane Acheson, recently called me from Florida where she is living permanently now, and invited me to join her on a safari to Africa, and then on another trip, a cruise around the Mediterranean. It is nice to be invited, but really, I have no interest as I am quite happy here in Essex leading my quiet cerebral life though I must admit, I do love Jane. I doubt if it will go beyond that, especially as I want to live in Essex, not Florida.

My life was so perfect with Joanne that I have never had to think very much about alternatives to living after her death. But I have thought a lot about Jane Acheson recently.

She and I have little in common except we both dance and party well together and enjoy each other's company. Otherwise, we disagree on just about anything philosophical. We've long since passed by the activities like skiing, sailing, and hiking, all of which she does not like. But it's not really important, as I don't do those things really anymore. She is a golfer, and I don't like that. And of course she lives in Florida, which I dislike. So there is no future. The gap is too wide. I must live with that as I am prepared to do.

I must say all that does not make me happy. But I have to be realistic. So I continue to live alone and stay where I am in Essex which I love even though she has often invited me down to Florida which I do not love. I do not see this ever changing.

Frank called me recently telling me that a friend of his knew about my business and was interested in buying it if I would consider selling. My initial reaction was positive, and after chatting with the prospective buyer, I started to put together some financial data for future discussion. As I worked on this data, I became very depressed, realizing that I was working on a plan to sell my baby.

If I sold the business and got nominally what it is worth, I would be able to put about $150,000 in the bank which is what I feel the business currently is worth. What would I do with it? I really don't know. My lifestyle couldn't be better, and without my business, I would simply not be as happy as I am. I don't need the money. So I came to the conclusion that I must not sell this business and communicated that to the buyer. I immediately felt a great sense of relief and joy, and I'm now able to go on doing what I like to do.

The current economy does not help but I am optimistic that things will improve, I feel, under the Democrats as our new president Obama gets going. Fortunately, I have arranged my assets so I have enough income to live comfortable with no threats of change. I must admit, I feel satisfied with my life.

Is there any hope for the satisfied man? To para-phrase an inscribed motto over the Denver Post Office main entry written by Fred Bonfis, founder of the Denver Post and later memorialized in the book Stampede to Timberline.

As I got deeper into the subject of the history of the Russell family and did more research, I learned a good deal about how many of us think about our forebears. It is sometimes comforting to some to think back in the past and find something special. Was there royalty or great wealth or wonderful contributions to society in literature, science, art, politics, but mostly, I think it's delusional. But we do like to know where we came from. Therefore, I started this book about our family. It has been interesting researching and writing it.

Of course, I am only going back to 1880, which was the year in which my father was born. So I haven't begun to search out all the relatives that came before, except in a much generalized way. I did discover that the Russell's have basically been professionals, gentry, doctors, scientists, or lawyers, and business people. Mostly they have been entrepreneurial and of an independent spirit. Oh yes, one of Joanne's uncles, Reggie, a doctor in the Jackson Clinic, was the son of a very wealthy woman, who married Dr Reginald Jackson and inherited quite a large estate from her family who earned it in the meatpacking industry. She was from the Armour family from Milwaukee. Their fortune and extensive lake-front property including Picnic Point, upon their deaths, was left to the University of Wisconsin. Aside from that, I found no wealth in the family that really has to be classified as economically middle-class, though able to get educated, provide well for their families, make a societal contribution and live the good life.

Research revealed the following about Joanne's grandfather, Dr James Jackson. He was father to Dr Arnold S. Jackson, Joanne's father.

Jackson, James Albert 1840-1921

Definition: physician, b. Wolverhampton, England. He moved with his family to the U.S. and to Wisconsin in 1853, settling in Madison. In 1858 he entered the Univ. of Wisconsin, but his training was interrupted by the Civil War, in which he served as hospital steward in the 8th Wisconsin Volunteer Infantry (1861-1864). Following the war, he entered Bellevue Hospital Medical College in New York City, graduated in 1866, and practiced medicine in Stoughton and De Pere before beginning his career in Madison. He was active in promoting medical societies in the state, was a founder of the Dane County Medical Society, and belonged to numerous professional organizations. He was best known as the founder of the Jackson Medical Clinic in Madison, which he organized with his sons in 1919. His son, Arnold S. Jackson, born in De

Pere, was also a prominent Madison physician. He attended the Univ. of Wisconsin, and graduated from the College of Physicians and Surgeons, Columbia Univ. (M.D., 1899). He was house surgeon at the Presbyterian Hospital in New York City (1900-1902), and in 1902 returned to Wisconsin to practice with his father. He was surgical preceptor for the Univ. of Wisconsin (1914-1924), and clinical professor of surgery at the university medical school (1924-1933). He also served as president of the State Medical Society (1933), and of the Western Surgical Association (1935). F. L. Holmes, et al., eds., Wis. (5 vols. Chicago, 1946); A. F. and B. Jackson, 300 Years American

(Madison, 1951); Who's Who in Amer., 20 (1938); Madison Democrat, Feb. 12, 1921; Madison Wis. State Journal, Sept. 8, 1939.

In another Internet search, I found the following on my former brother-in law, Henry Puharich. He was married to Joanne's sister, Virginia, until her death in 1975. He and Virginia often visited us when we lived in Worcester. They lived in Boothbay, Maine at the time where we visited them. Hank was founder and head of a research organization known as the Roundtable Foundation doing research in Extra Sensory Perception.

Hank and Virginia had three children Lani, Illyria, and Ditza.

The internet reveals the following about Henry K Puharich

Born   February 19, 1918 Chicago, Illinois

Died   January 3, 1995 Dobson, North Carolina

Residence   R. J. Reynolds Family Estate

Occupation   Inventor, Scientist, Physician

Andrija Puharich, MD, also known as Henry K. Puharich, (February 19, 1918—January 3, 1995), was a medical and parapsychological researcher, medical inventor and author, who is perhaps best known as the person who brought Uri Geller and Peter Hurkos to the United States for scientific investigation.

Bibliography

In 1947, Puharich graduated from the Northwestern University School of Medicine. His residency was completed at Permanente Hospital in California, where he specialized in Internal Medicine.

Of the many books Puharich wrote, he also wrote a supportive biography, Uri Geller. Before that he investigated favorably the Brazilian psychic surgeon José Arigó. He met the Dutch psychic Peter Hurkos and brought him to the United States to participate in scientific experiments in parapsychology. He encouraged a rational assessment of people said to exhibit paranormal faculties and applied scientific methods to investigations of what were their startling and often unpredictable and elusive skills or abilities.

Two of the most famous of Puharich's over 50 patents were devices that assist hearing—the "Means For Aiding Hearing" U.S. Patent 2,995,633 and "Method And Apparatus For Improving Neural Performance In Human Subjects By Electrotherapy" U.S. Patent 3,563,246 ". He was also granted a U.S. Patent 4,394,230 in 1983 for a "Method and Apparatus for Splitting Water Molecules." His research included studying the influence of extremely low frequency ELF electromagnetic wave emissions on the mind, and he invented several devices allegedly blocking or converting ELF waves to prevent harm.

Actually, in my experience, great wealth can be quite a burden. It sometimes leaves progeny insecure with the idea that they could never do as well as their parents. It also is a burden because we all feel that we owe something to society and the wealthy among us certainly owe the most. The obligations mount, as do the insecurities. Also, making it on our own is very satisfying. Starting out with wealth makes that almost impossible.

Then there is talent. Some are outstanding in their careers like Joanne's father, Arnold Jackson, who was an internationally recognized surgeon, who brought to his field several unique medical operative procedures. He was President of the International College of Physicians and Surgeons. However, in general, I was not able to find anyone in the family that could be considered exceptionally talented especially when one compares the contributions of some members of society.

I don't believe anyone in the Russell family has been involved in politics. One of Frank's children is married to the mayor of a southern city. Maybe that's an area that someday will open up to some of our children. Maybe Lauren, though now I have learned that she has accepted a position as an executive assistant to the president of an important firm in Oregon, Nike.

As I look back on my life, I have achieved everything I set out to attain. Maybe I set my sights too low. But I am not finished yet.

First, I was fortunate to have met at 18 and married at 21 the most wonderful wife for me that I could imagine. Joanne and I shared the perfect life of adventure and enjoyed a sincere mutual love for over 54 years until her death from pancreatic cancer at age 75 on April 14, 2001.

Second, Joanne and I raised 3 healthy successful children each of whom gained excellent educations and have created their worthwhile places in their communities, each conducting their own entrepreneurial businesses.

Third, I gained an excellent training in business as a senior corporate executive in several major international corporations with key responsibilities managing interesting and challenging businesses in both the USA and Europe for the first 20 years out of college.

Fourth, I have lived and worked in France and England as CEO of an American Public Company and have traveled extensively throughout the western world and in Japan.

Fifth, I have created and managed my own successful entrepreneurial activities, which have allowed me for 40 years to make my own decisions and run my own life without financial dependence on anyone else. My businesses that I have started and owned have included the Russell Agency, a Manufacturer's Representative Agency, Peter Storm, an international manufacturer and distributor of sportswear, Russell Yacht Charters, an international yacht charter agency, RAM Knitting, a manufacturer of knitwear, and Bill Russell's Mountain Tours, an International Tour Company which I continue to operate profitably, and currently I am trying to develop a new career as a writer.

I continue to enjoy good health for my age and live an interesting and comfortable life in the perfect antique village of Essex in a lovely antique character house built in 1830 and within walking distance of all town services and my yacht club. I am able to enjoy the beautiful Connecticut River in my boat.

I used to enjoy excellent canoeing, biking, and sailing on the beautiful Connecticut River in the 18-foot keel sloops maintained by the Essex Yacht Club, of which I am a long-time member, and can travel internationally first class at no cost as I wish. There is great deep woods hiking nearby and canoeing on the river in summer and excellent cross-country skiing in winter minutes from my home. My age has stopped all of this.

I am financially independent with a good income, have no debt, and enjoy the love and support of my family and friends.

I am working on my new career of creative writing and hope to publish my books in the future.

Is there anything better?

CHAPTER 35

An Inspiration

I t is New Year's Eve, 2008-9, and I just listened to various political speeches in the past presidential campaign we have just completed. Speeches were made by McCain and Obama both before the election, and following it. They made me very proud and inspired to be an American.

Certainly the most important event in my lifetime is the rise of the black race from total poverty and ignorance to positions of great leadership in our country. Our electorate has wisely chosen a black man to lead us and it made a statement that the world will not ignore. And that is that America is a true land of opportunity for people of all colors and all creeds without petty divisiveness and we want to bring this philosophy to all the peoples of the world that the American people value the black race.

It is an inspiration to me to see what is happening and I look forward to the coming years with great optimism that many of the problems that we face internationally will be alleviated by what we have represented as a true egalitarian philosophy towards all peoples of the world. They cry out for this and hunger for it, and we now are in a position to give it to them.

I've never had the privilege of knowing, a black person intimately. That is perhaps a shortcoming of my environment. My father always spoke of the equality of all men, and we believed him, and now to see it come to fruition is a true inspiration.

I also listened to the speeches made by the two candidates that both were well-qualified and particularly McCain on losing was truly magnanimous in his support of Obama. He is certainly a fine man though he did not offer what the people wanted and thus was not elected. He also chose the wrong running mate who was not qualified to run. That was bad judgment.

The major philosophers of our nation have always supported the equality of all mankind, and now to see it finally coming to fruition is truly inspiring to me. It foretells an era of great philosophical growth for mankind with the kind of leadership that our country is able to provide. President Obama has accepted a tremendous responsibility. I feel he is up to it and hope to be able to support him where I am able and certainly ask all citizens to do so as well.

Pres. Obama and wife, Michelle on a recent trip to Europe were a sensation. He is a natural leader. For the world to witness that the most powerful man in the world is black is going to mean a great deal to the millions of formerly oppressed people, who were looked upon in a demeaning manner simply because they were black.

Michelle, the first lady, too made a tremendous contribution in a speech she made to a group of inner-city school children. She explained to them that she came from humble circumstances from the ghetto of Chicago. The only reason she was able to emerge was through her ability to obtain a good education, which she did on her own with no help from anyone except her own energy and desire to be someone. She told the children that they also could be whatever they wanted to be. What an important message? Could any message to black children be more important?

CHAPTER 36

Ethics

We often hear ethics spoken of in a casual manner, and, perhaps, too many fail to realize its importance in a civilized society. Especially in business, ethics is fundamental. Business is by definition, organized to make a profit. Newspapers and television stations for example, frequently promote ideas that are questionable from an ethical point of view. These companies can only survive if they increase their circulation. The newspapers have to get read by more and more people. How to do this?

If I were to run down the street yelling love, love, love, no one would listen. Or if they did, they may want to commit me to an institution. If I were to run down the same street yelling murder, murder, murder. I would immediately get a lot of attention, and everybody would want to ask me questions and become involved.

That's the simple reason why newspapers have to print so much of what is ugly in life. Human beings seem to like to read about the ugliness of life. But ethics tells us, among other things, that profit only is not the most important motivation. Deciding on what is ethical, is one of management's most demanding jobs.

I was in the business that tried to convince women to use hair dye; we called it haircolor, and among other things bleach their hair. In my family that was anathema. Certainly Joanne never used products of this kind, nor did our mothers and I was very happy about that. Her minimal use of cosmetics made her ever more appealing to me and her gray hair in her later years was simply beautiful.

On the other hand, there are a lot of companies like Clairol who produce these products. But they do employ large numbers of people who need the income. It's a careful balance, and one that demands our attention.

The Center for Ethics and Business is an organization to provide an environment for discussing issues related to the necessity, difficulty, costs and rewards of conducting business ethically. Recognizing the special challenges connected with discussing ethical issues in a diverse global economy, the Center encourages a secular and philosophical approach to these matters. The primary program is Business Ethics Fortnight, an annual multi-week event held in the spring. Its centerpiece is an intercollegiate student team presentation competition.

"Do unto others as you would have others do unto you." That's probably one of the starting points of good ethics. There are others in a civilized society. I do believe we are coming to the point where the world is appreciating this to a greater extent. It probably has taken the atomic bomb to get us to the point where world wars, may never again occur. Now, perhaps we can concentrate on getting the religions to develop a meaningful understanding of what is important in a civilized life.

CHAPTER 37

Prayer in Schools

In an earlier reference in this book, I mentioned how I felt that prayer should never be allowed in any school, especially a public school. It is now against the law. We cannot allow religion to be supported in the schools. To permit prayer is confusing to young students, who are there to study science and not myths or superstitions.

Private institutions, of course, can do what they want. However, there is a fine line here. Unless you're speaking about a religious school, the balance of schools in our country are secular. Therefore it would seem out of place to allow prayer in any institution that professes a secular philosophy. Certainly no school receiving federal funding should be allowed to teach religion or permit prayer in school.

I recently had the privilege of attending my granddaughter, Lauren's, graduation at Yale University in New Haven. Following is an exchange of letters with the president of Yale, concerning prayer at the commencement exercises.

June 1, 2009

Richard Levin, President
Yale University
New Haven, Connecticut

Dear Dr Levin:

I had the great good fortune to attend my granddaughter's graduation last week from Yale.

The ceremonies were impressive, to say the least, with wonderful memories that graduates and family will carry with us for a lifetime.

I would like to make one comment, however, which will probably not be very popular. I am a Secular Humanist and therefore try to avoid all traditional religious ceremonies. I would think that an institution like Yale, with its emphasis on science, would not subject a secular audience to prayer and religious blessings.

Certainly, anyone can believe what they wish. But a science education has led me where I am philosophically, and I cannot deny it.

Maybe there is nothing that you or anyone can do about this, but I would hope eventually that science would prevail even at the great institution of Yale.

Thank you for your leadership.

Sincerely,
William F. Russell
President Levin replied:

June 18, 2009

Mr William F. Russell
3 Pratt Street
Essex, CT. 06426

Dear Mr. Russell:

Thank you for your letter of June 1, and for taking the time to write. I appreciate your comments about the religious elements of Yale's commencement and I am sorry that you are unhappy about their inclusion in the ceremony. Our commencement program reflects more than three centuries of tradition and history and includes a prayer, a blessing, and hymns, Some of which have been part of the ceremony since Yale's founding.

Congratulations on your granddaughter's graduation. You and your family must be very proud of her.

With best wishes,

Sincerely yours,
Richard C. Levin

June 21, 2009

Richard Levin, President
Yale University
105 Wall Street
New Haven, CT. 06520-8229

Dear President Levin:

Thank you for your letter of June 18.

Over the years I have been privileged to spend time frequently with my granddaughter and I can attest to the fact that she received an excellent university education at Yale and the family is very proud of her and that she graduated from Yale.

I would like to address the subject of tradition, if I may, as you relate that "prayers and blessings are a tradition at Yale commencement ceremonies" (paraphrased).

Tradition is important to all of us, of course. But we also know there are good traditions and bad traditions. Also, some traditions become outdated or irrelevant over time in the light of the revelations of new science. The subject recently has been addressed by many including Richard Dawkins, bestselling author and scientist,

I would like to suggest that Yale may wish to review the tradition of prayers and blessings at graduation ceremonies as they may no longer be acceptable to important numbers of your students and their parents in this modern world. This will only increase as the years pass.

Incidentally, I am a member of the Humanist Society of which there is a chapter at Yale. Had this society been in existence in the 18th century, it would probably have numbered our nation's founding fathers as supporters or members as they were all out spoken Deists who did not believe in prayer or its validity. One of the precepts of the Humanist Society is that prayer has no effect on anything nor does it have any value.

Sincerely,
William F. Russell

I did not receive further reply from Dr. Levin, nor do I expect one.

I did receive an abusive blast from son, Torrey, who said I was out of line to send such letters to the president of Yale that impinged on his and Lauren's reputation. On the contrary, it is my duty to send such letters where indicated. One of my objectives is to show the world the nonsense of prayer. You can talk to yourself if you want, but if you expect some higher power to make anything different or give you any advantage, you are wasting your breath.

Certainly we can all refer to many outdated traditions. There are also many traditions practiced today that should be outdated like the many forms of oppression of women in Muslim countries or the cutting off of hands of convicted thieves. Tradition, alone, is not a good enough reason to maintain prayer at Yale, or anywhere else. However, I am not going to further lecture Dr. Levin on the subject.

It does bring into focus the kinds of accepted ideas practiced throughout the world that should be examined critically, but are not. Many people know that prayer has no value. This has been supported by numerous research studies referred to earlier. But science alone will not answer this problem. Prayer is vitally needed by the majority of people to get through their day. If we take it away from them, we have to have something to replace it. The only answer to that is education, starting with the youngest members of society. The results will not be realized for generations.

CHAPTER 38

The Russell Children

Raising our family was one of the most rewarding experiences of my life. Two older boys and a younger daughter could not have been more perfect. We were a close family enjoying travel, and lots of adventure together around the world.

Lori especially was a gem to raise. She always did the right thing. She never seemed to have any problems. She always got top grades. Certainly, of the three children, she was easiest to raise.

By the time Lori was ready for college; she had already lived and gone to school in three different countries, the US, France, and England. She also had excellent grades in every school. So she could have gone anywhere and done anything. She did decide on Skidmore College in New York State and entered it as an art major. She described it as an upper-class girl's school of white Anglo-Saxon girls all of whom were born with a "silver spoon in their mouths". Lori said she didn't identify with those girls. As it turned out, her friends in college tended to be the "quota" black students from the ghetto brought in to balance the school's white members.

Lori was always an especially talented artist. We all thought that she would probably follow that career in life or maybe go into biological, anthropological, or ecological research. When she got into college she enrolled as an art major. But she felt that it was not significant enough for her and that it was really as she says, "self-indulgent" She really didn't see it as a valid statement for her life. Therefore, she changed her major to biology so she could better understand the world around her.

After two years at Skidmore, she transferred to the University of Michigan, where she felt she was in a much broader world of intellectual opportunity. It was at that time she changed her major to biology. Her most important focus was the world around her. She was always outside with her fingers in the mud, picking up insects looking at the birds, wondering what made the colors of the sky. She also learned to fly on her own and became a licensed pilot. She always exhibited great intellectual curiosity, independence, and individuality.

After college, Lori worked for Peter Storm, designing catalogs and artwork and helping in general to make this family company manufacturer of sports clothing well known in its field. However, she didn't like what she was doing. She was an outdoor girl spending all day in the studio designing ads and catalogs did not satisfy her as she wanted to be outdoors. Therefore, she decided to move to Colorado where she was born and where the skiing and all outdoor sports were so exceptional. Incidentally, she had become the best skier in the family by far.

During those years she ran the Grand Canyon four times, as well as other western rivers. Lori's life is really built around outdoor sports. Business, as an entrepreneur, though she is very good at it, is secondary.

Currently, with the bad economy, her construction business has ground to a halt so she is spending time helping her brother Torrey with telephone sales of his software computer products. She is also developing a successful gardening business and teaching at the local university. I am very proud of the way Lori has faced diversity and been able to move ahead successfully without complaining and make a fine living doing it her way.

Now Lori has returned to school to learn about solar heating. I am sure this will open up a new and exciting world for her and she will make a great success of this new and growing technology.

Bill was always easy to raise, and we had a lot of fun together with sailing, skiing, camping, and travel abroad. He received a good education with an undergraduate degree from the University of Wisconsin and a Masters from Columbia in finance, and after a couple of successful years working for Peter Storm as President went to work on Wall Street. He then started his own investment advisory company. He was divorced by Burgess after 24 years of marriage. He has re-married the lovely Janice. They live comfortably in Beaver Creek, Colorado where skiing is their first love. Bill and I frequently are involved in philosophical discussions on which, I admit, he outdoes me with his impressive depth of knowledge. He might be described as the closest to a philosopher and intellectual in the family. He has spent a lifetime trying to perfect "an invention" he calls, the flare craft, a boat that flies just above the surface of the water. He has invested large sums of time and money in this effort with minimal results at this writing. His dedication is commendable. Burgess meanwhile, continues to be one of my best friends.

Torrey, on the other hand, was difficult to raise. He managed to get expelled from several schools and has held many jobs. His early school work was not good but he did to get a master's degree from Babson Institute in Boston. I have learned not to raise any controversial or philosophical subjects with him to maintain an equitable relationship. He is married to wonderful, patient Barbara. They have one exceptional daughter, Lauren, who graduated from Yale and has done very well first in the public relations industry in Los Angeles and currently as an executive assistant to the president of a Nike division in Portland. She is currently working for Nike in Africa with under-privileged girls.

Torrey is currently involved in computer software sales, heading his own active company and was living in the Seattle area. He has recently moved to San Luis Obispo in California. He has developed exceptional software products and is a master of the computer. Unfortunately, Torrey has decided, at least for the time being, not to talk to me because I canceled the contract that was losing money for me drastically. I expect that, as in the past, he will eventually apologize for his emotional outburst.

In raising our children, Joanne and I had one unalterable point of view. That was, there was no other option but to obtain a college degree which

I happily was able to pay for on a current basis with ease. I mention this because the children of so many of my friends and family apparently did not have this rule which we felt was so important in the raising of our children.

CHAPTER 39

Why Can't We All Get Along?

We have often heard that question asked. There still does not seem to be a definitive answer. From the earliest development of life on earth, one species ate the other. We continue to see it today in the natural world in which such species as the brown and polar bears being able to mate but they fight and will eat each other at every opportunity.

When man first climbed out of the trees, territorial fighting was the norm. Over the millennia, humankind has continued their internecine battles. Throughout the middle Ages, city-states were in constant battle.

Why?

Much has been written on the subject. We do know that greed, hating others that look different, opposing different religious philosophies and many more provide reasons.

It is my belief that the single most influential reason is religion. It has caused most of the wars and much of the discontent in the world down through history.

The majority of the world seems to be unable to live without religion, however there may be more secularists than ever before in history. The rise in science in the last hundred years has been an important contributor to this phenomenon. Education, too, has contributed as well as improved communication. Today, 15% of our USA population admit to being atheists. It is much higher in Europe. I have heard as high as 80% in some Scandinavian countries.

The telephone and television were extremely helpful in starting this movement of communication throughout the world. Now computers and the Internet have delivered communication to the individual. It is difficult for despots and so-called religious leaders to hide the facts of life from the citizens when people can talk to free people elsewhere in the world.

More has been accomplished in the last hundred years through science than was in all the millennia previously, in the history of humankind. With the accelerated expansion of computer capability, we can only see an exponential growth in knowledge, as well as communication.

One scientist recently said, "There is no longer any science fiction." Today it seems anything is possible. Planetary travel lies before us. The secrets of creation of life and the universe may soon be revealed.

A New York Times editorial today states that a synthetic cell has been created. It's father is the computer. It brings us ever closer to creating life according to the article.

It is an exciting time to be alive.

CHAPTER 40

The Truth About Islam

by Bill Warner, Director,
Center for the Study of Political Islam

In an excellent essay, Bill Warner of ACT For America with disarming simplicity contends that Christian pastors must speak the truth about Islam, and that to date far too many of them are failing in this. Here is his paper:

> "We probably won't learn about the annihilation of Christianity in a church. You see, if you start with the facts of persecution, you might come to the point that you would ask the question: who is killing Christians? If the answer turns out to be Muslims, then a second question arises: Why do Muslims murder and persecute Christians? That answer can only be: Because Muslims follow the teachings of Islam.

Why are Christians in such denial about Islam? This is a critical question, since modern Western knowledge of Islam has a 14 century base of Christian scholarship. As the Church thought, so did the Western world. There are contributions from Jews, but, in the end, there is no real difference between the Islamic scholarship of Jews and the Christians, as they share the same limitations.

A LEGACY OF IGNORANCE

It started when Umar, the first Caliph, burst out of the Arabian Desert in the first universal jihad against a Christian Mediterranean civilization. When we read the earliest records, there is so much confusion about the conquerors that they called them Arabs, not Muslims. This began an intellectual construct to refer to Islam by the first invader's identity—the Turk, the Saracen, the Moor, the Arab—never, the Muslim.

It was five centuries after the first jihad passed before the Koran was translated into a Western language, Latin. Then it took another five centuries before there was another translation. Do you see a trend? The first translation of Mohammed's biography into English did not occur until the 17th century. The major Hadith author, Bukhari, is known in an English translation by a Muslim and that was done in the 20th century. This is a dreadful intellectual history. There were some good works in German, Italian and some other European languages, but the discussion about Islam took place mainly in academic realms.

The ignorance of Islam extends to the detailed history of the Islamic destruction of Christianity for 14 centuries.

This foundation of ignorance is what underlies the desert of Islamic studies at our universities. But, let's not only deal with the institutions of "higher" learning; they sold out to the Saudis in the sixties. Look at Christian schools' curriculum about Islam—think World Religions 101.

If the ministers of today were not taught about Islam and its history in college, where do they learn about it? Why would they know about it? Ignorance begets ignorance.

A LEGACY OF FEAR AND LOSS

But there is a far greater problem than intellectual ignorance. The real basis for Christian ignorance about the doctrine and history of Islam, is fear—primal fear, an in your DNA kind of fear.

Today, we cannot imagine the absolute massiveness of the Islamic jihad against the civilized world. The Middle East, Egypt, North Africa, Iraq, Syria, Lebanon, Spain, Persia (now Iran) all fell in about a century. Whole Christian regions that Christians would no longer recognize fell to Islam. And, not only were Christians annihilated, but Zoroastrians, Buddhists and Hindus all fell under the sword in the next century. When you think of Afghanistan, do you think of Buddhism?

The worst thing about this conquest was not the sword, but the doctrine of Islam, Sharia. The sword was the key to the top of government, and then came the Sharia. Sharia had a place for the Christian called the dhimmi. Dhimmis had no real civil rights, paid special taxes, and were semi-slaves, subject to the whims of Islam. Just like real slavery, there were bad times and better times, but in the end, Christianity, Buddhism and Hinduism vanished after a few centuries of being dhimmis.

Being a dhimmi was humiliating, impoverishing, degrading and eternal. This accounts for the law of Islamic saturation. When Islam can institute Sharia, the civilization will become completely Islamic. It is only a matter of time.

Lesson learned: Islam is the terminator of Christianity. After all this abuse, Christians have become the "abused wives of Islam". They will do anything not to upset the persecutor.

At this time the overwhelming majority of Christian leaders know nothing about the doctrine of Islam. They do not criticize Islam in public, not even in their own houses of worship. Not only are they unable to speak the truth about Islam, but, also they will not allow discussion about the topic. Ministers see that the history of 1400 years of being dhimmis, the annihilation of Christianity, and Islamic slavery is never mentioned, never talked about.

The only things that religious leaders will say about Islam is: "Same god, brothers in Abraham, Golden Age, tolerance, we have our sins—here, let us tell you, I know many nice Muslims, not all Muslims are . . . , those are extremists, you sound like a bigot . . ." My Muslim friends tell me wonderful things about Christians in the Koran and how they hate the murder of Christians. But, the Muslim friends never talk about how that Mohammed was friendly towards Christians, until he made them the jihad targets in his last year."

So what?

Only talking about the "good stuff" Islam and shutting our eyes to centuries of suffering caused by an Islamic doctrine of the Christian (and the Jew and the Hindu and the Buddhist and the atheist and the . . .) is not enough. We want to talk about annihilation. We want everybody to get a voice, including the victims. We must talk about the whole balance sheet. We have all heard about the assets, let's look at the debits.

DHIMMI LEADERSHIP

Why do religious leaders refuse to learn the doctrine and history of Islam? They are terrified of being called a bigot, an Islamophobe or intolerant. In business law, there is a concept of willful ignorance, and it can be a felony. Should we not hold our religious leaders to a higher standard than business leaders?

In the light of Islam, most of our leaders are ignorant, but the religious leaders (ministers, priests, rabbis and . . .) are the most disappointing. In their arrogant ignorance, religious leaders go to interfaith dialogs, and they insure that there is never a mention of persecution and dhimmitude. There is nothing negative that is brought up in front of the imam or Muslim Brotherhood representative. It is just all one big happy Abrahamic faith meeting. No Muslims are ever offended. No grievances are ever uttered. Meanwhile, overseas Christians (and Buddhists, Hindus and Jews) are persecuted and dying.

SOLUTIONS

Christians in the pews must wake up to the fact that tolerance is only half of a moral system. Tolerate what? Intolerance? Anything and everything? Tolerance and love that are only sentimental are immature. Christian leadership must include toughness and the heart of a warrior. And if the leaders will not lead, then those in the pews must.

What church gives three minutes each Sunday to recognize and pray for the murdered Christians? Find a way to make it happen.

What church brings in Christians from persecuted lands to speak to the church? Begin with Sunday school classes.

Is it not a fair demand for the pulpit to know the Islamic doctrine of the Christian and the Jew? Should a Christian leader not know both the Meccan and Medinan Koran? The Koran is about the same size as the New Testament. The Hadith and the Sira have been made readable. Go and read The Third Choice by Mark Durie, for the sake of humanity and the church. Form a study group. The foundations of Islam give anyone a basis in the doctrine of Islam as found in its texts.

Is it too much for Christian leadership to know the actual history of the destruction of Christianity in Turkey, Egypt, the Middle East, North Africa, and Eastern Europe? Look it up.

Should not a minister, at the very least, know the dictates of Sharia law in Christian-Muslim marriages? Google it.

These actions are doable and do not require heroic effort. Christians must plant small seeds in every church.

LAST REMARKS

Our universities, both secular and Christian, must teach the political doctrine and political history of Islam. Christian schools must teach the religious doctrine as well.

Some Christians may cry out that the main stream media is unfair to Christianity (and it is), but if Christians would strap on the armor of God, they will get more respect. Warriors are respected. Ignorance, pious platitudes and fear are not.

Oh, if you are a non-Christian, you get the same treatment with the same results. When it comes to Islam, there are Muslims and there are Kafirs. Don't think that Jews, humanists, atheists, pagans and all the rest will live in some new world where Christianity is annihilated and your special outlook on religion is going to be tolerated by the Sharia."

The above written by Bill Warner, Director, Center for the Study of Political Islam

Permalink   http://www.politicalislam.com/blog/saint-doonesbury/ copyright (c) CBSX, LLC, politicalislam.com

The big problem that is occurring wherever, Muslims achieve important pluralities in the populations is infiltration of their Islamic laws. Britain particularly, is undergoing a difficult time. The following article indicates the seriousness of this problem.

Inculcating British schoolchildren
by Soeren Kern, Senior Fellow for Transatlantic Relations.

In Cheshire, England two students at the Alsager High School were punished by their teacher for refusing to pray to Allah as part of their religious education class.

In Scotland, 30 non-Muslim children from the Parkview Primary School recently were required to visit the Bait ur Rehman Ahmadiyya mosque in the Yorkhill district of Glasgow (videos here and here). At the mosque, the children were instructed to recite the shahada, the Muslim declaration of faith.

British schools are increasingly dropping the Jewish Holocaust from history lessons to avoid offending Muslim pupils, according to a report entitled, Teaching Emotive and Controversial History, commissioned by the Department for Education and Skills.

British teachers are not permitted to discuss the medieval Crusades, in which Christians fought Muslim armies for control of Jerusalem: lessons often contradict what is taught in local mosques.

In West Yorkshire, the Park Road Junior Infant and Nursery School in Batley has banned stories featuring pigs, including "The Three Little Pigs," in case they offend Muslim children.

In Nottingham, the Greenwood Primary School cancelled a Christmas nativity play; it interfered with the Muslim festival of Eid al-Adha. In Scarborough, the Yorkshire Coast College removed the words Christmas and Easter from their calendar not to offend Muslims.

Schools across Britain are, in fact, increasingly banning pork from lunch menus to avoid offending Muslim students. Hundreds of schools have adopted a "no pork" policy, according to a recent report by the London-based *Daily Telegraph*.

The culinary restrictions join a long list of politically correct changes that gradually are bringing hundreds of British primary and secondary education into conformity with Islamic Sharia law.

CHAPTER 41

This I Believe

I believe in freedom and self-determination and that successful people must take full responsibility for their actions. Next I believe that science is a more relevant than religion ever could be.

Over the centuries, science and the church have seldom found unified opinions about the state of the world. Early scientists professing the world is not flat, and the sun did not rotate around the Earth were severely punished. The churches frequently opposed scientific revelation and most still do.

Today we have one of the most significant new developments in the history of medicine under the heading of Stem Cell Research which is actively opposed by many religions. This breakthrough in scientific knowledge could deliver potentially to mankind some of the greatest advances in the curing of debilitating diseases. Probably, it is not understood by many religious people. One does need a little background in biology to even discuss it.

Stem Cell research is said to be the most important scientific medical breakthrough in the history of medicine. It offers many opportunities to cure currently, so-called "incurable" diseases. The church is actively opposed to this vital research and is trying to get it outlawed. Just as the church in the 17th century placed Galileo under house arrest for the remainder of his life for supporting heliocentrism, the Copernican belief that the universe revolved around the sun.

Galileo's championing of Copernicanism was controversial within his lifetime, when a large majority of philosophers and astronomers still subscribed to the <u>geocentric</u> view that the Earth remains motionless at the centre of the universe. After 1610, when Galileo began supporting <u>heliocentrism</u> publicly, he met with bitter opposition from some philosophers and clerics, and two of the latter eventually denounced him to the <u>Roman Inquisition</u> early in 1615. Although he was cleared of any offence at that time, the <u>Catholic Church</u> nevertheless condemned heliocentrism as "false and contrary to Scripture" in February 1616, and Galileo was warned to abandon his support for it—which he promised to do. When he later defended his views in his most famous work, <u>*Dialogue Concerning the Two Chief World Systems*</u>, published in 1632, he was tried by the Inquisition, found "vehemently suspect of heresy," and forced to recant, and spent the rest of his life under house arrest which punishment was enforced by the Catholic Church.

The church has had a long history of negating science if it is not supported by Scripture. Can we permit the advancement of science to be blocked by these dark ages mythical philosophies? That Scripture in any way can foretell the future of what is right or wrong for the advancement of humanity is scientifically un-supportable? We must not allow these narrow parochial restrictions to be acceptable. Science must be encouraged to continue research to find answers to nature's questions which the church has never found.

"The only requirement for evil to triumph is for good people to do nothing." Edmund Burke

The millions of followers of Christianity, Jewdism, and Islam revere their "holy" books said to be direct messages from their gods. Though these religions profess to be peace loving, a close examination of both the Bible and the Koran reveal just the opposite as well as a total disregard for the civilized treatment of their fellow man.

It is highly questionable, in my opinion, that religion improves life here on earth. In fact, religion diminishes quality of life. Probably the most religious countries in the world are those that follow Islam. If one examines the quality of life in any of the Islamic countries, it is far below what is anywhere near reasonable and enjoyed in our Western world. Islamic people are still living in the 12ᵗʰ century, philosophically, and have a standard of living that would be unacceptable to most people in the modern Western world.

I believe that Islam has created burdens on their followers that make it impossible for them to deal adequately with problems of living in the contemporary world. They are hardly able to feed themselves. They often live in squalor. Their average lifespan is less than that of citizens of the Western world. They have made almost no scientific contributions to humankind in the modern history. The oppression of minorities and women in their society is unacceptable. Illiteracy is very high. They have limited freedoms. Their future is narrowed by heir religion. Islam has not helped to create a good life on this earth for their followers.

The people of Islam pray numerous times daily. I do not know what they request, but if they are seeking a good life and ask for it in their prayers, obviously, they are not getting their prayers answered. Not surprising as prayer has no effect on anything. Their religion has failed them.

Islam is a religion of death. They believe that this life is only temporary and the next life will be forever. They value death more than they do life.

> *In doing research for background material for this book, particularly in the area of freethinking, which some call Atheism; I could do no better than to refer to some of the greatest minds in history the world has ever known. I often find myself wondering why the majority of people in the world seem to need the dark ages myths and superstitions perpetuated in all religions. Why can't people live with science and reality? Is it just fear of the unknown and fear of death and of course lack of education and the under development of reason and logic and, of course, the brain-washing by their parents and Popes.*

We often refer to the Philosophy of Atheism as a better alternative to the Philosophy of Religion. As Sam Harris has so well suggested, it should be termed the Philosophy of Reason and Evidence. We do not speak of non-alchemist or non-astrologers or non-racists. Is it not the same?

Some of the greatest intellects of history were either Atheists, Agnostics, or Deists. None believed in an afterlife or that prayer had any effect on anything. Here is a small list—a tiny portion of those who were freethinkers and disbelievers.

John Dewey
Bertrand Russell
Albert Einstein
Thomas Paine
Benjamin Franklin
Thomas Edison
Epicurus
Charles Darwin
Clarence Darrow
Richard Dawkins
Thomas Jefferson
Robert Green Ingersoll
Abraham Lincoln
Aldous Huxley
Salman Rushdie
Luther Burbank
Galileo
Mark Twain

I am proud to be included as a member of such a group.

Quotations from Muslim leaders about killing Christians:

> "Those who know nothing about Islam pretend that Islam counsels against war. Those people are witless. Islam says: 'Kill all the unbelievers just as they would kill you all!' Does this mean that Muslims should sit back until they are devoured by the infidel? Islam says: 'Kill them, put them to the sword

and scatter them.' Islam says: 'Whatever good there is exists thanks to the sword.' The sword is the key to Paradise, which can be opened only for the Holy Warriors! Does all this mean that Islam is a religion that prevents men from waging war? I spit upon those foolish souls who make such a claim." (Ayatollah Ruhollah Khomeini)

"In the Muslim community, the holy war is a religious duty, because of the universalism of the Muslim mission and the obligation to convert everybody to Islam either by persuasion or force. The other religious groups (Christianity and Judaism) did not have a universal mission, and the holy war was not a religious duty to them, save only for purposes of defense. (Ibn Khaldun, The Muqadimmah: Ail Introduction to History, Islamic historian, 1377 AD)

"Islam makes it incumbent on all adult males to prepare themselves for the conquest of countries so that the writ of Islam is obeyed in every country in the world." Ayatollah Ruhollah Khomeini, Iranian Shiite mullah)

"the religion of Islam could be above all, so that all areas of life could be guided by Islam, and so that the earth could be cleansed from unbelief" (The Islamic Council in Chechnya)

"The foremost duty of Islam is to depose the government and society of unbelievers (jahiliyyah) from the leadership of man." (Sayyid Qutb, Egyptian)

"Uniting the five pillars of Islam is the principle Jihad (lit. struggle). In Islam a Muslim must struggle against himself and his habits to submit fully to God. He must also struggle to guide his family, relatives, and friends to bring them to Islam and to convey the message of Islam itself. Since Islam is totalistic, Muslims wherever they may be, must struggle and sacrifice their energy, time, and material resources to establish Muslim congregations, mosques, madrassas (religious schools) for the maintenance and spread of Islam. Where

Muslims make up a substantial fraction of the population, they must struggle to establish the Islamic Shari'ah (law) as their rule for living, with the aim to ultimately establish a full Islamic state in which Islam would be the ruling ideology and system. To understand this last point is very important for it is part and parcel of Islam to seek its full manifestation and where Muslims fail politically or economically, they also fail spiritually. It is innate to Islam to be militantly uncompromising with alien systems since all sovereignty and glory belongs to God, to the Prophets (PBUH) and to the believers." (Spirit of Toronto, Ontario, Canada: 1834-1984, Lindsay Holton, 1983 AD, Foreword by David Crombie, MP: Secretary of State and Minister of Multiculturalism, Islam—A Dynamic Stability, by Camel Xerri Abdullah Idris, Islamic Center Toronto Jami Mosque, p282-293)

Suicide bombers openly call themselves terrorists with pride since the Koran calls for Muslims to act as terrorists in Koran 8:12. "I will instill terror into the hearts of the unbelievers: smite ye above their necks and smite all their finger-tips off them".

The Bible

In my experience, most people I have contacted who say they believe in the Bible, have not read the Bible. Or at best, at Sunday school as children they were exposed to brief sections. I have not read the Bible in its entirety, but I have done some considerable research which I have noted below and I hope you will find it of interest.

A Short History of the Bible

The stories of the Bible evolved slowly over centuries before the existence of organized religions. Many belief cults spread stories, mostly verbal, and myths probably handed down only by oral tradition from generation to generation before people wrote them down. Many of the stories originally came from Egyptian and Sumerian cults. All of these early religions practiced polytheism, including the early Hebrews. Some of the oldest records of the stories that later entered the Old Testament came from thousands of small cylinder seals depicting creation stories, excavated from the Mesopotamia period. These early artifacts and artworks (dated as early as 2500 B.C.) established the basis for the Garden of Eden stories a least a thousand years before it impacted Hebrew mythology.

Virtually every human civilization in the Middle East, before and through Biblical times, practiced some form of female goddess worship. Archeologists have confirmed that the earliest law, government, medicine, agriculture, architecture, metallurgy, wheeled vehicles, ceramics, textiles and written language had initially developed in societies that worshiped a Goddess. Later the goddesses became more war-like with the influence of the northern invaders who slowly replaced the goddesses with their mountain male war gods. So why doesn't the Bible mention anything about the Goddess? In fact it does, but in disguise from converting the name of the goddesses to masculine terms. Many times "Gods" in the Bible refers to goddesses. Ashtoreth, or Asherah, named of masculine gender, for example, actually refers to Astarte—the Great Goddess. The Old Testament doesn't even have a word for Goddess. The goddesses, sometimes, refers to the Hebrew word "Elohim" (masculine plural form) which later religionists mistranslated into the singular "God." The Bible authors converted the ancient goddess symbols into icons of evil. As such, the snake, serpents, tree of knowledge, horns (of the bull), became associated with Satan. The end result gave women the status of inferiority, a result which we still see to this day.

The New Testament has even fewer surviving texts. Scholars think that not until years after Jesus' alleged death that its authors wrote the Gospels. There exists no evidence that the New Testament came from the purported original apostles or anyone else that had seen the alleged Jesus. Although the oldest surviving Christian texts came from Paul, he had never seen the earthly Jesus. There occurs nothing in Paul's letters that either hints at the existence of the Gospels or even of a need for such memoirs of Jesus Christ. The oldest copy of the New Testament yet found consists of a tiny fragment from the Gospel of John. Scholars dated the little flake of papyrus from the period style of its handwriting to around the first half of the 2nd century. The language of most of the new testament consists of old Greek.

There has existed over a hundred different versions of the Bible, written in most of the languages of the time including Greek, Hebrew and Latin. Some versions left out certain biblical stories and others contained added stories. The completed versions of the old and new testament probably got finished at around the period 200-300 although many disputed the authenticity of some books which later ended up as Apocrypha For example, the book of Ecclesiasticus appears in the Catholic Bible but not in Protestant versions.

So the idea of the Bible as a single, sacred unalterable corpus of texts began in heresy and later extended and used by churchmen in their efforts to define orthodoxy. One of the Bible's most influential editors, Irenaeus of Lyon, decided that there should only exist four Gospels like the four zones of the world, the four winds, the four divisions of man's estate, and the four forms of the first living creatures—the lion of Mark, the calf of Luke, the man of Matthew, and the eagle of John. In a single stroke, Irenaeus had delineated the sacred book of the Christian church and left out the other Gospels. Irenaeus also wrote what Christianity did not include, and in this way Christianity became an orthodox faith. A work of Irenaeus, Against the Heresies, became the starting point for later inquisitions.

In the early 1500's the German heretic, Martin Luther, almost single handedly caused the final split from the Roman Catholic church and created the beginnings of the Protestant revolution. This split still influences violence to this day. He translated the Bible into German which further spread Protestantism. Luther also helped spread anti-Jewish sentiments with his preaching and books such as his "The Jews and their lies," all supported through his interpretation of the Bible. One should not forget that Hitler (a Christian and great admirer of Luther) and his holocaust probably could not have occurred without his influence and the support of Bible believing German Christians.

Today we still have dozens of Bible translation versions, with Bible scholars still arguing over the meaning and proper translations of words and phrases. The following shows just a few of the most popular versions:

King James Version (KJV)

The New King James Version (NKJV)

Modern King James Version [Green's Translation] (MKJV)

Literal Translation Version [Green] (LITV)

International Standard Version (ISV)

The New International Version (NIV)

English Standard Version (ESV)

New English Bible (NEB)

American Standard Version (ASV)

New American Standard Bible (NASB)

Revised Standard Version (RSV)

New Revised Standard Version (NRSV) Contemporary English Version (CEV)

Today's English Version (TEV)

The Living Bible (LB)

New Century Version (NC)

New Life Version (NLV)

New Living Translation (NLT)

Young's Literal Translation (YLT)

Revised Young's Literal Translation (RYLT)

John Darby's New Translation

Weymouth New Testament Translation

The Bible is filled with murder and mayhem. It is a book of sadism and war and treachery. Classical in its oppression of women, anti-Semitism, support of slavery and disregard for minorities. Hardly a book to be revered. Here are a few quotations from the Bible. Decide for yourself if these ideas fit your idea of a civilized way of life.

Boil and Eat Your Son

"And the king said unto her, What aileth thee? And she answered, This woman said unto me, Give thy son, that we may eat him to day, and we will eat my son tomorrow. So we boiled my son, and did eat him: and I said unto her on the next day, Give thy son, that we may eat him: and she hath hid her son . . . ." (II Kings 6:28-29)

Death To Adulterers

We have little reason to think that violence inspired by
Bibles and other religious texts will ever cease. One only has
to look at the religious wars around the world to see belief's
everlasting destructive potential. One only has to look at the
Protestant-Catholic uprising in Ireland, the conflicts in the
middle east with Jews fighting Moslems & Christians, the
Gulf war, Sudan's civil war between Christians and Islamics,
the Bosnia conflicts, and the war in Iraq. The desperate acts
of fanatical individuals who have killed for their beliefs of
Jesus, Mohammed, God or Satan would create a death list
unmatched by any other method in history. The "Holy" Bible
supports the notion of war and destruction, not only as a
prophesy but as a moral necessity. If we wish to become a
peaceful species, it may well serve us to understand the forces
of belief that keep us in continual conflict and why the Bible
has such a strong hold on the minds of people around the
world.

"that committeth adultery with another man's wife, even
he that committeth adultery with his neighbor's wife, the
adulterer and the adulteress shall surely be put to death. And
the man that lieth with his father's wife hath uncovered his
father's nakedness: both of them shall surely be put to death;
their blood shall be upon them." (Leviticus 20:10-11)

God's Threat To Kill

"And Moses said, Thus saith the LORD, About midnight
will I go out into the midst of Egypt: And all the firstborn
in the land of Egypt shall die, from the firstborn of Pharaoh
that sitteth upon his throne, even unto the firstborn of the
maidservant that is behind the mill; and all the firstborn of
beasts." (Exodus 11:4-5)

Godly Mass Murder

"And he smote the men of Bethshemesh, because they had looked into the ark of the LORD, even he smote of the people fifty thousand and threescore and ten men: and the people lamented, because the LORD had smitten many of the people with a great slaughter." (I Samuel 6:19)

Kill All Unbelievers

"And that prophet, or that dreamer of dreams, shall be put to death; because he hath spoken to turn you away from the LORD your God . . ." (Deuteronomy 13: 5)

"If thy brother, the son of thy mother, or thy son, or thy daughter, or the wife of thy bosom, or thy friend, which is as thine own soul, entice thee secretly, saying, Let us go and serve other gods, which thou hast not known, thou, nor thy fathers;" (Deuteronomy 13: 6)

"Thou shalt not consent unto him, nor hearken unto him; neither shall thine eye pity him, neither shalt thou spare, neither shalt thou conceal him: But thou shalt surely kill him; thine hand shall be first upon him to put him to death, and afterwards the hand of all the people." (Deuteronomy 13:8-9)

"Thou shalt surely smite the inhabitants of that city with the edge of the sword, destroying it utterly, and all that is therein, and the cattle thereof, with the edge of the sword." (Deuteronomy 13:15)

Female Inferiority

"But I would have you know, that the head of every man is Christ; and the head of the woman is the man; and the head of Christ is God." (I Corinthians 11:3)

"For the man is not of the woman; but the woman of the man. Neither was the man created for the woman; but the woman for the man." (I Corinthians 11:8-9)

Kill The Witches!

"Thou shalt not suffer a witch to live. Whoever lieth with a beast shall surely be put to death. He that sacrificeth unto any god, save to the LORD only, he shall be utterly destroyed." (Exodus 22:18-20)

Silence The Woman!

"Let the women learn in silence with all subjection. But I suffer not a woman to teach, nor to usurp authority over the man, but to be in silence. For Adam was first formed, then Eve. And Adam was not deceived, but the woman being deceived was in the transgression." (I Timothy 2:11-14)

Stone The Woman!

"If a man be found lying with a woman married to an husband, and a man find her in the city, and lie with her;" (Deuteronomy 22:22)

"Then ye shall bring them both out unto the gate of that city, and ye shall stone them with stones that they die; the damsel, because she cried not, being in the city; and the man, because he hath humbled his neighbors' wife: so thou shalt put away evil from among you." (Deuteronomy 22:24)

Wives, Submit Yourselves!

"Wives, submit yourselves unto your own husbands, as unto the Lord. For the husband is the head of the wife, even as Christ is the head of the church: and he is the saviour of the body. Therefore as the church is subject unto Christ, so let the wives be to their own husbands in everything." (Ephesians 5:22-24)

Women Shall Not Speak

"Let your women keep silence in the churches: for it is not permitted unto them to speak; but they are commanded to be under obedience, as also saith the law. And if they will learn anything, let them ask their husbands at home: for it is a shame for women to speak in the church." (I Corinthians 14:34-35)

The Wicked Woman

"Give me any plague, but the plague of the heart: and any wickedness, but the wickedness of a woman." (Eccles. 25:13)

"Of the woman came the beginning of sin, and through her we all die." (Eccles. 25:22)

"If she go not as thou wouldest have her, cut her off from thy flesh, and give her a bill of divorce, and let her go." (Eccles. 25: 26)

"The whoredom of a woman may be known in her haughty looks and eyelids. If thy daughter be shameless, keep her in straitly, lest she abuse herself through overmuch liberty." (Eccles. 26:9-10)

"A silent and loving woman is a gift of the Lord: and there is nothing so much worth as a mind well instructed. A shamefaced and faithful woman is a double grace, and her continent mind cannot be valued." (Eccles. 26:14-15)

Happy To Kill Children

"Happy shall he be, that taketh and dasheth thy little ones against the stones." (Psalms 137:9, KJV)

"How blessed will be the one who seizes and dashes your little ones Against the rock." (Psalms 137:9, New American Bible)

"Happy the man who shall seize and smash your little ones against the rock!" (Psalms 137:9, New American Bible)

"a blessing on anyone who seizes your babies and shatters them against a rock!" (Psalms 137:9, Jerusalem Bible)

God's Threat To Kill

"And Moses said, Thus saith the LORD, About midnight will I go out into the midst of Egypt: And all the firstborn in the land of Egypt shall die, from the firstborn of Pharaoh that sitteth upon his throne, even unto the firstborn of the maidservant that is behind the mill; and all the firstborn of beasts." (Exodus 11:4-5)

Kill All Unbelievers

"And that prophet, or that dreamer of dreams, shall be put to death; because he hath spoken to turn you away from the LORD your God . . ." (Deuteronomy 13: 5)

"If thy brother, the son of thy mother, or thy son, or thy daughter, or the wife of thy bosom, or thy friend, which is as thine own soul, entice thee secretly, saying, Let us go and serve other gods, which thou hast not known, thou, nor thy fathers;" (Deuteronomy 13: 6)

"Thou shalt not consent unto him, nor hearken unto him; neither shall thine eye pity him, neither shalt thou spare, neither shalt thou conceal him: But thou shalt surely kill him; thine hand shall be first upon him to put him to death, and afterwards the hand of all the people." (Deuteronomy 13:8-9)

"Thou shalt surely smite the inhabitants of that city with the edge of the sword, destroying it utterly, and all that is therein, and the cattle thereof, with the edge of the sword." (Deuteronomy 13:15)

Serpent Jews

"Ye serpents, ye generation of vipers, how can ye escape the damnation of hell?" (Matthew 23:33)

Comment

Chapter 23 describes the famous diatribe of Jesus against the Jewish leaders. Such biblical words has, for centuries, given believers justification for Jewish hatred. This verse, spoken by the alleged Jesus himself, compares the unbelieving Jews with the serpent devil.

Synagogues Of Satan

"But this thou hast, that thou hatest the deeds of the Nicolaitanes, which I also hate." (Revelation 2:6)

"I know thy works, and tribulation, and poverty, (but thou art rich) and I know the blasphemy of them which say they are Jews, and are not, but are the synagogue of Satan." (Revelation 2:9)

"So hast thou also them that hold the doctrine of the Nicolaitanes, which the thing I hate." (Revelation 2:15)

"Behold, I will make them of the synagogue of Satan, which say they are Jews, and are not, but do lie; behold, I will make them to come and worship before thy feet, and to know that I have loved thee." (Revelation 3:9)

Comment

These verses by Jesus has fueled the engine of anti-Semitism throughout Europe and the rest of the world for centuries. Unfortunately many believers (as did Hitler) today still justify their hatred of Jews based on Scripture.

Let us work towards a new world where we are not influenced by the many ancient scriptures telling myths and superstitions in all religions leading the faithful in ways inimical to the realization and fulfillment of The Good Life.

Competition

Competition is essential to progress in a civilized world. Competition in philosophies, in business, in community organization, in all human activities. Without competition, civilization will not progress. The fundamental of competitive progress is illustrated graphically with the current Olympiad in Great Britain. The world's greatest athletes compete and winners are chosen. Not everyone can win. But the spirit of good fellowship exists with the losers congratulating the winners and civilization progresses. It must be the same with all other facets of a civilized competitive life. We must be open-minded about examining the best elements of all the philosophies of life without demanding dominance of one. Dogma, which states that our idea is better than yours and will dominate cannot be allowed. We must be open-minded examining all philosophies, so that each idea can bring betterment to our lives. But competition is at the root. Let's compete with ideas but not demand dominance. Selecting the ideas that work the best. Down through history, we've moved from dictators to monarchies to democracy. It seems obvious that we are making progress even though there are some ideas that are creating disruptive problems like Islam.

Innovation

I recently watched a current edition of the televised Charlie Rose show. It happened to be on the subject of Innovation and was really very apropos and inspiring.

Rose had two guests. The first was Larry Page, cofounder and CEO of Google. The second was Mark Andreesen, founder and CEO of Netscape, a web browser and software innovator.

Both of these men are bright beyond belief and have such a handle on the subject of innovation that it is inspiring.

Page discussed the development and the details, progress, and objectives, long-term, of Google. Basically, in one sentence, it is to make all of the information of the world available to everybody as they are a sophisticated search engine for computers.

Andreesen spoke about the opportunities in the world today. He knows more about the high-tech world than anyone I've ever heard speak. It was inspiring to listen to him. He spoke of the contribution that Mark Zuckerberg has made with Facebook. That is to bring the entire world together.

An important development will be what today is called the iPhone. It used to be called a cell phone. The latter will soon be discontinued as everyone will have an iPhone, which he says is really a misnomer. This device is really a miniature micro-sized computer that does everything and yet it's small enough to put in your shirt pocket. He thinks everyone in the world will have one.

One of the important contributions that this technology will make is that every farmer in the world will now know, in advance, the real market value of his crop and the current crop market demand before he goes to market or even plants a particular crop. He will also know about weather forecasts. This knowledge will allow him to be a more efficient farmer and a more profitable business man.

Knowledge is power and this knowledge was never before available to the average farmer throughout the world. The pocket computer will provide this for him. Andreesen claims that this will increase the world's food supply measurably as well as the farmer's profits.

It got me thinking about innovation in general. We can go back to the so-called holy scriptures like the bible and koran written about 2000 years ago. Written by desert nomads who would be considered ignoramuses by today's standards. The wheelbarrow was high-tech in those days and the world was flat.

It's interesting when we see, for example, countries in Africa where peasants are still carrying loads on their heads instead of in a wheelbarrow. They still haven't even accepted this wheelbarrow technology. If you don't keep up with technology, you're doomed to live in the past. That's, of course, the problem with the Islamic world.

Then we move ahead rapidly to innovations like the printing press, running water, central heating, electricity, automobiles, airplanes, telephones, television, computers, android phones and what's next? Andreesen prophesies we will have computer-driven cars so even a blind man can drive to the store and that's coming very soon.

Innovation in technology is finally available to us all and we all benefit through its use. If we don't take advantage of it, we are doomed to live less than fulfilling lives.

Since only the hard-core reader will have managed to get this far, I feel comfortable making the following statement:

I am now 86 years old and I must say I'm pretty happy about the whole thing . . . I'm referring to my life. I've accomplished everything I wanted to. I had a successful corporate business career, a successful marriage of 54 years, a successful entrepreneurial career, raised and educated three fine children and enjoy excellent health living in the perfect village and in the perfect house. And my living is about as close to luxurious as one could make it with a daily housekeeper, most of my meals eaten out as I please, and plenty of opportunity to do anything I want whenever I want to, including world travel as I am financially independent. It's just plain bragging but I followed all of my rules my father taught me on how to lead the good life and hope that you will also.

I only have one serious concern and that is the encroachment of Islam on the world. The next book I am writing on the subject details the problems the world faces with Islam. I'm not optimistic that the people living in our world, let's say 30 to 50 years from now will be able to do anything about it. It's going to be a very sad world if it happens. Civilization, as we know it, will suffer and the world may return to the dark ages. Let's hope that my book, along with many others will somehow influence people as they must stop the expansion of Islam if they wish to maintain the civilized freedoms to which our western world has become accustomed.

William F. Russell, Author
Essex, Connecticut July 2012

END

CHAPTER 42

About The Author

The author was born in New York City in November 1925 the eldest of three children of Dr. and Mrs. Frank H Russell. Dr. Frank Russell was house surgeon of the Hotel Astor on Times Square where the family lived until 1930. Mrs. Charlotte Russell was an opera singer who performed in New York at Carnegie. Boston in Symphony Hall, and Los Angeles at the Hollywood bowl. The family also lived in Riverdale and on Central Park West.

Dr. Russell bought a medical practice and private hospital in Worcester Massachusetts in 1938. The family moved there and lived there until Dr Russell died in 1955.

It was here that William developed an interest in the outdoors after joining the Boy Scouts, including camping, hiking, white-water canoeing, mountaineering, and skiing. He became a troop leader and a Life Scout. He was also Master Counselor of the Worcester chapter order of DeMolay. He volunteered in the U.S. Army Air Corps and served during World War II during 1944 and 45.

Following the war William matriculated at Clark University in premed studies. He continued at the University of Colorado in Boulder where he graduated with a BS in 1950.

He married Joanne Jackson, daughter of Dr. Arnold S Jackson President of the Jackson Clinic of Madison Wisconsin. Joanne graduated with a BS from the University of Wisconsin with a major in chemistry.

William, while a student at the University of Colorado worked part-time as a ski instructor at Arapahoe Basin and also held other part-time jobs in direct sales to supplement his income to help support his growing family.

On graduation in 1950 he decided to abandon medical studies and started as a salesman for Physicians and Surgeons surgical supply company of Denver. His territory was the Rocky Mountain states including Colorado, Wyoming, Montana, and Utah. He later became sales manager and ultimately president of this company.

He then became VP marketing manager with Noreen Incorporated of Denver, manufacturer of hair care products sold to the drug and variety market. He later joined Clairol in New York as a group product manager and was responsible for the development and marketing of Loving Care, Nice and Easy, and Silk and Silver.

He later was promoted to President and CEO of Clairol de Paris SA with headquarters and manufacturing in Paris, France and president and CEO of Clairol Limited of London England.

He also held positions of VP, Director-General of consumer products of American Cyanamid of Wayne New Jersey and New York. Following that he was VP, Director of Marketing of the Gillette Safety Razor company in Boston.

Entrepreneurism was always his first love so he left the corporate world in 1970 and started his own business. Among the several businesses he started and managed were Peter Storm Limited, manufacturer of sportswear, RAM knitting, sweater manufacturer, Russell Yacht Charters, an international yacht chartering company, and Bill Russell's Mountain Tours, conducting hiking and skiing tours in the Swiss Alps and throughout Europe and the UK. This last company is still in operation.

William is currently concentrating on developing his writing skills and has currently completed work on a second book which exposes The Threat of Islam to world civilization. Books are in publication.

He says he is an antique, living in an antique house in the antique village of Essex Connecticut where he enjoys a lifelong interest in yachting as a member of the Essex Yacht Club cruising on the beautiful Connecticut River. "Old age is not bad when one considers the alternative."

My Antique House In My Antique Village of Essex

Sincerely,
William Russell